THE COMPLETE

RETIREMENT PLANNING

BOOK

Also by Peter A. Dickinson

The Fires of Autumn: Sexual Activity in the Middle and Later Years
The Illustrated Encyclopedia of Better Health (coauthor)
The Wealth Management Handbook (coauthor)
Sunbelt Retirement
Retirement Edens: Outside the Sunbelt
Travel and Retirement Edens Abroad

PETER A. DICKINSON is the founding editor of *Harvest Years* (now *Fifty Plus*) and *The Retirement Letter, The Money Newsletter for Mature People.* He is the author of several books, including *The Fires of Autumn (Sexual Activity in the Middle and Later Years), The Complete Retirement Planning Book, Sunbelt Retirement, Retirement Edens: Outside the Sunbelt,* and *Travel and Retirement Edens Abroad.* He has served as a Special Investigator for the U.S. Senate Special Committee on Aging, is a consultant to major corporations, and conducts seminars, films, and expositions on retirement planning and living.

THE COMPLETE

RETIREMENT

PLANNING BOOK

Revised Edition

PETER A. DICKINSON

E. P. DUTTON, INC.   NEW YORK

Published in the United States by E. P. Dutton, Inc.,
2 Park Avenue, New York, N.Y. 10016
Library of Congress Catalog Card Number: 83-71776

ISBN: 0-525-93304-2 (cloth) 0-525-48081-1 (DP)

Published simultaneously in Canada by Fitzhenry & Whiteside, Limited, Toronto

W

10 9 8 7 6 5 4 3 2 1

Second Edition

This book is dedicated
to those who want to
add more life to their years
as well as
more years to their life.

CONTENTS

PREFACE:

DON'T

CALL IT

RETIREMENT

"Retirement! What a distressful word! It smacks of retreat, withdrawal, seclusion, removal from circulation, elastic stockings, and Windsor rockers. I wish my status were called 'refirement' instead of retirement, because I'm still mobile, and my engine still functions rather well."

I agree with this man, who obviously isn't *retired* in the conventional sense. And I approve when he says that he would replace the word "retirement" with a more apt description of the later years—the "Elective Years"— to indicate that at last you can *choose* your way of life rather than having it programmed for you.

After researching and writing about retirement for over 23 years, I realized that the prevailing concept governing retirement is all wrong. Retirement isn't idleness, letting down, or letting go; rather, it is a time we can opt for second careers, different life-styles, and new dreams. With retirement ages lowering, early retirements rising, and more opportunities opening up for all ages, now is the time to start to do what we've always really wanted to do—even if we are preparing for a conventional retirement date.

At age 45 I decided that wherever I wanted to go in this life I didn't have to take the 8:03 A.M. train to get there. So I left my job as founding editor of *Harvest Years* (now *Fifty-Plus* magazine) and launched a new career, new activities, and a new philosophy that have made me happier, healthier, and wealthier.

I don't call it retirement—I call it "renewment."

Why wait for a conventional retirement date? Why not start right *now* to prepare for something better?

Worried about money? Concerned about health? Don't know what to do with your spare time? Not sure how or where you'd like to live? Worried about the future?

This book tells how you can make and save enough money to retire today or 10 years from tomorrow. You'll explore ways to guarantee better health, gain rewards for spending leisure time, find housing that is as personal as your dreams and as practical as your pocketbook, enrich your present as well as assure your future.

This book offers the *practical advice* of experts and the *personal experience* of people like you and me. It tells what I did, what I learned, and what hundreds of people told me about bridging the gap—financially, physically, and mentally—between an uncertain today and a more secure tomorrow when Social Security, Medicare, and a pension will smooth the way. You'll enjoy philosophizing as well as planning, and you'll find new pursuits to nourish the mind and feed the soul.

Enjoy your trip through this book. I'll help you avoid the pitfalls and seize the unexpected pleasure of your journey to retirement—and a life of your *choice*.

This book could not have been written without the cooperation of the scores of men and women who shared their experiences with me so that others might benefit. I am also deeply indebted to those gerontologists, sociologists, doctors, lawyers, and other professionals in the field of retirement planning and living who shared their research findings with me. And my special thanks to Irene Donelson, coauthor of *When You Need a Lawyer* and *Married Today, Single Tomorrow*, and William P. Dumont, mentor and associate, who offered much help and information; to Frederick Jung, M.D., who fact-checked the "Health Means Wealth" section; to Kenneth Donelson, attorney at law, who fact-checked "Your Changing Legal Needs" section of this book; and to Brigitte W. Dickinson, who, as reference librarian and wife, provided much information and offered much encouragement for this book.

                                                    PETER A. DICKINSON

Larchmont, New York
January 1984

PART I

INTRODUCTION:

OUT

OF A RUT

Why seek something better than a conventional retirement? The liveliest persons I've known were those who *forced* themselves out of a rut that was leading nowhere except a dead-end retirement and found a new direction.

The dullest persons I've met were those who just "hung on" until they could grasp their pension checks, then wondered why the payoff didn't buy health and happiness.

Striving is surviving; stagnation is dying.

This book is for those who seek a better life-style at any stage of mature living. Call it retirement or "renewment," you don't have to cast your new life-style in image-shattering molds. Here's how some people did it:

Margaret Smith wanted a more active social life. She was a bachelor woman with a good job but poor friendships. Several years before retirement she scouted resort areas of Florida, finally settling on Vero Beach. She cultivated the friendships of people who regularly vacationed there or who were retired. She bought a cottage, using it as her vacation and entertainment headquarters, renting it the rest of the year. When she's ready for retirement, she'll have a new home, new friends, and a new life-style waiting for her.

The Roger Bartons wanted to maintain their social status. They had always enjoyed the prestige of their social set, but they realized that retirement would offer few occasions for such enrichment. Also, they wouldn't have much money for lavish entertaining. A few years before retirement they both joined a local branch of a prestigious national service organization. Roger used his leverage as a working executive to elevate himself and his wife to top-rung jobs in this group. When they retire, they'll be secure in their place in the community.

Frank Markowitz wanted to become financially independent. He started as a clerk in his firm and 20 years later was still far from the top. His wife, Sarah, worked as a bookkeeper and secretary. So they decided to pool their talents to set up a husband-and-wife business team. Sarah got up a prospect list, researched leads, and set up files. Frank expanded his contacts with potential customers. When retirement arrives, they'll be able to launch their new business.

There's no reason why you, too, can't start a new life-style. And you'll have the time to test and develop it today, polish and perfect it tomorrow.

The Prime Time for Shifting Gears

Somewhere between ages 35 and 55 most of us reach one of those revealing crossroads of life—instead of reaching out for rewards, we start probing in for values. Life is a series of milestones. In younger days you rush past the markers, your eye on the next. But as you approach middle years, you can slow down . . . reflect on where you've been; deliberate on where you're going.

A recent editorial in the *Boston Globe* suggested the value of finding a new life-style:

> *Work has its place. Putting one foot in front of the other will get you to the grave in the end . . . But it is through change that the unexpected likeness of unlike experiences is revealed . . . if dropping out on the production line means dropping in on the human race, we're all for it—and no strings attached.*

Remember that we have this advantage: no one has defined a proper role for the later years—*we can do what we want when we want.*

Planning the Trip of Your Dreams

Embarking on a new life-style should be the trip of your dreams—your reward for a lifetime of work. But sometimes it turns into a trip of pitfalls, detours, and dead ends.

You can avoid the pitfalls and accentuate the possibilities if you realize: (1) You can't shut off your motor without coasting or going downhill; (2) You must *plan* any trip in advance.

Look back on your last big trip. Half the fun was *planning;* you got guidebooks and maps, planned where you wanted to go, and made reservations. The further ahead you planned and the more money you saved—the more you enjoyed the trip. There may have been unexpected adventures along the way, but if you were prepared, you turned potentially bad dreams into pleasant memories.

Planning invites a challenge—exploring of new frontiers. Someone once said: "Challenges are opportunities in work clothes." Challenges *create* opportunities; we don't get the most out of life unless we respond to a challenge. A new life-style gives you that sort of challenge—something to aim at and something to strive for. And the secret of a full response to a challenge is to *plan* for it.

For instance:

■ It's not *where* you live but *how* you live that determines how much money you need. Simplify your life today, and you'll have more money tomorrow.

■ Start *now* on a program of enjoyable exercise, proper diet, and sufficient rest, and you'll be happier and healthier today and tomorrow.

■ Start *now* to develop a hobby, service project, second career. You can enjoy it today and perfect it tomorrow.

Make Decisions While You've Still Got the Answers

You've already made many decisions and experienced many changes to get where you are; you're well equipped to make decisions to get where you're going.

Retirement or "renewment" shouldn't be the crushing change it is for most people. Change exacts a toll; the more abrupt the change, the more costly the toll. In his book *Future Shock*, Alvin Toffler warns there may be definite limits to the change that any one of us can adapt to in a short time span. Dr. Robert N. Butler, author of *Why Survive? Being Old in America*, says: "Human beings need the freedom to *live with change*, to invent and reinvent themselves a number of times throughout their lives. By loosening up life, we enlarge the value of the gift of life."

The older we are, the more experience we've had with change—in our jobs, our families, our bodies. We should be old enough to know, young enough to do. As one middle-aged philosopher told me: "You feel you have lived long enough to have learned a few things that nobody can learn earlier. That's the reward and that's the excitement. I now see things in books, in people, in music, that I attribute largely to my present age."

Unhappy older persons are the ones who identified with what they did, not who they were. They worked, married, and raised families by following orders, not asking questions. When I've asked retirees what they missed most about work, the majority answered "money," with friendships and other rewards far down the line. When I've asked them if they suffered financial hardships in the impact year of retirement, most said, "No." And when I questioned them about their adjustment to retirement, 35 percent said it had turned out better than expected, only 5 percent said it had turned out worse, and the rest said it turned out about the way they expected.

I draw these conclusions: (1) If you work mainly to make money, if you retire with enough money, you'll not miss work; (2) while you might tolerate and even enjoy work friends, they didn't choose you, and you didn't choose them; (3) no matter what doubts you have before retirement, you'll be better off after. Consider:

BEFORE RETIREMENT	AFTER RETIREMENT
Letting others dictate your life	Living life as you want
Regulated by work schedules	Setting your own pace
Structured leisure time	Doing what you want—and when
Eating when you must	Eating when you need or want to
Being nice to fellow workers	Choosing your own friends
Heavy tax burdens	Lighter tax burdens
Business expenses	Reduced leisure expenses
Worrying about getting ahead	Happy with what you've got

In short, whatever your situation now, it will be better when you make the change.

HOW YOUR NEEDS AND WANTS CHANGE OVER THE DECADES

The Fabulous Forties—more options and opportunities for second careers, new life-styles, new relationships. The forties is also the decade of mid-life crisis and shifting gears. Some challenges and opportunities for this decade:

MONEY	HEALTH	LEISURE	HOUSING	LEGAL
Building a nest egg for kid's college, retirement, estate, dream trips, aging parents; need to find growth investments; life insurance needs still high.	Physical changes in eyesight and hearing; increasing concern with internal health; possible selecting of nursing home for aging parents.	Increasing value on quality of time spent; taking dream trips and second honeymoons.	A bigger house for size or prestige; looking for "ideal" vacation-retirement location; turning parts of home into office or shop.	Preparing wills and setting up estate plans; establishing trusts and guardianships; setting up a business; deaths or divorce that affect wills, ownerships.

The Fortunate Fifties—the nailing-down decade when you have it "all together." Winding up past needs and wants; settling down for the future. A pleasant autumn or afternoon of life when inner contentment replaces outer turmoil. Some needs and wants:

MONEY	HEALTH	LEISURE	HOUSING	LEGAL
Switching from growth to income investments; settling debts; reexamining insurance needs; saving rather than spending; loans to kids and inheritances from relatives.	Internal health problems (heart, diabetes, arthritis, cancer) may increase.	Considering early retirement to escape pressures or fulfill unrealized dreams; emphasizing internal values rather than external rewards.	Serious thoughts about "empty nest" and retirement housing; whether to move or stay put; fixing up housing for more comfortable living.	Changes in wills and estate planning; final arrangements for older parents; arranging matters for self and children.

The Sensible Sixties—the true "settling in" decade when people make final plans for the rest of their lives. The decade when most retirements take place. New questions of Social Security, Medicare, pensions, retirement housing arise. Some other changes:

MONEY	HEALTH	LEISURE	HOUSING	LEGAL
When to retire and take Social Security and pension; converting life insurance; freeing up inflation value of home; new state and federal tax advantages; tapping hidden value of collectibles; reducing business-related expenses.	Maintenance and prevention health goals; less job-related stress and more enjoyable activities; "retirement shock" for those not adequately prepared; Medicare will cover health insurance needs.	Establishing a retirement lifestyle; finding rewarding new leisure activities that replace work satisfactions; new activities for those who are or who will become single (most women over 65 are single).	Either improving present housing or finding new housing that becomes recreation center, office or workshop, perhaps convalescent ward. Option of getting less expensive housing in less expensive area.	New legal problems may arise involving pensions, Social Security, Medicare; late or new marriage; setting up a retirement business; buying or selling housing; taking care of ill or incompetent relative.

The Settled Seventies—this may be the final decade when a person can really enjoy life. But if you've lived this long, you should be in good shape to enjoy the rest of your years. And you still have time to reach any remaining life goals.

MONEY	HEALTH	LEISURE	HOUSING	LEGAL
Annuities make the most sense at this age; decisions including whether or not to have someone else manage your finances, investments, business.	Maintenance should be stressed as should prevention of the killer diseases like heart and blood problems; cancer.	Finding less physically demanding activities; writing or taping the family history; mending fences and building bridges with relatives and friends.	Considering life-care housing that provides shelter, meals, recreation, medical care; perhaps nursing home for spouse, relatives or friends.	Final arrangements for wills, estate, funeral; gift-giving to minimize estate taxes.

The longer you live the longer you may be expected to live, as shown in these latest figures from the U.S. National Center for Health Statistics:

EXPECTATION OF LIFE AT VARIOUS AGES
IN THE UNITED STATES 1980

AGE	WHITE			ALL OTHER			TOTAL		
	MALE	FEMALE	TOTAL	MALE	FEMALE	TOTAL	MALE	FEMALE	TOTAL
0............	70.5	78.1	74.3	65.3	74.0	69.6	69.8	77.5	73.6
1............	70.4	77.9	74.1	65.7	74.3	70.0	69.8	77.4	73.6
5............	66.6	74.0	70.3	62.0	70.6	66.2	66.0	73.6	69.8
10............	61.7	69.1	65.4	57.1	65.7	61.4	61.1	68.7	64.9
15............	56.8	64.2	60.5	52.2	60.7	56.5	56.2	63.7	60.0
20............	52.2	59.4	55.8	47.6	55.5	51.7	51.6	58.9	55.3
25............	47.7	54.5	51.1	43.3	51.1	47.2	47.1	54.1	50.6
30............	43.1	49.7	46.4	39.0	46.4	42.7	42.6	49.2	45.9
35............	38.5	44.9	41.7	34.8	41.7	38.3	38.0	44.4	41.3
40............	33.8	40.1	37.0	30.6	37.1	33.9	33.5	39.7	36.6
45............	29.3	35.4	32.4	26.7	32.8	29.7	29.0	35.1	32.1
50............	25.1	30.9	28.0	22.9	28.6	25.7	24.8	30.6	27.8
55............	21.1	26.5	23.9	19.5	24.8	22.1	20.9	26.3	23.7
60............	17.4	22.4	20.0	16.7	21.2	19.0	17.3	22.2	19.9
65............	14.1	18.5	16.5	14.1	18.1	16.2	14.1	18.4	16.4
70............	11.2	14.9	13.3	11.6	14.9	13.3	11.2	14.9	13.3
75............	8.7	11.5	10.3	9.4	12.5	11.1	8.7	11.6	10.4
80............	6.8	8.8	8.1	8.7	11.5	10.3	7.0	9.0	8.2
85 and over ...	5.4	6.8	6.3	8.1	10.5	9.6	5.6	7.0	6.5

Source: National Center for Health Statistics, U.S. Department of Health and Human Services.

At any age a woman averages three to eight years more life expectancy than a man of the same age. At the "usual" retirement age of 65, a man might have over 14 more years life expectancy while a woman has over 18 more years. Those who are now in their twenties and thirties can expect to live to ages 85 to 100. Cell research indicates that most of us have a life potential of 110 to 120 vigorous, healthy years. If science could eliminate the number-one killer—major cardiovascular-renal disease—life expectancy for both sexes would jump an average of 15 to 25 years. So whatever planning you do, take into account your *increasing* life expectancy.

Plenty of Prime Time Left

Age 55 soon will become the *prime* age. It will soon be the "normal" retirement age, when you can view life clearly over the past, present, and future.

The median age in this country is moving from thirty toward the forties. Those of us now in our mid-fifties already make most of the decisions and issue most of the orders. We not only cast three quarters of the ballots in any election (enough to swing it as a group), but we are the most active group in national, state, and local politics—as workers or candidates.

The mid-fifties and older contain over 40 million persons today; before the end of the century there will be more than 50 million persons over age 55, and thanks to zero population growth, this group will be the biggest and most influential, healthiest, best educated, and most attuned to leisure activities of all groups in America. We pacesetters will want more options open to us based on ability, not age. And we will be concerned with what we may have missed in life as well as what we have achieved.

Already we've won improvements in housing, medical care, and Social Security, and we're getting more attention than ever in the newspapers and other media. There's more emphasis on the "quality of life" rather than on the "quantity." And there's more concern with leisure time, individual freedom, rights and responsibilities for all ages. So *now*'s the time to start planning to get our share of the rewards in the offing.

How Do You Get Started?

Here are seven things you can be doing *right now:*

1. *Investigate the possibilities of living elsewhere.* We all dream of some place where the costs are lower and the climate milder . . . perhaps someplace where we can start a new life. *Now*—during vacations, long weekends, time off—start reading up and exploring these places. The more places you visit, the more certain you'll be whether you want to move or stay put.

2. *Review your present life insurance.* Most of us took out policies when we were younger to protect a growing family. But with the family grown and many expenses over, we probably don't need as much protection as we once did. Also, if you have straight life, whole life, or endowment policies, you are building up *cash value* as well as insurance protection. Unfortunately, the cash value is (probably) growing at less than 5 percent annually. Even if you had to take a "loan" at 5 or 6 percent to borrow on this money, you could reinvest it at 10 to 13 percent and make about 7 percent annually on your own money. In any event, at least consider *reducing* the amount of insurance premiums you pay, and putting the cash value to better work for you.

3. *Review your present investments.* When you were younger, you probably invested for *growth* (capital gains) rather than for *income*. But as we

grow older, we should be more concerned with *safety* as well as income . . . and less concerned about growth (we have fewer years to worry about keeping ahead of inflation). Simply by starting to switch your investments from growth to income, you'll have more money for today as well as tomorrow.

4. *Consider a retirement job.* Not something you must do to produce money, but something you *want* to do that provides income—as well as pleasure. No matter what your skills, interests, background, there are more *opportunities and options* for second careers, small businesses, part-time or temporary jobs, time-sharing or flexible-time work schedules. So no matter what you are doing now, consider doing something else that you really *want* to do tomorrow. You can get a second wind through a second career or job. If it's deeply satisfying, you'll find that making money is no longer important. And by organizing your life around your own standards, you'll find that you can cut down on expenses without sacrificing life-style. You can usually earn enough money to bridge the gap between the present and the time when you can start drawing Social Security and a pension. Most important, you can start preparing yourself *now* for the opportunities that lie ahead.

5. *Find something in retirement to get up in the morning for.* If you don't have a desirable retirement job, you should have *something worth doing* on each day's agenda. It could be a bridge party, golf game, or hobby. But it should be something that you *want* to do and will pay you a tangible *reward* that will satisfy some basic need or want.

6. *Start cutting down on "indulgences."* Some of the money you're spending right now is for "instant gratification" (perhaps food or drink) because you "owe it to yourself" after a hard day at the office. But if you're doing something you really *want* to do, you'll be getting "instant gratification" from "doing your thing." Once you realize this, you can start cutting down on some needless expenses.

7. *Try retirement.* Once you know what you want to do and how much it is going to cost, *now* is the time to rehearse, experiment, and practice with retirement. In any new venture you usually make a number of mistakes; *now's* the time to get the mistakes out of the way so you can sail into a successful retirement.

Whom Should You Involve in Your Retirement Planning?

Consider the points above, and depending upon what you do, you may have to involve your insurance agent, banker, doctor, lawyer, financial adviser. But you *must* involve your spouse, roommate, closest friend. A good relationship should be a good partnership. However, approaching retirement often puts a strain on a relationship. For instance:

■ A man who might feel he's losing prestige might start demanding excessive attention. And a spouse might respond with nagging.

■ A man who's been wrapped up in a job and a woman who's been wrapped up in raising a family might find they have fewer interests in common and fewer ties that bind in retirement.

But you're going to *need* each other more than ever before in retirement . . . need to talk to each other and plan together.

How, Then, Can You Ease Any Strains of Approaching Retirement?

You can take these steps to positive action:

■ *Plan your finances.* A good relationship should be a good business partnership. Planning finances is something you can get a handle on, plan together, and get positive results from that will pay off today as well as tomorrow. By planning your finances together, you'll not only provide a nest egg to cushion the stress of retirement, you'll set the stage for further planning together.

■ *Plan common interests* to replace those you may lose. This could be a service project, volunteer activity, a small business or even a social venture that will give you something to do together and to talk about together.

■ *Plan separate activities.* It's even more important to assure the *privacy* of each person in a retirement situation—especially if you're going to be at home together a lot. People should have a den, study, workshop, studio, or sewing room, where they can close the door and be alone. And people should have "days off" when they can go separate ways and do "their thing."

Planning for Singles and for Those Who Will Become So . . .

A 20-year-old woman who marries a 22-year-old man will probably outlive him by eight years. And by age 65, a woman might outlive her husband by some 20 years. At present, there are only 67.6 men per 100 women among persons 65 years and older.

Widows in the United States outnumber widowers almost five to one (approximately 10 million widows for over 2 million widowers), and most widows and many widowers don't remarry.

Whether widowed, divorced, or unmarried, older "singles" have a variety of life-styles open to them. They can move into singles apartments, buy homes and rent out rooms to other singles, live in "foster homes," and even set up communes. In Winter Park, Florida, some 60 seniors—ranging in age from fifties to nineties—live in four homes as families, paying a younger couple to manage the homes and do most of the work. The arrangement has worked out so well that a group of Winter Park citizens formed Share-a-Home of America, Inc. to collect money to set up homes in other communities.

Probably the saddest singles I've known were widows who had moved with a retired husband to some "Shangri-la." Before they had a chance to make friends, their husbands died and left them strangers in a strange environment. But even these widows can adjust and prosper if they plan for their future wisely—by cultivating themselves and their interests as well as saving their money. Many widows find new outlets once they have rid themselves of their grief and realize they have more freedom and opportunity than ever before. The key to happiness in your future is to plan for it now.

Phase Out . . . Phase In

The average retirement age is dropping, and many employees and employers are anticipating retirement at age 55. Some 96 percent of pension plans have "escape hatches" for early retirement, and over half those now collecting Social Security are under 65.

These young, vigorous retirees are getting a second wind for a second career. Above all, your second career should be the *one career* you want above all others. It should satisfy your dreams and reward your pocketbook. And if you have a pension and savings to cushion you, your second career could be the one that you *want* to do, not *must* do to make money.

If you choose a deeply satisfying second career, you'll find that making money is no longer of paramount importance. By organizing your life around your own standards, you'll find ways to cut down or eliminate nonessential material goods. You can also earn or save enough money *now* to bridge the financial gap between the present and the time you start drawing Social Security and a pension. Most important, you can start preparing yourself now for the *opportunities* that lie ahead—both psychological and financial.

Here are some guidelines about what you should have *now* for a successful early retirement:

■ An income of at least $12,000 (from all sources) for yourself and your spouse, and proportionately more in succeeding years to keep ahead of inflation. Singles need at least 75 percent of what a couple needs.

- Major financial obligations (mortgages, children's education, installment payments) either paid off or under control.

- At least $12,000 in savings or investments.

- Counseling or some study in advance of retirement.

- A second career or socially useful part-time occupation, preferably one that pays.

When you add up your assets, you may find that you'll have more income and benefits than you realize. And if you start planning *now* and use the information on *finances, health, leisure, housing,* and *legal* matters in this book, you'll be prepared for "renewment" or retirement at any age.

Mistakes Some People Make

1. *Planning too late.* "If you've left your mid-forties behind you, your financial life plan is overdue," says St. Petersburg, Florida, attorney James E. Elliott, a specialist in estate planning. He adds that you should have determined your net worth—how fast it's been growing, and how much income it's likely to produce in the future. If your net worth isn't growing fast enough, or if there's no margin for safety against inflation built into it, you should find ways to put it on target.

2. *Planning for too short a time.* You'll probably live longer than you think. If you arrange to liquidate your finances over a period of time (withdrawing from a mutual fund or savings account), you might find yourself running out of money before running out of time. You must arrange your finances to provide income now and in the future.

3. *Not setting definite goals.* Unless you set definite goals, you won't reach them. Avoid piecemeal planning that doesn't coordinate your retirement goals, tax status, wills, trusts, life and health insurance, and investments.

4. *Not matching goals to personality and temperament.* If you're a conservative family man, you're not likely to become a "swinging senior." Your investments, activities, housing, and location should reflect *who you are* as much as *what you want.*

5. *Not spending time to save money.* Time is money; money is time. The more you have of one, the less you need the other. If you'll have *less money* in the future, then spend *more time* now planning how to spend, make, or save money. In many instances, investing only a little time saves a lot of money. You'll be happier and healthier when you spend time to save money; it pays off in your pocketbook, your doctor's office, and in your pleasure at home.

Steps to Positive Action

1. *Define your concepts of "renewment" and retirement.* Understand the meaning, purpose, and problems so you'll be prepared to meet challenges and take advantage of opportunities.

2. *Make decisions based on fact*—rather than on hunches or guesses. Decisions based on facts will help you tailor a workable plan for *you.*

3. *Keep an open mind.* Nothing is cut and dried, especially this most adventurous part of life. You'll have many opportunities that you'll be able to turn to your advantage—if you're prepared for them.

4. *Maintain harmonious relationships*—with your spouse, relatives, friends, neighbors. By planning with those nearest to you and who will be involved in your decisions, you create challenges and opportunities for shared experiences.

5. *Keep your plans flexible.* There'll always be an intriguing side road that you'll not want to pass by. By knowing the main routes through your retirement, you'll feel more confident in exploring intriguing byways.

Remember, you're going to have more *time, freedom,* and *opportunity* than ever before. You can go *where* you want, *when* you want, *how* you want, and with whom you want.

You'll have many *happier tomorrows*—if you start your *retirement planning today!*

PART II.

HEALTH MEANS
WEALTH

When I was younger, I was surprised when my surveys revealed that older people were more concerned with their health than their wealth. Now that I'm older I understand—our want for things money buys fades, while our need for good health intensifies. We can always make money; we can't always buy good health.

Doctors say that as you grow older you should be on a pleasant plateau—looking back on a vigorous youth, enjoying an active present, and preparing for a ripe old age. You should be able to do what you really need and want to do.

Best yet, you should have many years ahead to practice good health habits that broaden this plateau. All it takes is a dollars-and-sense approach to enjoyable exercise, nutritious food, relaxation, and stimulating activities that make you think, feel, and look better.

In many ways you *are* as old as you think and feel. Consider these points: We age piecemeal, each organ separately rather than uniformly; no disease results just from growing older. You may have the heart of a 25-year-old and the kidneys of a 50-year-old. Your hearing may be as keen as a teen-ager's but your eyesight as dim as a centenarian's. It's not how "old" the calendar says you are—you're as old as your heart, arteries, and other essential organs.

Physically we mature between ages 25 and 30, when the body reaches its maximum stature and strength. Up to this time, body tissues and cells have constantly rebuilt and renewed themselves. From age 30 on, nutrition, rest, exercise, and stress influence the length of time your body maintains a balance between wearing down and building up. This happens at various intervals. For instance, your vision may be sharpest at age 25, but your eye loses its ability to focus rapidly after age 40. Your hearing may be sharpest at about age 10; then it diminishes as you grow older. Your sensitivity to taste and smell lessen after age 60. There's a decline in strength and agility,

17

although it is slow and gradual and even includes some gratifying plateaus. At age 50 a man still has four fifths of the muscle strength he had when he was 25. And as you grow older, what you want to do depends less on physical strength and more on skilled muscular action.

Your mind actually improves during the middle and later years. For example, some years ago, Dr. William A. Owens, Jr., a psychologist at Iowa State College, compared mental-ability scores of middle-aged men to the scores they had as college freshmen and found that the new scores were higher on general-information quizzes as well as on tests requiring practical judgment. And at Columbia Teacher's College, Dr. Irving Lorge found that people in their seventies could learn Russian and shorthand as easily as their younger classmates.

Doctors tell me that the reason more people don't live longer and better is that they aren't willing to follow a program of diet, exercise, rest, and recreation—coupled with moderation. Perhaps we should all heed the wisdom of those who lived to be 100 years old and more: they ate simple but well-balanced meals (just enough food to keep living); they maintained their own pace of daily activities (kept busy without hurrying or straining); they took care of themselves when ill and rested when tired.

LIVING LONGER AND ENJOYING IT MORE

Ben Franklin once said: "All would live long but none would be old." We die because our body cells lose their ability to reproduce and because the connective tissues that hold our organs together lose some of their natural elasticity. The body thus loses some of its reserve to fight off the degenerative diseases that finally kill us—heart disease, cancer, atherosclerosis, hypertension.

We seem to have a biological clock ticking inside us that tells how long we're going to live. Statistics show that women tend to live three to eight years longer than men; offspring from young mothers tend to have a better chance for long life; blacks aged 70 and over have a better chance of longevity than whites; long life tends to run in families. If all four of your grandparents lived to be more than 80, you're likely to live until about age 90 or older.

Ancestry seems to play a part. Studies show that persons from Northern European stock have a longer life expectancy than those with Middle or Southern European ancestry. The Swedes have the longest life expectancy, followed by the Norwegians, Dutch, Icelanders, and Danes. The British and Germans also tend to live long. (Interestingly enough, in the United States people of Scandinavian or Northern European ancestry, inhabiting the coldest parts of the country—Nebraska, North and South Dakota, Minnesota, and so on—lived longest.)

The late Dr. Stephen Jewett, professor emeritus of the Department of Psychiatry, New York Medical College, found these other common characteristics among long-living people: they were married, enjoyed a good sex life, were of average height, had superior native intelligence, were calm and relaxed, were either self-employed or enjoyed a great deal of independence and freedom, enjoyed life without artificial stimulation, were adaptable and open-minded about religion, were moderate eaters and sleepers, and drank and smoked moderately.

As for occupations, the Metropolitan Life Insurance Company analyzed the mortality rates of prominent men over age 45 and found that the best record for longevity was held by scientists, with college professors, administrators, and clergymen next. Military officials and artists, illustrators, and sculptors had mortality rates just below the average.

The worst longevity rates—with mortality rates twice as high as all the rest—were held by correspondents and journalists. Editors, authors, writers, critics, and historians were not as bad, but their mortality rate, as a group, was nearly 30 percent higher than the average. Government officials were nearly 20 percent higher than the average; physicians and surgeons had a death rate about 10 percent higher; business executives and lawyers were close to average.

What Factors Threaten Longer Life?

Dr. Bernard Cohen of the University of Pittsburgh has developed these "risk factors," which tend to shorten life expectancy (LER = Life Expectancy Reductions) by the number of days indicated and threaten longevity.

ACTIVITY OR RISK	DAYS LER	ACTIVITY OR RISK	DAYS LER
being unmarried	2000	grade school dropout	800
cigarette smoking	1600	unskilled laborer	700
30 lb. overweight	900	diet drinks	2

Increasingly computers are being used to appraise health hazards. Participants list their habits on questionnaires and note the presence or absence of certain physical abnormalities and mental attitudes. Then a computer compares the responses with the health status of others of the same age and sex and predicts the risk of the individual becoming seriously ill or dying of various ailments.

You can get *Health Risk Appraisals: An Inventory,* which summarizes 29 appraisal services offered by state and local health departments, health insurers, private groups, and university medical centers by writing to National Health Information Clearinghouse, P.O. Box 1133, Washington, DC 20013. The list is free.

For $20 to $40 you can get a personal-risk profile computerized by General Health Inc., 1046 Potomac St. NW, Washington, DC 20007 (call toll-free 800/424-2775). The analysis program of the federal Center for Disease Control includes 37 questions that compare your health-risk age with your actual age and tells you how to modify certain health habits. For a free sample profile, a booklet on how to interpret the results, and information on where the program is being offered in your area, write to Charles Althafer, Center for Health Promotion and Education, CDC, Atlanta, GA 30333.

Is Life-Style Linked to Life-Span?

A study of the long life of 7,000 Californians (age 80 and up) revealed that they:

- Get 7 to 8 hours of sleep per night.

- Eat breakfast regularly.

- Don't eat between meals.

- Keep within a few pounds of recommended ideal weight.

- Engage frequently in active sports or exercise.

- Drink moderately or not at all.

- Don't smoke.

And Dr. Robert J. Samp, who conducted a study for the University of Wisconsin of more than 2,000 Americans who lived longer than average, added these factors:

- Accommodate yourself to life's challenges.

- Avoid prolonged stress.

- Develop outside interests.

- Keep working at either paid or volunteer activities.

- Eat and drink sparingly, but with enjoyment.

And, above all, he adds: "Don't fight your enemies; outlive them."

To see how these and other factors affect your chances for a longer, happier life, fill in the quiz below. Part I of the quiz is designed to help you know yourself, your inherited strengths and weaknesses better. This information plus your own personal health records will help your doctor give you the best possible advice and guidance.

Part II is designed to help you evaluate your daily habits and attitudes. Rejoice in the pluses and let the minuses lead you to an improved life-style. You—and only you—can add more life to your years and more years to your life.

Note: respond *only* to those statements that apply most nearly to your situation.

		+	−
• *Heredity*			
1. For each parent or grandparent who lived to age 80	+3	___	___
2. For each parent or grandparent who lived to age 70	+2	___	___
3. For each parent or grandparent who lived to age 60	+1	___	___
4. For each parent or grandparent who died (not including deaths caused by accident, war, etc.) before age 50	−3	___	___
5. For each parent or grandparent who died before age 60	−2	___	___
6. For each parent or grandparent whose cause of death and age at time of death, except accidental, you do not know	−3	___	___
TOTALS		___	___
• *Family Health History*		+	−
1. Two or more immediate relatives (parents, grandparents, brothers, sisters) with a history of heart disease	−3	___	___
2. One immediate relative with heart disease	−1	___	___
3. No history of heart disease	+3	___	___
4. Two or more immediate relatives with a history of cancer	−3	___	___
5. One immediate relative with a history of cancer	−1	___	___
6. No family history of cancer	+3	___	___
7. Two or more immediate relatives with a history of diabetes	−3	___	___
8. One member of immediate family with diabetes	−1	___	___
9. No family history of diabetes	+3	___	___
10. Two or more immediate relatives with a history of high blood pressure	−3	___	___

		+	−
11. One member of immediate family with a history of high blood pressure	−1	___	___
12. No family history of high blood pressure	+3	___	___
13. Two or more immediate relatives with a history of chronic respiratory diseases	−3	___	___
14. One member of immediate family with a history of chronic respiratory disease	−1	___	___
15. No family history of respiratory diseases	+3	___	___
TOTALS		___	___

Score

Plus score in Heredity and in Health History, you are most fortunate.

Minus score in Heredity, as we said earlier, much progress has been made and there is much you can do to add years to your life.

Minus score in Health History, forewarned is forearmed; these are the areas in which you should exercise the most care. Let your doctor know, too.

Be sure your children have a record of the family health history, too.

Now take Part II of the quiz to see how you can improve your health habits to make the most of your retirement years.

		+	−
● Exercise			
1. One hour daily (or at least 6 days a week) of brisk walking, swimming, volley ball, bicycling, tennis, dancing	+3	___	___
2. Three or more hours daily of moderate exercise such as gardening, golf, household chores, etc.	+3	___	___
3. Both of above	+3	___	___
4. Half of either of above	+1	___	___
5. Half of both	+2	___	___
6. Sedentary	−3	___	___
● Proper Rest		+	−
1. Normally sleep 6–8 hours per day (total)	+3	___	___
2. Siesta as part of total	+2	___	___
3. Considerably less than 6 or more than 8 hours per day	−3	___	___
TOTALS		___	___

● *Eating Habits*   +   −

1. Make sure you have the recommended number of servings of food from each of the major food groups every day   +3   ____   ____

2. Often fail to plan meals that include the recommended number of servings of food from each of the major food groups   −3   ____   ____

3. Know what these major food groups are and the recommended number of servings   +3   ____   ____

4. Never consider these food groups when planning meals   −3   ____   ____

5. Watch intake of saturated fats   +3   ____   ____

6. Don't watch intake of saturated fats   −3   ____   ____

7. Watch intake of salt   +3   ____   ____

8. Don't pay attention to how much salt you use in cooking, at the table, or in processed foods   −3   ____   ____

9. Watch how much sugar you consume daily   +3   ____   ____

10. Pay no attention to sugar consumption   −3   ____   ____

11. Read labels on packaging and reject products that contain unnecessary amounts of salts, fats, sugar, and chemical additives   +3   ____   ____

12. Never read the labels   −3   ____   ____

13. Have a sensible meal schedule and eat at about the same time each day most of the time   +3   ____   ____

14. Grab something to eat when you feel like it   −3   ____   ____

15. Eat in a pleasant atmosphere   +1   ____   ____

16. Have a program of proper dental care so you can enjoy fresh fruits, raw vegetables, and a variety of meats   +3   ____   ____

17. Having neglected proper dental care, eat only soft foods   −3   ____   ____

18. Make it a practice to eat slowly and chew thoroughly   +2   ____   ____

19. Gulp it down as fast as possible   −2   ____   ____

20. Take supplemental vitamins if recommended   +3   ____   ____

21. Eat things you like and keep variety in your diet   +3   ____   ____

22. Just have the same old thing because it's easier   −3   ____   ____

23. Usually have 3 or fewer servings of beverages containing caffeine per day   +3   ____   ____

24. Four or 5 servings of beverages that contain caffeine per day   −1   ____   ____

25. Six or more servings of caffeine beverages daily   −3   ____   ____

		+	−
26.	Never eat "junk food"	+3	___ ___
27.	Eat some "junk food" but watch total consumption	−1	___ ___
28.	Eat lots of "junk food"	−3	___ ___
	TOTALS		___ ___

● *Weight*

		+	−
1.	Most of your life you have been within 5 pounds of your ideal weight	+3	___ ___
2.	For the last 5 years you have been within 5 pounds of ideal weight	+2	___ ___
3.	More than 10 pounds from ideal weight	−1	___ ___
4.	More than 20 pounds from ideal weight	−3	___ ___
5.	Check weight regularly	+1	___ ___
	TOTALS		

● *Alcoholic Beverages*

		+	−
1.	Usually have one or two drinks a day	+3	___ ___
2.	Average 3 a day	−2	___ ___
3.	Usually have 4 or more	−3	___ ___
4.	Never touch a drop	−1	___ ___
	TOTALS		___ ___

● *Smoking*

		+	−
1.	No smoking for the last 6 years or more	+3	___ ___
2.	One pack, low tar, low nicotine, or less daily	−1	___ ___
3.	Two packs, low tar, low nicotine, daily	−2	___ ___
4.	One pack or less regular cigarettes	−2	___ ___
5.	Two or more packs regular cigarettes daily	−3	___ ___
6.	Smoke a pipe only	−1	___ ___
7.	Cigars, no more than 6 a day	−1	___ ___
8.	Seven or more cigars daily	−2	___ ___
	TOTALS		___ ___

● *Safety*   +   –
1. Home maintained with an eye to safety, uncluttered halls, handrails on stairs, etc. +3 ____ ____

2. Proper lighting and ventilation with refreshingly cool, comfortable temperature +3 ____ ____

3. Haven't given home a safety check in years −3 ____ ____

4. Always use seat belts when driving or riding in a car +3 ____ ____

5. Sometimes use seat belts +1 ____ ____

6. Never use seat belts −3 ____ ____

7. Drive a car after taking drugs or other medications −3 ____ ____

8. Drive a car after drinking −3 ____ ____

9. Never drive after taking drugs or other medications +3 ____ ____

10. Never drive after drinking +3 ____ ____

      TOTALS

● *Mental Health*   +   –
1. Live with family or friend(s) +3 ____ ____

2. Live alone with a pet +3 ____ ____

3. Live alone, but with daily in-person contact with family and friends +2 ____ ____

4. Live alone, have little personal contact with others −3 ____ ____

5. Have a variety of activities and interests +3 ____ ____

6. Keep adding new interests and making new friends +3 ____ ____

7. Haven't added any new activities, interests or friends in the last year −3 ____ ____

8. Have a full- or part-time paid or voluntary occupation +3 ____ ____

9. Have no outside responsibilities −3 ____ ____

10. Have a feeling of self-respect, self-worth, and that you are important to others +3 ____ ____

11. Feel that nobody needs you −3 ____ ____

12. Sense of humor +3 ____ ____

13. Usually optimistic +3 ____ ____

14. Like people +3 ____ ____

15. Enjoy a little flirtation once in a while +3 ____ ____

		+	−
16. Often depressed, sad, have crying spells	−3	___	___
17. Often bored	−3	___	___
18. Usually watch television more than 4 hours per day	−3	___	___
19. Occupation causes stress	−3	___	___
20. Other conditions cause stress	−2	___	___
21. Major change in life-style	−3	___	___
22. Loss of close tie	−3	___	___
23. Trouble with any "authority"	−3	___	___
24. Satisfied with life-style	+3	___	___
25. Balance work with play	+3	___	___
26. Change what we can, accept what we can't change	+3	___	___
27. Have a live-and-let-live attitude	+3	___	___
28. Often do something nice for someone	+3	___	___
29. Often do something nice for yourself	+3	___	___
30. Often tense, worried, have feelings of guilt or failure	−3	___	___
31. Rarely have feelings of guilt or failure	+3	___	___
TOTALS		___	___

● *Doctors*

		+	−
1. Visit doctor about any problems that arise and have complete checkups periodically	+3	___	___
2. Visit doctor only when ill	−2	___	___
3. Visit dentist at least annually	+3	___	___
4. Visit dentist only when in pain	−3	___	___
5. Have eyes checked, including glaucoma test, annually	+3	___	___
6. Fail to have eyes checked	−3	___	___
7. Have hearing checked periodically	+3	___	___
8. Fail to have hearing checked	−3	___	___
9. Take good care of feet, including proper shoes	+3	___	___

		+	−
10.	Remember your posture	+3	—— ——
11.	Take good care of skin	+3	—— ——
12.	Get recommended immunizations	+3	—— ——
13.	Know the 7 danger signs of cancer and watch for them	+3	—— ——
14.	Be aware of physical changes and check them if they persist	+3	—— ——
15.	If you have any doubts, get a second opinion	+3	—— ——
16.	Ignore doctor's orders if you don't like them	−3	—— ——
17.	Ignore symptoms and hope they'll go away	−3	—— ——
	TOTALS		—— ——

		+	−
	● *Costs*		
1.	Have a reasonable amount of insurance coverage	+3	—— ——
2.	Make a list of things to ask your doctor before your visit to get the most from your appointment	+2	—— ——
3.	Ask for generic drugs where possible	+3	—— ——
4.	Ask to have expiration date put on label of all prescriptions and check for and discard expired medicines regularly	+3	—— ——
5.	Take advantage of free screenings and tests	+3	—— ——
6.	Substitute good food and exercise for drugs as much as possible	+3	—— ——
7.	Believe that preventive medicine costs less and does more, and live accordingly	+3	—— ——
	TOTALS		—— ——

Scoring

125 and over	Excellent: keep up the good work.
100–124	Good: review for ideas you can use
75–100	Fair: room for improvement, check your minus scores to see where
74 or less	Poor: make a list of your minus scores and start today to improve your life-style.

REPORT DEBUNKS THE MYTHS OF AGING

The National Institute of Aging has published findings of the Gerontology Research Center that debunk some old medical ideas:

■ While obviously a health hazard, obesity has consistently been somewhat overrated as a life-shortening factor. There also appears to be a large gray area in the correlation between obesity and diabetes, and especially in the standards for the diagnosis of diabetes.

■ More than any age group, old people use day-dreaming as a mechanism for solving day-to-day problems. They retain a sense of optimism, a strong ability to cope, and remarkably stable personality traits.

■ In lung tests, people who smoke appear to be 10 years older than they really are. Two years after quitting, however, their lungs recover and register near normal.

■ Healthy older men maintain their production of sex hormones at levels found in younger men and some of them continue to enjoy active sex lives well into old age. Some older men, however, lose interest in sex. As far as the researchers can tell, it isn't a physical problem.

AN OUNCE OF PREVENTION

. . . is worth at least a dollar of cure. Adults age 65 and over spend *three times* ($2,400 a year versus $800) what adults 19 to 64 spend on medical bills. Even with Medicare the out-of-pocket expense is great: Medicare pays *only about 40 percent* of the elderly person's medical bill (75 percent of the average hospital bill, 55 percent of physician's bills, 3 percent for home health care, 3 percent for nursing homes). And as health-care costs are rising about *three times* faster than the average consumer price index, the average medical bill for the elderly is estimated to rise to some $5,000 annually in 1985.

The sad part is that a study of hospital patients by Massachusetts General Hospital shows that *three out of five* patients could have stayed out of the hospital and healthy if they had followed the "ounce-of-prevention" adage. Prevention and detection become all the more important as we grow older, as we're more likely to develop *internal illnesses* that become chronic and disabling rather than external illnesses that heal more quickly. And although a *complete* annual check isn't necessary in most cases (see section on cutting health-care costs), it does pay to know when to see a doctor.

What If You Don't Have a Doctor?

If you've moved recently or must find a new doctor, telephone your county medical society and ask if their listings include internists who specialize in geriatrics (the medical science of aging). Another way to find a good doctor is to call a nearby medical school or accredited hospital (preferably one affiliated with a local university medical school) and ask for a list of internists or general practitioners who are on its staff as attending physicians. Generally, the best doctors are affiliated with accredited hospitals and medical schools in a teaching, consulting, or other staff capacity.

You could also find a doctor through the American Academy of Family Physicians. Write to them at 1740 West 92nd St., Kansas City, MO 64114, and ask for a list of members in your area.

An alternative to finding a private doctor is to seek out a group medical practice in which specialists pool their talents and expensive equipment and offer a group rate. Some group plans are affiliated with the American Group Practice Association, P.O. Box 949, Alexandria, VA 22313. You might also investigate Health Maintenance Organizations (HMOs), which emphasize *preventive medicine.* No two HMOs work alike, but to join one, you sign up with a participating health insurer (Blue Cross or other health insurance company) and pay a monthly premium. Almost all HMOs have arrangements with Medicare to receive payment for covered services.

You don't necessarily pay less for HMO coverage, but you tend to use the services more. Drug bills at HMOs range between 25 and 30 percent less than at neighborhood pharmacies. And a before-and-after study of 1,000 Medicaid patients enrolled in an HMO showed that hospital admissions were reduced 30 percent, days in the hospital, 32 percent, and visits to doctors, 15 percent. *The average patient saved 21 percent by being enrolled in the HMO.* If you can't locate an HMO near you, write HMO Program, 12420 Parklawn Dr., Rockville, MD 20857.

Once you've signed up with a doctor (in private or group practice) *discuss fees*—many doctors tailor their bills to what they think the patient can afford. And if you're enrolled under Medicare, find doctors who *accept Medicare assignments.* That means they'll accept 80 percent of the prevailing rates set by Medicare for services in their area. If they don't accept Medicare assignments, Medicare will pay you only 80 percent of the prevailing rates, and you must pay any excess that the doctor chooses to bill you for.

What to Tell Your Doctor

Be completely frank with your doctor, answer questions as directly as possible, and give all the information that might be helpful. Mention any drugs you might be taking—including tranquilizers, aspirin, and sleeping tablets or aids. Mixing drugs (even prescription ones) is dangerous; sleeping tablets or aids when mixed with alcohol will make you a lot drunker or sleepier; aspirin may decrease the effectiveness of some antigout pills; nose drops may counteract drugs taken to lower blood pressure; and laxatives, vitamin pills, and antacid pills may be dangerous unless prescribed.

When you get instructions from the doctor, make sure you understand them and follow them. Hopefully, by following this advice, you'll stay healthy and well. However, if you are home and feel ill, call your doctor when:

- Symptoms are too severe to endure.

- Apparently minor symptoms persist for more than a few days.

- Symptoms return repeatedly.

- In doubt.

Summed up: Call the doctor when there's *severity . . . persistence . . . repetition . . . doubt.*

HOW TO KEEP YOUR BODY TUNED UP

Physically, your body should be like a well-tuned and broken-in car. It should be running smoothly, with plenty of passing power and cruising miles left. Some of us may have reached a certain milestone with most parts functioning smoothly; others may have a bit of carbon in the valves. But whatever the condition of the physical machine at checkup time, there's something you can do to improve it—and a lot you can do to smooth the rest of the journey.

That Suit of Armor That Protects You from Within and Without

Your skin tells more about your "age" than your birth certificate. Your skin is an organ—like your heart and liver—that protects you from external disease and hazards while sealing in the vital fluids you need to keep living. Skin changes not only alter your appearance but could signal internal health warnings, so it's important to know how to take care of your skin for both appearance and health's sake.

WHAT'S NORMAL. As we grow older, the oil and sweat glands slow down, causing the skin to become dry, wrinkle, and itch. The skin may lack some of its former elasticity and tone, causing us to sag in places and look "older." "Liver spots" tiny red tags, and donut-shaped or oval growths may also appear. However, age itself doesn't age skin. Among prime agers: exposure to sunlight and weather and hereditary and racial characteristics.

WHAT'S NOT NORMAL. The growths mentioned above are benign (harmless). But as we grow older, we're more susceptible to malignant growths like cancer. *Basal cell cancer* starts with a small fleshy nodule, usually on the face. It may take several months to reach one-half to one inch in diameter, but in about a year it begins to ulcerate and bleed. Then it forms a crust, which it sheds at intervals, leaving another ulcer. If you notice anything like this, see your doctor, as he can usually remove the ulcer with a local operation.

SQUAMOUS CELL CANCER lesions may appear on the lips, mouth, and genitalia, and they tend to spread and increase in size. Horny growths in exposed areas—face, ears, neck, and scalp—may be forerunners of squamous cell cancer. Again, your doctor can treat and operate effectively.

MALIGNANT MELANOMA, a dangerous form of skin cancer, is usually preceded by a small, flat brown or black spot on the skin that enlarges, bleeds, ulcerates, or darkens. While commonly referred to as "moles," if they become malignant, chances for survival after five years tumble depressingly. Most common sites for malignant moles are on the palms, soles of the feet, and genitals.

What can you do to protect your skin:

■ *Stay out of the sun.* Even small amounts of sun may make your skin look leathery, thick, and wrinkled. And sun may be the prime cause of the above skin cancers. The more sunbathing you do, the sooner your skin may become aged and cancer-prone. If you must sunbathe, try to find sunscreen solutions containing pure PABA (para-aminobenzoic acid) that dry quickly and leave a clear film on the skin that screens out harmful ultraviolet rays.

■ *Don't wash too often,* especially with harsh soaps or detergents that remove the skin's natural film and cause it to dry. The production of natural body oils decreases with age; *don't* bathe daily, and when you do bathe, use bath oil or apply a body lotion afterward.

■ *Replace some of the lost oils* by using emollient creams. Women should use makeup that contains a balance of pigment and cream. Fortunately, the makeup that feels and looks best is probably the best for you. Both men and women can use nonallergenic *cover-all creams* that mask mild skin disfigurements and blemishes. Pay particular attention to the area around the eyes—

this area tends to sag and wrinkle more quickly than the rest of the face and is among the first to show signs of aging.

Protecting Your Precious Vision

Although it's *normal* for eyesight to diminish after age 40, my eyes started bothering me even before then (when the eye usually loses its elasticity and ability, especially for close work). I started to see halos around lights, and my vision blurred; I was in danger of going blind.

WHAT'S NOT NORMAL. If, like me, you have had any sudden change in vision, need frequent changes of glasses, have loss of side vision or blurred or foggy vision, you may be in trouble.

At least one in 50 persons over age 40 has *glaucoma* (pressure within the eye interfering with blood vessels and nerve fibers) like me, and at least one million others have it and don't know it. Chronic glaucoma is called the "thief that steals in the night." Acute glaucoma develops suddenly, with severe pain and reduced vision; the most common kind, chronic glaucoma (which I have) steals upon you so gradually that you may suffer permanent loss of vision before you're aware of it. Once detected, your doctor can prescribe eye drops that reduce the pressure and check the disease. My problem was caught so early that I haven't suffered any vision loss, and my eyes are better than those of most persons my age. Instead of regular glasses I just use simple magnifying spectacles.

When General Douglas MacArthur made his famous "Old Soldiers Never Die" speech before Congress, he demonstrated his "youth" by removing his glasses when reading his text. What many people didn't realize was that this suddenly "improved" vision occurs just before the eye becomes cloudy with *cataracts.* Cataracts develop when the protein molecules in the lens degenerate, causing the lens to get cloudy. If the clouding is slight and doesn't interfere with vision, the doctor may not need to operate. Until a few years ago, doctors removed the lens of the eye to remove the cataract. Now they can insert a tiny needle into the eye to clean out the degenerated protein without removing the lens capsule, or they may insert a plastic lens to replace the diseased one. Such surgery is safe and effective at least 95 percent of the time.

If you suspect any eye trouble, go first to an *ophthalmologist*—a medical doctor (look for the M.D. after his name)—who is qualified to treat and operate on eyes and to prescribe proper lenses for glasses. An *optometrist* is a licensed, nonmedical practitioner who examines eyes and sells and fits glasses but cannot treat diseases of the eye. An *optician* sells and fits glasses usually from the prescription of the ophthalmologist.

What you can do to prevent eye trouble:

■ *Keep clean.* Dirty hands or towels carry germs that can cause eye infections.

■ *Get enough sleep and rest.* When you're tired, your eyes suffer; when you do too much close work, you strain your eyes. Rest them for a moment by focusing on a distant object.

■ *Use good reading habits.* Place a lamp with at least a 100-watt bulb slightly to the back and to one side. Angle the light to avoid glare.

For further information you can contact these organizations: National Association for the Visually Handicapped, 305 East 24th St., New York, NY 10010; American Foundation for the Blind, 15 West 16th St., New York, NY 10011; Library of Congress Services for the Blind, 1291 Taylor St. NW, Washington, DC 20542.

Help for the Hard of Hearing

Samuel Jackson, age 52, started finding it hard to follow a group conversation or one in a noisy background. He also had difficulty understanding words with an *s* or *th* sound.

Sam, like most people over 50, was experiencing some hearing loss— usually starting with high-pitched sounds. This loss happens first to those exposed to noise, but sooner or later all of us will experience some hearing trouble.

WHAT'S NORMAL: Some hearing loss may be caused by wax, diseases of the eardrum, and abnormalities such as *otosclerosis*, a bony growth that may close the "window" to the inner ear. An ear doctor (otologist) can treat these conditions by removing wax from the ear, repairing or replacing eardrums, removing bony growths, and loosening or removing fixed ear bones.

WHAT'S NOT NORMAL: Disease, drugs, blows, and falls may cause *nerve defects* that are harder if not impossible to cure. An operation or a hearing aid may be effective in some cases, but if you need a hearing aid, make sure your doctor refers you to a nonprofit hearing clinic (see below) where you are fitted individually. A recent National Institutes of Health survey showed that most older persons who bought hearing aids directly from dealers rather than through a hearing clinic soon discontinued using them.

What you can do to prevent hearing loss:

- *"Don't stick anything smaller* than your elbow in your ear" is a good rule of thumb, but if you must remove wax from the opening of the ear canal, use a cotton applicator.

- *Stay away from noise.* Anything over 90 decibels is dangerous: jackhammers, jet airplanes, rock-and-roll bands.

- *Get your hearing checked* if people seem to be mumbling, or if you find it harder to understand words with an *s* or *th* sound.

For the address of speech and hearing center nearest you, write the American Speech-Language-Hearing Association, 10801 Rockville Pike, Rockville, MD 20852. Other sources of information include the American Council of Otolaryngology, Suite 602, 1100 17th St. NW, Washington, DC 20036; the National Institute of Neurological and Communicative Disorders and Strokes, Rm. 8A-06, Bldg. 31, Bethesda, MD 20205; Better Hearing Institute, 1430 K St. NW, Washington, DC 20005. For information on hearing aids, you can send for a free copy of the booklet *Hearing Aids* by writing to Consumer Information Center, Dept. 582J, Pueblo, CO 81009. Also contact Office of Consumer Affairs, FDA, 5600 Fishers Lane, Rockville, MD 20857.

"Your Aching Back" Isn't Funny

If you're *not* one of the 70 million persons who have suffered severe back pain, you may be next. Almost all of us who are middle aged and older have suffered from this wrenching pain; 7 million people are hobbling around right now with this problem, 2 million more join the "ranks" each year. I've thrown out my back four times, each time because I lifted something the wrong way. What I and countless others haven't realized is that man really shouldn't be standing. Nature intended us to walk on all fours, and by middle age our back muscles, forced into this unnatural posture and weakened by inactivity and normal wear and tear, begin to complain.

WHAT'S NORMAL. Dull aches and pains—especially upon rising in the morning—aren't unusual because your joints are stiff from lying still. Obesity, tumors, arthritis, tension, anxiety, and depression add pressure and pain to the back. As we grow older, the water content of the gelatinous matter of the shock-absorbing disks of the back falls from about 88 percent water to about 70 percent and loses much of its compressibility, rendering the back more susceptible to strain. We also tend to become narrower in the shoulders and wider in the waist, causing extra strain on the back.

WHAT'S NOT NORMAL. You can "slip" your disk (actually, it ruptures or herniates) in over 100 ways—usually by lifting something the wrong way. When this happens, the ruptured-disk material bulges, exerting pressure on the nerves and triggering severe pains in the lower back and down to the toes. Nature "splints" the back by throwing muscles into spasms—this hurts, but it helps. If the pain is so severe that you can't or don't dare move, it's best to get into bed and have a bed board placed under the mattress to help support your back. A jigger of your favorite pain-killer might help, as might aspirin, heat (from a heating pad or hot bath), and gentle massage. After about three days you should be able to hobble around, especially if you use your arms to take pressure off your legs and back. Your doctor can't do much for a slipped disk except offer sympathy and perhaps administer a pain-killer or muscle relaxant such as ethyl chloride, often given to athletes. Only as a last resort is he likely to operate.

What you can do to prevent back trouble:

■ *Exercise is your best prevention*—especially swimming and walking. Also try some special exercises to strengthen your back muscles. When sitting, pull in your stomach and buttock muscles. Or lie on your back on the floor. Squeeze buttocks together and tighten abdominal muscles while flattening back against the floor. Hold position a few seconds, then relax. Stretching and crawling also strengthen back muscles, and some YMCAs around the country offer special back exercises.

■ *Be careful how you lift.* Use your leg muscles (stronger than back muscles) by placing your feet close to the base of the object, bending your knees outward, and pushing up with your legs. Use your arms to lift yourself out of a chair or bed. When you lift something, keep it close to your body. The farther away the object, the greater the strain on your back.

■ *Sit and stand erect.* An "easy" chair exerts the greatest pressure on your spine; standing produces twice as much pressure as lying down. For least pressure, lie flat on your back, your knees propped up. When sitting, prefer a straight-backed chair to keep your back erect. Reclining chairs that keep your legs propped up also help. Don't sit in any one position too long; when you're on a long auto, plane, or train ride, get up every half hour or so to stretch and take pressure off your back.

One consolation about growing older: Your spine stiffens, making it harder to bend over—but protecting your back.

Your Feet May Be Killing You

The next time someone says, "My feet are killing me," he may be right. Your feet are farthest from the center of your blood supply, and circulatory diseases as well as arthritis and diabetes often show up first in the feet.

WHAT'S NORMAL. Although it isn't unusual if your feet hurt after a hard day of standing and walking, don't accept such aches and pains as "normal." Find out if the pain is a sign of some ailment. Untreated foot problems could cause headaches, fatigue, lower-back and shoulder pain.

WHAT'S NOT NORMAL. Warning signs of serious foot disorders include continued cramping of the calf muscles, pain in the arch and toes, and unusually cold feet—especially if the skin is bluish. Brittle or thickened toenails or burning, tingling, and numbness may also signal circulatory disease or internal illness.

Diabetes may first show up as a foot ulcer. Arthritis can cause bunions and swollen, tender, and red joints in the foot. Heart disorders may cause swelling of the feet and ankles.

Ill-fitting shoes probably cause most foot problems. Avoid pumps, high heels, and narrow shoes. The best shoe is moderately broad across the instep, has a straight inner border, and a moderately low heel. Shoes should extend one half to three quarters of an inch beyond the longest toe, *Don't buy shoes in the morning*; feet swell during the day, and the shoe that fits in the morning will be too tight at night.

How you can prevent foot problems:

■ *Bathe feet with warm—not hot—water.* Dry thoroughly, especially between the toes. If the skin is dry or scaly, lubricate with lanolin or olive oil. Medicated powder is also helpful, but avoid commercial preparations containing harsh chemicals.

■ *Trim toenails straight across and not too short.*

■ *Keep your feet warm and dry.* Wear a pair of heavy woolen socks if your feet are cold.

■ *See a podiatrist* (foot doctor) if you experience any unusual problems. Most foot problems are "covered conditions" under Medicare except for

"routine foot care and the treatment of flat feet, sprains, or partial disloca-
tions."

■ *For further information*: American Podiatry Association, 20 Chevy Chase
Circle NW, Washington, DC 20015.

How to Keep Your Teeth Smiling

Every time I've *not* seen my dentist "at least twice a year" it's cost me
money. Until my mid-thirties, cavities multiplied as the weeks went by. Now
it's periodontal disease—pyorrhea—that affects my gums and bones, causing
extensive damage if I don't have my teeth cleaned every six months (although
I brush them after every meal).

WHAT'S NORMAL. By age 65, about one half the population have no
natural teeth. After age 50, over half of us have some form of periodontal
disease; by age 65 almost all of us have pyorrhea.

Periodontal disease begins when a sticky film called dental "plaque"
forms on the teeth. Soft at first, this deposit soon hardens into a cementlike
crust (calculus) that becomes a breeding ground for many bacteria. If not
removed, the bacteria-laden crust irritates the gums, causing them to become
red and swollen and bleed when you brush your teeth. Should you not treat
the inflammation (gingivitis), it spreads along the roots, and the gums
separate from the teeth to form pockets that fill up with more food particles
and bacteria. As the disease progresses, it weakens the bone support for the
teeth; the affected teeth begin to loosen and drift from their normal position;
and finally—unless the disease is treated in time—the teeth must be removed.

WHAT'S NOT NORMAL. It's not normal or usually necessary to remove
your teeth; prevent periodontal disease and avoid dentists who want to pull
all your teeth. Once you lose a tooth, other teeth begin to loosen and drift.
Above all, before having teeth pulled, consult an *independent* exodontist who
specializes in extractions.

How to prevent teeth problems:

■ *Brush after every meal.* Use a soft brush, brushing at a 45-degree angle to
"vibrate" along the gum lines. To make sure you brush effectively, buy
"disclosing tablets" that show where you've missed. If your toothbrush isn't
doing the job (a good cleaning will wear out a brush in about a month), use
unwaxed dental floss. Brush your tongue, too; it harbors tooth-decaying

bacteria. A saltwater rinse helps retard bacteria growth and toughens raw gums.

■ *Use fluoride tooth paste* to strengthen tooth enamel and drink fluoridated water to reduce tooth decay. Fluoride also strengthens bones.

■ *See your dentist at least twice a year* to have your teeth cleaned and x-rayed. If you lose a tooth, replace it promptly so adjacent teeth won't drift.

■ *If you need to find a dentist*, get names from your family physician or from the faculty of a nearby university school of dentistry. Avoid dentists not willing to provide emergency care and discuss fees. Check to see if your insurance covers dental care; insurance may be expensive, but it could save money in the long run.

■ *For further information*: American Dental Association, 211 E. Chicago Ave., Chicago, IL 60611

Sexual Activity: A Case of Mind over Matter

In my earlier book *The Fires of Autumn: Sexual Activity in the Middle and Later Years*, I exploded some myths and explored some truths about sexual activity after age 45. Among my findings:

■ Whatever you do sexually in the middle and later years, it doesn't matter—if you don't mind.

■ Sexuality—how you feel about yourself and others as a man or woman—can shift from sex as a physical activity to sexuality as an emotional experience.

■ The main ingredient for a satisfactory sexual life in the later years is reasonably good health and a willing and available partner. There's nothing physically that happens to cause you to lose interest in sex. While it may take a middle-aged man longer to get an erection, he usually has more control over his eventual ejaculation than when he was younger. And if an older man has sex only when he really *wants* to, he can keep on indefinitely. While it may take longer for an older woman to secrete vaginal lubrication, adequate sexual foreplay brings it on. And although orgasms may be shorter and less frequent, they're still satisfying.

Interestingly enough, my surveys reveal that 15 percent of older women actually show *increased* sexual interest as they grow older. I found only one woman who stopped having sex because *she* had lost interest; most women stop because the man becomes ill, loses interest, or becomes impotent.

Why might men lose sexual interest as they grow older? The causes I found were: (1) monotonous sexual relations; (2) preoccupation with the job; (3) mental and physical fatigue; (4) too much food and drink (Shakespeare said: "Too much drink provokes the desire but takes away the performance"); (5) physical handicaps and illnesses; (6) fear of failure (or pressure to perform).

The menopause, now happening to most women around age 50, is *not* the end but often the beginning of sexual activity and freedom for most women. Although 50 percent may suffer hot flashes and other symptoms during menopause, these usually bother only those women who have nothing else to think about. Estrogen therapy and creams can supply lubrication to dry skin and mucus membranes and improve vaginal lubrication, but consult your gynecologist or doctor about what's best for you.

While men may go through some sort of "psychological menopause" in middle age, nothing physical happens to hamper their ability to perform.

Physical changes (operations) in or around the sex organs may hamper sexual activity. Some women who have had hysterectomies may feel (or their husbands make them feel) "desexed" or like mere "shells of women." But in many instances, it can be like taking out the nursery and leaving in the playpen. Many men over age 50 complain of prostate problems, but this is often controlled by drugs and massage. Refined techniques make prostate surgery neither more nor less dangerous than other types of surgery.

Other findings I reported:

■ The sexier you are when younger, the sexier you'll be when older. Sex keeps hormone levels up; an occasional orgasm or ejaculation is like sipping at the Fountain of Youth.

■ Neither ejaculation nor orgasm depletes the body. Emission of semen is no more a loss than the loss of saliva. Before semen is discharged, it has been stored and is out of circulation. Once discharged, it is quickly replaced. And studies by Masters and Johnson show that women can have as many as 50 orgasms an hour without becoming satiated.

■ Simultaneous orgasms are nice but not necessary. Women are capable of multiple orgasms and should have several before the man has his "grande finale." Also, a woman has an orgasm usually because the *clitoris* has been stimulated sufficiently, not just because of vaginal penetration.

■ There's no such thing as the "ideal" sexual position. The penis rarely comes in contact with the clitoris. Thus, various positions recommended to increase penile contact are superfluous or impossible. The "female on top" and the side-by-side position, however, do offer more clitoral stimulation than other positions.

■ Ideally, both partners should be relaxed and physically ready for the act. Many older couples find that sex is better in the morning when they're refreshed than in the evening when they're more likely to be fatigued. Dr. Adel Ismail of the Endocrinological Research Unit in Edinburgh, Scotland, found that a man's highest sexual hormone levels occur between 4:00 A.M. and noon, while his lowest occur around 8:00 P.M.

■ Masturbation should be tolerated if not "encouraged." Dr. Lester W. Dearborn, marriage consultant, in pointing out the role of masturbation in the lives of the single and widowed says: "It is hoped that those interested in the field of geriatrics will . . . encourage the aging to accept masturbation as a perfectly valid outlet when there is a need and no other means of gratification are available." Medical authorities now agree that masturbation—no matter how frequently practiced—produces no harmful physical effects.

There are many other ways to express our *sexuality* besides physical sex. Some of the most attractive women I interviewed were in their sixties— well-groomed, poised, walking gracefully, and talking softly. Some of the most vital men were retirees who showed their masculinity with gallant gestures—their concern for their loved one—and their neat appearance. By displaying their sexuality, they reached out to others and interchanged "charm" with "sex appeal." They raised the *art* of loving above the *act* of loving.

Dr. Mary S. Calderone, executive director of the Sex Information and Education Council of the United States, told me: "As human beings at any stage of life, we long for other human beings to respond to us and to be responsive with—whether in touch, shared pleasures, joy, sorrows, intellectual interchange, or from time to time in sexual responsiveness at many levels, including the purely physical." She added that these needs include touching, kissing, embracing, and many other forms of verbal and nonverbal sexual communication.

If there's one thing we oldsters can learn from the youngsters it is that displays of affection—words, body contact, touching—are natural forms of communication. If we learn to touch, hold, and stroke for *these pleasures alone*—without other commitments—we will feel freer to signal for more physical activity if that's what we want. Intimacy shouldn't be equated with sex; we should be able to have an intimate relationship without having a sexual one.

Maurice Chevalier once said: "There are ten thousand ways of loving. The main thing is to choose the ones that suit you the best." Whatever you do in the middle and later years, it doesn't matter—if you don't mind. By expressing your sexuality, you'll find that the Fires of Autumn are just as warm as—and a lot more comforting than—the Fires of Spring.

What Happens When One Becomes a Widow or a Widower?

By age 65, a woman might outlive her husband by some 20 years. At present, there are some 147 women over age 65 for every 100 men; widows in the United States outnumber widowers more than four to one.

But whether widowed, divorced, or unmarried, older "singles" have a variety of life-styles open to them. They can move into singles apartments, buy homes and rent out rooms for other singles, live in "foster homes," and even set up communes.

Many widows find new outlets once they have rid themselves of grief and realize that they have more freedom and opportunity than ever before. The key to happiness in your future is to plan for it now. Here are some tips while husband and wife are both alive:

1. *Develop individual interests* so you'll have something to fall back on if you find yourself alone.

2. *Make final arrangements*—including funeral arrangements—wills, all other papers (tax records, Social Security information, insurance policies, investments) organized in a safe place.

3. *List "who gets what"*—besides items passed through wills, personal and household possessions should be tagged or listed so there is no question about who are the recipients.

4. *Know whom to turn to for help.* It could be your spiritual adviser, doctor, lawyer, banker, insurance agent, relative, friend . . . anyone who will help you get over the adjustment period.

Besides community and state resources for widows and widowers, here are some national organizations that can help:

■ The Widowed Persons Service of the National Retired Teachers Association-American Association of Retired Persons (NRTA-AARP), 1909 K St. NW, Washington, DC 20049.

■ Parents Without Partners, 7910 Woodmont Ave., Bethesda, MD 20014, has chapters throughout the country and organizes social events for those who have children.

Some of the largest local groups include:

■ Widow and Widower Outreach Program, Jewish Family Service Agency, 1600 Scott St., San Francisco, CA 94115.

■ Widow/Widower Outreach Program, Ravenswood Hospital Medical Center, 1920 W. Wilson Ave., Chicago, IL 60640.

■ Tulsa Widowed Persons Service, 222 East 5th St., Tulsa, OK 74103.

■ Widows and Widowers Family Service, 470 Mamaroneck Ave., White Plains, NY 10605.

Some good books on the subject include:

■ *Widow* by Lynn Caine (New York: Bantam Books, 1975).

■ *Helping Each Other in Widowhood* by Phyllis Silverman (New York: Health Science Publishing, 1974).

■ *When You're a Widow* by Clarissa Start (St. Louis: Concordia Publishing, 1973).

What Are Successful Ingredients for a Late or Second Marriage?

Dr. Walter C. McKain of the University of Connecticut says the five characteristics to look for in a mate in a late or second marriage are: (1) enthusiasm, (2) ability to accept responsibility, (3) a feeling that the person's life is useful and important, (4) pride in appearance, and (5) a cheerful, optimistic mood. Dr. James Persons, a family counselor and professor emeritus at the Andrus Gerontological Center, University of Southern California, adds: "Talk, talk and more talk. The couple must be bathed in talk. It is the only way to really share a relationship."

Besides communication, Dr. Peterson offers these other guidelines:

1. A couple should know each other well before deciding to marry.
2. It is important that children and friends approve. If children are worried about losing an inheritance, you can solve this with a prenuptial agreement (see "Your Legal Rights and Responsibilities").

3.   A couple should not live in the same house whether either one lived before. The ghosts of former spouses may put too great a strain on the new relationship.

4.   An older widow or widower should not remarry before she or he has completed the grieving process for the former partner. "There must be a growing distance from the spouse who died," says Dr. Peterson.

How Can I Mend Fences with My Children?

You might use approaching retirement as an excuse to write to your children, telling them about your plans. Don't scare them off with the prospect that you might tap them for money, but keep them guessing about how much money you have—or might leave. "Big Daddy" with a mysterious hoard of money is as intriguing to grown children as Santa Claus is to starry-eyed youngsters.

And to help get along with your children, here are some "don'ts":

1.   *Don't try to boss them.* If they want your advice and opinion, they'll ask for it.

2.   *Don't meddle.* Any infringement on privacy should be considered a meddlesome act.

3.   *Don't demand age preference.* Just because you've lived longer than the rest, doesn't mean you get special privileges.

4.   *Don't seek sympathy.* The mother or father who uses "you don't love me" to get sympathy doesn't deserve any.

5.   *Don't talk too much.* Excessive talking—especially about yourself—marks you as a bore at any age.

6.   *Don't harp on the past.* They probably didn't do it better in your day, and the younger generation is interested mainly in the present—and future—*not* the past. As much as you don't owe them anything, they don't owe you anything, either. The best way to treat each other is with mutual respect and admiration—just like people and friends of any age.

THE STATE OF YOUR MIND AFFECTS
THE CONDITION OF YOUR BODY

Plato said: "He who is of a calm and happy nature will hardly feel the pressure of age, but to him who is of an opposite disposition, youth and age are equally a burden." About 100 years ago Mark Twain added: "Whatever a man's age, he can reduce it several years by putting a brightly-colored flower in his buttonhole." To which actress Billie Burke added: "Age doesn't matter unless you're a cheese."

Doctors have long recognized the link between a healthy mind and a healthy body. The American Medical Association (AMA) stated at a White House Conference on Aging that many of the medical ills affecting older people are the product of emotional complications that disturb normal physical processes, intensify diseases, and interfere with healing. The AMA added "Encouraging older persons to assume functioning, valuable roles in the family and community will reduce their emotional problems and improve their general health." Doctors add that extreme emotions cause high blood pressure and strokes; worry brings on ulcers and heart disease; emotions may even form a base for cancer.

One of my neighbors, Samm Sinclair Baker, has written numerous books on health and happiness and has combined the two in a recent book, *Conscious Happiness*. The book is inspiring and informative, especially the chapter "How to Grow Older Enthusiastically, Exultantly, Ecstatically." In this chapter Samm states: "You are as young as your enthusiasms, as old as your disinterest. It's not how old you are but how you are old." Samm adds that you age by deserting your interests, ideas, exertion, and while old age wrinkles the skin, giving up enthusiasms and eagerness for living and participating wrinkles the soul.

A gerontologist, Dr. Robert N. Butler, who wrote the recent *Why Survive? Being Old in America*, found older people seem to regret most what they did *not* do rather than what they did. He adds: "All too many have allowed themselves the kind of identity which has led them to several modes of unsatisfactory coping." He suggests that it is essential that there be greater freedom to rebel against what no longer "fits" and less fixed identity.

We may be perpetuating the myth that "old dogs can't learn new tricks." What we really mean is that we're afraid to compete with youngsters in a youth-worshiping society. But if we have sufficient interest, motives, and self-confidence, we can continue to learn and stimulate our intellects if we really want to—at any age.

For most people, the maximum creative activity takes place during middle age. Painters, architects, musicians, and writers have been most creative in their forties; presidents, college presidents, and popes have all been men past middle age (late fifties to nineties). And the years 45 to 60 can be the time of greatest creative opportunity. We who have adapted to life successfully in middle age have both emotional and mental flexibility that not only allows us to cope with change but to *institute* change.

In middle age we have the opportunities—the necessities—to change with changing conditions. If we're willing to give up old attitudes that don't enhance living, we're ready for change. Enthusiasm, curiosity, and wonder fuel a youthful attitude to living at any age or stage of life.

Stress: It Can Cure or Kill

If you were walking down a railroad track and suddenly saw a train bearing down upon you, your adrenal glands would pump andrenalin into your bloodstream, your heart would start to race, your blood pressure would soar, and you'd leap faster and farther than you ever did before. In short, you'd be reacting to *stress.*

Stress is your body's physical, mental, and chemical reaction to any event or circumstance that frightens, excites, confuses, or endangers you. "Stress isn't a dirty word," says Dr. Richard A. Kern, professor of medicine emeritus, Temple University School of Medicine (Philadelphia, Pennsylvania). "Stresses which can be endured and do not exceed man's power to react are potent factors in building mind and body as well as character. If there hadn't been stresses to overcome, we'd all still be jellyfishes."

Dr. Hans Selye, director of the Institute of Experimental Medicine and Surgery, University of Montreal, calls stress the "spice of life" that makes us work harder and more creatively. However, he emphasizes the need to find the *right kind* of stress for the right length of time and at the level that's best for you. Otherwise, he says, "stress becomes distress, taking its toll on mind and body and probably hastens aging."

Boredom causes stress. It's not uncommon for those of us who are middle-aged and older to want to "call it quits." But Dr. Daniel J. Levinson, Yale University psychologist, feels that we should use this unsettled period to try for something new. He explains: "There's more here than just survival. If you try for the big changes, you may fail miserably. On the other hand, if you don't try for the big changes, you'll feel dead in a few years because you'll be stagnant."

Stagnation, boredom, and other stresses cause or aggravate heart disease, menstrual disorders, migraine headaches, asthma, skin ailments, and all sorts of digestive troubles. Studies have shown that some 60 percent of patients in surgical wards for nonelective surgery were people who had suffered a major stress (loss) within six months prior to surgery. The death rate of widows and widowers is 10 times higher during the first year of bereavement than for others their age. One doctor summed it up: "Fifty percent of all sick people need prayer more than pills, aspiration more than aspirin, meditation more than medication."

All of us are subject to stresses caused by love, hate, biological and physical changes (diminished eyesight and hearing, more sensitive skin, slower reactions), and environmental changes (air pollution and excessive noise); the worst stresses are those over which we have no control, such as the death of a spouse or retirement. Dr. Thomas Holmes, professor of psychiatry at the University of Washington, devised a stress chart in which he ranks stresses according to their impact. Add up your score of stress-related events during the past year; if you've accumulated 200 to 300 stress points, you have a better than even chance of developing a stress-related illness. If you score below 150 you're fairly "safe," but those who exceed 300 stress points are likely to become seriously ill with heart attacks, depression, or disruptive illnesses.

How to Minimize Stress

"Flight" (momentary retreat) is often better than "fight" for stress. *Just doing something* helps minimize the stress, but if there's too much stress on any part of you, you need *diversion*; if there's too much on the whole, you need rest.

Don't wait until you're about to "explode"—you might do something rash that will increase tension. Diversion prevents explosions. One study of persons hospitalized because of mental disorders showed that 57 percent had no planned recreation or creative activities during the year prior to hospitalization. In contrast, only 10 percent of well-adjusted subjects had no purposeful activities. Rest generally eases stress because human beings, like automobile tires, last longer when they wear evenly over a long period of time. So try a change of pace or a change of scene.

Learn to recognize when you're tense, and learn how to relax. Sit on the edge of a straight wooden chair, your knees about 12 inches apart, your legs slanting 6 to 12 inches in front of the chair. Sit up very straight, then let yourself collapse like a rag doll, your head forward, your spine rounded, your hands coming to rest on your knees. Then say to yourself: "My right arm is heavy, my right arm is heavy . . ." Repeat this for about 20 seconds, concentrating on your arm from the armpit to fingertips. Then make a fist, bend your arms, take a deep breath, and open your eyes. Do this with the rest of the body, and you'll soon learn to relax all parts.

Other ways to minimize stress:

■ *Take one thing at a time.* Sir William Osler once said: "The load of tomorrow, added to that of yesterday, carried today, makes even the strongest falter." Concentrate on one thing at a time—one day at a time.

RATE YOUR STRESS LEVEL THIS YEAR

EVENT	VALUE	YOUR SCORE	EVENT	VALUE	YOUR SCORE
Death of spouse	100	_____	Trouble with in-laws	29	_____
Divorce	73	_____	Outstanding personal achievement	28	_____
Marital separation	65	_____	Spouse begins or stops work	26	_____
Jail term	63	_____	Starting or finishing school	26	_____
Death of close family member	63	_____	Change in living conditions	25	_____
Personal injury or illness	53	_____	Revision of personal habits	24	_____
Marriage	50	_____	Trouble with boss	23	_____
Fired from work	47	_____	Change in work hours, conditions	20	_____
Marital reconciliation	45	_____	Change in residence	20	_____
Retirement	45	_____	Change in schools	20	_____
Change in family member's health	44	_____	Change in recreational habits	19	_____
Pregnancy	40	_____	Change in church activities	19	_____
Sex difficulties	39	_____	Change in social activities	18	_____
Addition to family	39	_____	Mortgage or loan under $10,000	17	_____
Business readjustment	39	_____	Change in sleeping habits	16	_____
Change in financial status	38	_____	Change in number of family gatherings	15	_____
Death of close friend	37	_____	Change in eating habits	15	_____
Change to different line of work	36	_____	Vacation	13	_____
Change in number of marital arguments	35	_____	Christmas season	12	_____
Mortgage or loan over $10,000	31	_____	Minor violation of the law	11	_____
Foreclosure of mortgage or loan	30	_____	Total		_____
Change in work responsibilities	29	_____			
Son or daughter leaving home	29	_____			

■ *Find someone to talk to.* Just "getting it off your chest" to a sympathetic listener (one whose judgment you respect) will lighten your load and help gain new perspective.

■ *Consult your physician.* He or she may be able to relieve your tension with medication, or refer you for psychotherapy.

Do Older People Get "Senile"?

Senility is a word commonly used to describe a large number of conditions with an equally large number of causes, many of which respond to proper treatment. And many of the "symptoms"—forgetfulness, confusion, and certain other personality and behavioral changes—can be prevented by following a few simple rules. Actually, there are only two common incurable forms of mental impairment in old age: *multi-infarct dementia and Alzheimer's disease.* But even in these cases, doctors can prescribe drugs that can lessen agitation, anxiety, and depression. And the best way to *prevent* some of the symptoms associated with these diseases is to keep the mind and body active. Careful attention to physical fitness, including a balanced diet, can go a long way toward protecting health. Certain physical and mental changes should be considered normal; in most cases they may just signify an overload of facts and shouldn't be classified as "senility."

In fact, less than 5 percent of older people end up in institutions of any kind, and many of those classified as senile are more emotionally sick than mentally ill.

INTERNAL HEALTH PROBLEMS IN THE
MIDDLE AND LATER YEARS

The longer we live, the more we're subjected to stresses and diseases from within and without. We're more subject to chronic internal diseases, including arthritis, cancer, diabetes, heart and related blood diseases. Physically, we have lower resistance and respond more slowly and less positively to therapy; psychologically, we may not be in the mood to follow preventive health programs.

Below are some facts about internal health problems—what they are, what causes them, how to prevent them—that I've gleaned from leading medical authorities.

Arthritis May Get You—So Better Watch Out

Arthritis covers over 100 related illnesses. The word is derived from *arthros* meaning joint, and *itis*, meaning inflammation.

WHAT'S NORMAL. We may all develop *osteoarthritis* if we live long enough. This is caused by normal wear and tear on the joints. Osteoarthritis usually develops in any joint subjected to years of abuse: the knee or hip joint of someone who is overweight; joints injured in an accident or sports; joints subjected to unusual stresses and strains in work or play; hidden defects at birth. Osteoarthritis is usually mild, and pain is moderate; it generally starts in the hip, knee, shoulder, or back. There's rarely inflammation.

WHAT'S NOT NORMAL. *Rheumatoid arthritis*—often called "the great crippler"—strikes at any age (most commonly between 20 and 35 years of age) and is three times more common in women than in men. Early symptoms may include weakness, fever, loss of appetite, loss of weight, persistent pain and stiffness on arising, pain, stiffness, or tenderness in one or more joints (especially the neck, lower back, and knees), and tingling sensations in the fingertips, hands, and feet. Skin, especially of the hands, may be cold and clammy. The patient might feel depressed and doesn't look well. One or more joints become inflamed and swollen.

HOW YOU CAN PREVENT ARTHRITIS. The exact cause of arthritis isn't known, but it tends to run in families, in those who are overweight and/or with poor posture, and in those subject to emotional upsets, tensions, and shocks. (Symptoms sometimes begin after a disturbing event.) *Early diagnosis is vital.* Laboratory tests can detect bacteria that invade joints, and steps can be taken to prevent rheumatoid arthritis; X rays can also give clear pictures of typical joint damage in osteoarthritis, and proper treatment can be prescribed.

WHAT THE DOCTOR CAN DO FOR YOU. While the doctor can't "cure" arthritis, he can prescribe common pain-killers like aspirin and aspirin supplements (naproxen, ibuprofen), as well as gold salts and cortisone, to reduce the pain and swelling. He may also prescribe exercises, rest, and perhaps a reducing diet to relieve symptoms. While heat (hot baths, hydrotherapy, paraffin-wax applications) may help in some cases, it's not necessarily true that moving to a warmer climate will help the disease. Surgery may help, and doctors now rebuild hips and knees with metal-and-plastic devices and even restore normal finger function with rubber finger joints. They can also remove inflamed tissue from a joint before it does extensive damage. A word of caution: The pain and stiffness and swelling of rheumatoid arthritis may suddenly subside (remission) and disappear for months or years. The disease is still there, and damage has been done, but you may think you're "cured." Many "quacks" take advantage of these natural remissions by claiming a "cure" and trying to sell you anything from filtered seawater to magnetic (or copper) bracelets; from radium baths to musical vibrations.

There's no cure for arthritis, but in the hands of a competent doctor, you can get proper diagnosis and relief.

For further information: The Arthritis Foundation, 3400 Peachtree St., Atlanta, GA 30326; National Institute of Arthritis, Diabetes and Digestive and Kidney Diseases, NIH, Bldg. 31, Rm. 9A04, Bethesda, MD 20205.

The Hopeful Side of Cancer

While we may be more likely to get cancer as we grow older, the older we get, the greater the chance that scientists will have found a cancer "cure." Even though a universal cure isn't in sight, new treatments alleviate certain kinds of cancers and promise relief for others.

WHAT'S NORMAL. Cancer itself is *not* normal. It's an abnormal growth of malignant cells that spreads and invades normal tissue. The cells divide and reproduce themselves, and the cancer grows.

WHAT'S NOT NORMAL. The Cancer Society says these are the alarm signals that should send you immediately to your doctor: (1) an unusual bleeding or discharge; (2) a lump or thickening in the breast or elsewhere; (3) a sore that does not heal; (4) a change in bowel or bladder habits; (5) a persistent hoarseness or cough; (6) indigestion or difficulty in swallowing; (7) a change in a wart or mole.

HOW TO AVOID CANCER. Many factors could cause cancer: frictional and chemical irritations such as cigarette smoking; irritation of the skin and mouth (such as poor dentures); exposure to sun, X rays, or chemical and radioactive elements; a diet high in animal fats, alcohol, food additives. Common cancer sites are the lips, mouth, stomach, intestines, rectum, liver, lungs, breasts, kidneys, bladder, skin, uterus, and prostate. Because many sites are internal, it's important to have a medical checkup each year regardless of how you feel. To prevent both internal and external cancers, follow these simple rules: Stop smoking cigarettes (a leading cause of lung cancer); avoid unnecessary exposure to X rays, chemicals and sun; cut down on high-cholesterol foods (animal fats and eggs) that may be a cause in colon-rectal cancer.

WHAT THE DOCTOR CAN DO FOR YOU. Improved detection, including laboratory tests and heat-sensing techniques *(thermography),* now enable doctors to detect cancer earlier. *The sooner it's found, the better the chance of its being arrested and cured.*

Although surgery and/or X rays eliminate most cancerous tumors, doctors have still other weapons: *chemotherapy* (massive doses of several drugs); *immunotherapy* (triggering the body's own defense mechanisms to fight against the malignant cells); *radiotherapy* (radioactive isotopes and machines producing beams of electron volt energy).

For further information: American Cancer Society, 777 Third Ave., New York, NY 10017; Office of Cancer Communications, Bldg. 31, Rm. 4B39, National Cancer Institute, Bethesda, MD 20205; Cancer Care, 1 Park Ave., New York, NY 10016. Also, you can call the Cancer Information Service at 800/638-6694 (in Maryland 800/492-6600).

Diabetes—The Complicated Disease

Your chances of getting diabetes increase with age, yet you may not be aware of it until it leads to such complications as heart and blood-vessel changes and damage to the eyes. However, there's a lot you can do to avoid diabetes and to resume a normal life if it does strike.

WHAT'S NORMAL. Normally, the body changes carbohydrate foods—sugars and starches—into a form of sugar called "glucose." The body may burn it right away to supply heat or energy, or it may store the glucose in a slightly different form for use later on.

WHAT'S NOT NORMAL. If the pancreas can't produce enough insulin (necessary for storage and reconversion of glucose), the body can't make use of the carbohydrates that enter the blood in the form of glucose. It then accumulates in the blood until the surplus passes through the kidneys into the urine.

When this happens, you may have one or more of these symptoms: excessive thirst and urination, hunger, loss of weight, easy tiring, slow healing of cuts and bruises, changes in vision, intense itching, pain in fingers and toes, drowsiness, and (in men) sexual impotency. A simple blood sugar or urine test can detect the diabetes.

WHAT YOU CAN DO TO AVOID DIABETES. Anyone can get diabetes, but it most often strikes people with diabetic relatives, persons over age 40 (women more often than men), and people who are overweight. While you can't control most of these factors, you can get a health examination that includes a test for diabetes.

WHAT THE DOCTOR CAN DO FOR YOU. If tests show you have diabetes, the doctor may prescribe a diet that limits your intake of sweets. He may also prescribe exercise to help use up the sugar and reduce insulin need, as well as insulin by injection or oral diabetic pills (although some oral diabetic pills have fallen into disfavor). Through these relatively simple treatments and by following rules for sensible living, most diabetics resume normal activities and lives.

For further information: The American Diabetes Association, 2 Park Ave., New York, NY 10016.

Be Careful—It's Your Heart

Gil Hodges, a manager of the New York Mets, and Chuck Hughes, a wide receiver for the Detroit Lions, were vigorous men in their prime when they were felled by sudden heart attacks—and died within seconds. The saddest part is that this shouldn't have happened because doctors say there should be no such thing as a "sudden" heart attack.

WHAT'S NORMAL. Your heart is the strongest, toughest muscle in your body, and it has a complete maintenance and repair system, enabling many heart-disease victims to continue long and useful lives. The good news about heart attacks is that those of us in our forties and fifties are less likely to suffer heart attacks than our counterparts 10 years ago.

Although heart disease (which could mean any of 20-odd diseases of the heart and blood vessels) isn't necessarily a product of aging, some heart and blood-vessel diseases become more acute as we grow older. The heart may become flabbier, pumping less blood; the heart muscle may suffer an oxygen shortage during exercise; the heart valves may acquire a form of "biological rust"—cholesterol and calcium deposits—causing the heart to work harder.

However, your odds of having a heart attack are only about 1 in 20 to 50 if your weight and blood pressure are normal, your blood cholesterol is average or low, you don't smoke cigarettes or have diabetes, you're moderately active, have a normal electrocardiogram, and no damage to your kidneys or thyroid gland. But if you're abnormal in any one factor above, you multiply your risks two to eight times. And if you have any three abnormalities, you multiply your risks thirty times, making you a prime target for heart disease.

WHAT'S NOT NORMAL. Chest pains—including the so-called stitch—usually don't signal a heart attack. Heart attacks often start as some form of "indigestion," and the pain is usually described as a pressure or squeezing pain in the center of the chest, behind the breastbone. The pain may spread to the shoulders, arm, neck, or jaw and is often accompanied by sweating. The person usually feels sick and is short of breath. When this happens, get the patient into a comfortable position—in bed or even lying on the ground or floor—and offer a jigger of whiskey, Scotch, brandy, or a tranquilizer. Reading or watching TV may be diverting. Call the doctor immediately; if one isn't available, and symptoms increase, get the patient to a hospital emergency room at once; seconds count.

WHAT THE DOCTOR CAN DO FOR YOU. Over half the country's hospitals now have coronary-care units with around-the-clock monitoring devices showing each patient's heart rhythm on a screen visible from a central nursing station. Physicians and nurses control emergencies with drugs, electrical means to restart or replace the heart, mouth-to-mouth breathing, and other means of artificial respiration.

After the immediate danger is over, treatment usually consists of bed rest, diet (low-fat, -cholesterol, and -sodium, no tobacco and minimal alcohol), drugs, and possibly surgery (open-heart, bypass, heart transplants). After a heart attack, most patients are able to resume normal working and marital relations.

WHAT YOU CAN DO TO PREVENT HEART DISEASE. Doctors gave me these sensible rules to reduce your chances of a heart attack:

■ *Keep your weight down.* A pound of fat contains 25 miles of blood vessels, adding extra burdens to your heart.

■ *Control your cholesterol intake.* Cut down on high-cholesterol foods like butter, cheese, beef, pork, lamb, and chocolate, and substitute foods like veal, chicken, fish, low-fat milk, and vegetable oil.

■ *Cut out cigarettes.* Heavy smokers suffer three times as many heart attacks as pipe or cigar smokers (if they don't inhale).

■ *Exercise.* Inactive people suffer more heart attacks than active people. Continuous, vigorous, rhythmic exercise like walking, cycling, or swimming improves the pumping action of the heart and produces a reserve collateral circulation system that pumps blood to your heart in an emergency. You can even engage in a new form of exercise, *cardiovascular training* (CVT), that gives your heart the exercise it needs without straining it. Some 200 clinics, hospitals, and university medical centers have CVT programs; if your physician recommends the course, you may be covered by insurance or you may deduct it from your taxes, especially if you are a postcardiac patient.

■ *Stress.* Undue tension and pressure contribute to raising blood-pressure levels. High blood pressure places a severe strain on your heart, slowly forcing it to fail. If you're under a lot of strain, don't get overly tired—the combination makes you doubly prone to heart disease.

For further information: American Heart Association, 7320 Greenville Ave., Dallas, TX 75231.

ACTIVITIES FOR FUN AND FITNESS

Before age 40 you exercise to improve your performance. After age 40, you exercise to *improve your chances of survival.*

In researching this book, I interviewed a 74-year-old man who jogs for fun and to stave off arthritis . . . a 59-year-old doctor who skis to help ward off heart disease . . . an 83-year-old woman who still plays championship tennis for fun and health. These people know the best way to keep healthy is to be lively; the more active you are, the healthier you are.

Doctors say that enjoyable physical-fitness activities make you feel and think better, lose excess weight, fight disease better and recover faster from illness, and stay younger. Your body gets weak and tired from *not* using it. Activity supplies energy, removes waste, and promotes rest in the tissues supplying the skeletal, muscular, arterial, and nervous systems. It also improves your posture, back, digestion, and bowel functions, as well as stimulates your brain by getting it more oxygen, and improves your lungs' capacity and efficiency. Activity also makes you sleep better.

You'll not only look and feel healthier if you exercise, you'll be more relaxed and have less mental strain and stress. Dr. Herbert A. deVries, a physiologist at the University of Southern California, found that 15 minutes of moderate exercise is more effective than a tranquilizer in reducing nervous tension and eliminating the physical effects of stress.

Enjoyable activity leads to longer life. You've probably heard the saying, "The larger the beltline, the shorter the lifeline." Overweight contributes to heart disease, high blood pressure, and other ailments. If you are overweight by 10 percent, your chances of surviving the next 20 years are 15 percent less than if your weight were ideal; if you are 20 percent overweight, your chances are 25 percent less; if you are 30 percent overweight, 45 percent less.

While exercise alone can't keep off weight, it does help burn up calories. You must burn 3,500 calories to lose a pound of fat. But even if you burn only 100 calories daily doing some pleasant activity, you will lose 10 pounds in a year. Don't worry about "cellulite," which is just ordinary fat causing the skin to "dimple." Exercise won't take this "dimpling" away, but it will improve skin and muscle tone to make it less noticeable.

How much exercise is enough? Enough so that you feel pleasantly tired when you want to go to bed but not so much that it causes you to lose sleep. Doctors say you may be exercising too strenuously if: (1) your heart doesn't stop pounding within 10 minutes after exercise; (2) breathing is still hard after 10 minutes; (3) you're shaky for more than 30 minutes afterward; (4) you can't sleep well afterward; (5) your fatigue (not muscle soreness) continues into the next day.

The type of exercise doesn't matter as long as it's suited to your age and body, you like it and continue it regularly, and you keep it up. It's the cumulative effect of regular exercise that pays off.

What kind of activities are best for you? Dr. Samuel M. Fox, former president of the American College of Cardiologists, suggests that the best kind of activity builds you up to a steady level of exertion and involves as many muscles as possible. The best activities in the later years include bicycling, tennis, badminton, skating, swimming, brisk walking, vigorous dancing. Activities to *avoid* after age 40 include those that require surges of output such as weight lifting, push-ups, squat thrusts, and deep-knee bends.

Other experts say that if you're starting an activity after age 50, avoid running or highly competitive sports unless you get your doctor's OK. You can, however, swim, cycle, walk, play golf, and engage in other less strenuous sports without medical supervision. If you're over age 60, you can indulge in these same sports as long as you don't jog, run, or even run in place— unless you started these activities earlier in life and have maintained them.

The following activities are recommended by the International Committee on the Standardization of Physical Fitness Assessments for mature adults, 50 and over: archery, badminton, bowling, putting, golf, curling, table tennis, deck tennis, shuffleboard, volleyball, horseshoes, croquet, darts, boccie, billiards, tennis, swimming, boating, sailing, trail walking, gardening, bicycling, skating, dancing, shooting, fishing, horseback riding. For specific fitness programs the committee recommends:

For physical fitness and work capacity—walking and fishing
For general health—swimming
For appearance—walking and volleyball
For physical recreation—tennis, swimming, fishing, and volleyball.

(If you're in doubt as to your fitness for any sport or activity, get your doctor's advice.)

Adding it up, the best and easiest all-round activities (which you can do most of the year) are walking and swimming.

Prepare your body for vigorous exercise by warming up. The U.S. Administration on Aging booklet, "The Fitness Challenge in the Later Years," states: "A warm-up period should be performed by starting lightly with a continuous rhythmical activity such as walking, gradually increasing the intensity until your pulse rate, breathing, and body temperature are elevated. It is also desirable to do some easy stretching, pulling, and rotating exercises during the warm-up period."

Effective warm-up exercises include raising the arms over the head, placing the hands behind the head and behind the back, and straightleg raises while lying down.

The Wonders of Walking

The famous heart specialist, the late Dr. Paul Dudley White, said: "A five-mile walk is better for the health of anyone not already too ill to walk, than all the medicine and philosophy in the world."

Health authorities say that walking is as natural to the human body as breathing. It's a muscular symphony involving all the foot, leg, and hip muscles, and many of the back muscles. And the abdominal muscles, along with the diaphragm and rib muscles, tend to contract and support their share of the weight when you walk.

Walking makes other muscles automatically step up their action—you strengthen your shoulder and neck muscles as you hold your head erect; you exercise your eyes as you look about. In short, walking supplies exactly the type of physical activity you need to tighten up your body muscles and produce that reserve collateral-circulation system for your heart.

Try to make walking a part of your daily routine. Walk instead of ride to the train or bus station, restaurant, place of work, or recreation. Larry Lewis, a San Francisco waiter who passed away recently at the age of 106, started each day at 4:00 A.M. with a 3-mile walk through Golden Gate Park, then jogged home—a distance of 6.7 miles. He then walked another 3 miles to his job at the St. Francis Hotel, where he walked, walked, walked . . .

For brisk walking, you can join walking tours sponsored by hiking, garden, and outdoor clubs, and museums, as well as guided walking and hiking tours into magnificent wilderness areas. For further information, write to Appalachian Trail Conference, P.O. Box 236, Harpers Ferry, WV 25425; Wilderness Society, 9901 Pennsylvania Ave. NW, Washington, DC 20006; Sierra Club, 530 Bush St., San Francisco, CA 94108.

To get the most from walking, hold your head squarely above your shoulders, keep your abdomen flat and your back straight. Keep your toes pointed straight ahead, and take long easy strides. For most people over age 50, a 45-minute brisk walk is as beneficial as a 30-minute jog.

Getting into Swimming

You're never too old, nor is it ever too cold, to go swimming. Philip Severin, a neighbor who is 81, swims every month of the year outdoors (except when the water freezes over in February). Despite a collapsed lung, he swims vigorously and breathes deeply because he feels the salt air and water are good for him. He then takes a nap in the air (hot or cold) and is renewed for eight more hours of activity.

Swimming is a healthy, enjoyable activity that should be enjoyed year round. I swim at beaches in summer and indoor pools in winter. When I swim, I spur all my muscles into action. I use my arms and legs continuouly and strengthen my back and abdominal muscles—increasing my lung power and burning up calories in the process. But for maximum benefit you must swim vigorously enough to offer resistance to the water—"paddling around" just isn't enough.

Spinning Wheels to Health

Cycling, like walking, fits into everyday living; you can cycle to work, to the market, or to recreation centers. Cycling uses the same leg muscles as does walking, linking leg strength to good muscle tone of the arms, back, and abdomen. It also helps extend the lung capacity—especially necessary to those with emphysema. And physical-fitness studies show that cycling at between 9 and 10 miles per hour burns up 7 calories per minute, the average calorie consumption for canoeing, tennis, or vigorous dancing.

After a month of cycling, your heart action improves, and you'll have attained the proper balance of oxygen you need.

For club riding and touring, write to League of American Wheelmen, P.O. Box 988, Baltimore, MD 21203. For books on cycling, see *How to Choose and Use a Bicycle Without Doing Something Dumb*, ed. Anne C. Hicks (Villanova, Pa.: Tobey Publishing, 1973) and *The Practical Book of Bicycling*, rev. ed., by Francis Call and Merle Dowd (New York: E. P. Dutton, 1981).

Put More Health into Your Games

Authorities claim that most games or sports don't provide the best exercise. According to researchers at the Physical Fitness Laboratory of the

University of Illinois, the trouble with most games is that the action is intermittent—starting and stopping—a burst of energy and then a wait. The bowler swings a ball for 2.5 seconds and gets about one minute of actual muscular work per game. Golf is a succession of pause, swing, walk (or often a ride) to the next pause, swing, walk, and so on. You also spend a lot of time merely standing and waiting for the foursome ahead and for your partners. Tennis is starting and stopping; so is handball. No game, it seems, has the tension-releasing pattern essential for continuous, vigorous, rhythmic motion. However, in the sections that follow, we'll examine favorite activities to see how you can get top enjoyment—and healthful benefits—from them.

The Goodies of Golf

If you want to look and feel like a Lee Trevino, do what he does. Get out on the golf course and stride vigorously, lifting your head and chest. Throw out your arms and legs as you stride—you'll feel great!

Dr. Warren K. Guild, a past president of the American College of Sports Medicine, says: "Playing a round of golf does enable you to breathe a little more deeply, utilizing your pulmonary and cardiac capacity more than if you sat around playing bridge. If you walk briskly between shots, it can be good recreational and beneficial sport."

Tennis, Everyone!

One of the fittest men I know is Ed Everett, 72, who still plays singles tennis every day. Ed is exceptional, but I've known other people who have taken up tennis in their fifties and gotten both enjoyment and pleasurable exercise from it.

People with cardiac or some other organic weakness should follow their doctor's advice about playing tennis, but those who are fit enough for the game will find that they use all their muscles when the ball is in play. As more oxygen goes to the tissues, the circulatory system becomes more efficient. Even the start-and-stop strain on the heart, joints, and muscles can improve circulatory fitness.

The Benefits in Bowling

Dr. Morris Fishbein, editor (emeritus) of the *Journal of the American Medical Association*, believes bowling combines grace and ease for healthy exercise and relaxing fun. Says Dr. Fishbein: "Bowling produces better coordination of vision and mind with practically all the muscles of the body. Research has shown that such activity may relieve the postural backache often associated with long hours of sitting in an office chair."

Bowling also provides a relaxing change of pace. Stanford University researchers, who polled 260 bowlers, found that 7 out of 8 felt more relaxed after bowling. Many even said they purposely bowled to forget their worries.

Skiing Your Way to Better Health

Skiing for better health? Dr. Merritt H. Stiles, now in his seventies, learned to ski at age 55 because he became convinced not only of its pleasure but of its medical benefits. Skiing is beneficial because it is sustained and prolonged; the exercise could help prevent heart disease and help the patient after a coronary. However, no one of advanced age should really take up skiing without a physical examination.

Can you really learn to ski in the later years? One instructor told me: "The American ski-teaching techniques have advanced so tremendously in the last few years that we can now take an older person and teach him the sport in six lessons."

You're never too old to begin an activity or to exercise. Besides the Senior Olympics, many seniors are continuing such strenuous sports as baseball in their seventies, eighties, even nineties. In St. Petersburg, Florida, the Three-Quarter Century Softball club pits the "Kids" against the "Kubs." All players are at least 75 years old, and a star outfielder is 88. Another active hustler has a pacemaker in his heart, but he keeps it a secret. "The hell with it," he told me. "If I'm going to go, just have them stop the game and haul me away." These men are in excellent physical shape, they train for their games, and they maintain an active social and physical life, both on and off the field.

Even seniors who haven't exercised in the past are now taking part in "Preventive Care" programs started by Lawrence Frankel, 70, of Charleston, West Virginia. Frankel's program involves group participation for one hour, three times a week, in stretching, bending, and dancing to music. Seniors also do the exercises at home—all it takes is a sawed-off piece of broom handle for arm exercises and two 1-pound cans of vegetables for weights.

For further information, contact the Frankel Foundation, Virginia at Brooks St., Charleston, WV 25301; for a free list of information sources and free or low-cost publications that describe exercise programs, write to:

Exercise, National Institute on Aging, Bldg. 31, Room 5C35, Bethesda, MD 20205. Also, write to National Association for Human Development, 1750 Pennsylvania Ave. NW, Washington, DC 20006, for a list of medically approved exercise and diet books for older people.

FOOD FOR GOOD EATING AND BEST HEALTH

A good diet adds years to your life and life to your years. Leading nutritionists and dietitians point out that in many respects we are what we eat—eating the right foods in the right amounts keeps us active, helps ward off illness, and slows down aging.

While we need the same basic nutrients as we grow older, we do face special problems. We need to:

1. Select food more carefully to include adequate proteins, vitamins, and minerals, while cutting down on weight-producing calories;
2. Avoid bad eating habits—eat regular meals and don't snack;
3. Get the most nutritious food for the least money and learn new techniques to stretch meals, to use leftovers, and to substitute lower-priced items with the same nutritional value for higher-priced foods.

CHART I, 1.
BASIC FOUR FOOD GROUPS*

VEGETABLE-FRUIT GROUP

FOODS INCLUDED:
All vegetables and fruits.

Good Sources of Vitamin C—Grapefruit or grapefruit juice; orange or orange juice; cantaloupe; guava; mango; papaya; raw strawberries; broccoli; brussels sprouts; green pepper; sweet red pepper.

Other Sources—Honeydew melon; lemon; tangerine or tangerine juice; watermelon; asparagus tips; raw cabbage; cauliflower; collards; garden cress; kale; kohlrabi; mustard greens; potatoes and sweet potatoes cooked in the jacket; rutabagas; spinach; tomatoes or tomato juice; turnip greens.

Sources of Vitamin A—Dark-green and deep-yellow vegetables and a few fruits, namely: apricots, broccoli, cantaloupe, carrots, chard, collards, cress, kale, mango, persimmon, pumpkin, spinach, sweet potatoes, turnip greens and other dark-green leaves, winter squash.

---

*Prepared by the Consumer and Food Economics Institute, Agricultural Research Service, U.S. Department of Agriculture.

AMOUNTS RECOMMENDED:
Choose four or more servings every day, including:
One serving of a good source of vitamin C.
One serving, at least every other day, of a source of vitamin A. If the food chosen for vitamin C is also a good source of vitamin A, the additional serving of a vitamin A food may be omitted.

The remaining one to three or more servings may be of any vegetable or fruit.
Count as one serving: ½ cup of vegetable or fruit; or a portion as ordinarily served.

MEAT GROUP

FOODS INCLUDED:
Beef; veal; lamb; pork; variety meats, such as liver, heart, kidney; poultry and eggs; shellfish or fish. As alternates—dry beans, dry peas, lentils, nuts, peanuts, peanut butter.

AMOUNTS RECOMMENDED:
Choose two or more servings every day.
Count as a serving: two to three ounces (not including bone weight) cooked lean meat, poultry or fish. Count as alternates for ½ serving meat or fish: one egg; ½ cup cooked dry beans or peas, or lentils; or two tablespoons peanut butter.

MILK GROUP

FOODS INCLUDED:
Milk—fluid whole, evaporated, skim, dry, buttermilk.
Cheese—cottage; cream; cheddar-type—natural or processed.
Ice cream.

AMOUNTS RECOMMENDED:
The recommended amount for adults is two or more 8-ounce cups. Cheese and ice cream may replace part of the milk.

BREAD-CEREAL GROUP

FOODS INCLUDED:
All breads and cereals that are whole grain, enriched or restored; *check labels to be sure.*
Specifically, this group includes: breads; cereals; cornmeal; crackers; flour; grits; macaroni and spaghetti; noodles; rice; rolled oats; and baked goods if made with whole-grain or enriched flour. Parboiled rice and wheat also may be included in this group.

AMOUNTS RECOMMENDED:
Choose four servings or more daily. If no cereals are chosen, have an extra serving of breads or baked goods which will make at least five servings from this group daily.
Count as one serving: one slice of bread; one ounce ready-to-eat cereal; ½ to ¾ cup cooked cereal, cornmeal, grits, macaroni, noodles, rice or spaghetti.

How Can We Get the Essential Nutrients?

A good rule is first to eat recommended servings from the Basic Four Food Groups (Chart I,1) established by the National Research Council. Then, eat other foods you like, as long as you don't go over the recommended daily caloric intake. The average man in the 55- to 75-year age group should consume 2,200 calories per day; the average woman in the same age group, 1,600 calories a day. This is a drop of between 500 and 600 calories a day from what you needed at age 25. As you grow older, your physical activity decreases, and your metabolism slows, causing body fats to build up at a much higher rate, making you more prone to hardening of the arteries and certain heart conditions, and necessitating a reduction of caloric intake.

What Should We Emphasize in Our Diets?

Medical authorities say that a desirable diet in the later years is *high in proteins*, *moderate in carbohydrates*, and relatively *low in fats*. The diet should be rich in all vitamins and essential minerals and provide sufficient iron and calcium. The fluid intake should be generous; tea and coffee are acceptable except in specific instances; and *judicious* use of alcohol may be beneficial.

The overweight person is more likely to develop arthritis, cancer, diabetes, heart disease, high blood pressure, kidney trouble, and other fatal and disabling disorders than a person of normal weight. Excess weight also brings fatigue, muscle pain, irritability—the same symptoms you might have if you had to carry a 20-pound weight on your back all the time.

Look at the weight chart on page 63 to determine your ideal weight. Ideally, you should weigh now about the same as you did when you were 25. But the older we get, the less efficiently we burn up calories and the more food turns to fat. Moderately active people should consume only about 15 calories per pound of desired weight—at 150 pounds this would be no more than 2,250 calories a day. And for every pound of weight you want to lose, you should eventually eliminate 3,500 calories.

Although nutritionists emphasize *protein* in our diets, most of us eat more protein daily than we need (0.42 grams of protein per pound of weight; a man weighing 154 pounds needs 65 grams protein daily; a woman weighing 128 pounds needs 55 grams daily). Most of us feel we should get this protein from meat—a complete protein because all eight essential amino acids are present in the proper proportion—but far less expensive sources of protein, ranking in quality with the leanest cuts of fresh beef, are dried beans and peas. And you can satisfy your protein needs by mixing meat with these plant

CHART OF DESIRABLE WEIGHTS FOR MEN AND WOMEN OVER AGE 25

The "ideal weight" for a long life has been adjusted upward by the Metropolitan Life Insurance Company. The latest (1983) tables show an average increase in recommended weight of 13 pounds for short men, 7 pounds for men of medium height, and 2 pounds for tall men. The average increase for short women is 10 pounds, 8 pounds for women of medium height, and 3 pounds for tall women. Just why rising weights are having fewer adverse effects on life-span is not entirely clear, but speculation is that the increasing health-consciousness of Americans may be lowering risks for certain diseases.

Following are 1983 Metropolitan Life Insurance Company weight tables by height and size of frame, for people aged 25 to 59, in shoes and wearing 5 pounds of indoor clothing for men, 3 pounds for women.

MEN

HEIGHT	SMALL	MEDIUM	LARGE
5' 2"	128-134	131-141	138-150
5' 3"	130-136	133-143	140-153
5' 4"	132-138	135-145	142-156
5' 5"	134-140	137-148	144-160
5' 6"	136-142	139-151	146-164
5' 7"	138-145	142-154	149-168
5' 8"	140-148	145-157	152-172
5' 9"	142-151	148-160	155-176
5'10"	144-154	151-163	158-180
5'11"	146-157	154-166	161-184
6' 0"	149-160	157-170	164-188
6' 1"	152-164	160-174	168-192
6' 2"	155-168	164-178	172-197
6' 3"	158-172	167-182	176-202
6' 4"	162-176	171-187	181-207

WOMEN

HEIGHT	SMALL	MEDIUM	LARGE
4'10"	102-111	109-121	118-131
4'11"	103-113	111-123	120-134
5' 0"	104-115	113-126	122-137
5' 1"	106-118	115-129	125-140
5' 2"	108-121	118-132	128-143
5' 3"	111-124	121-135	131-147
5' 4"	114-127	124-138	134-151
5' 5"	117-130	127-141	137-155
5' 6"	120-133	130-144	140-159
5' 7"	123-136	133-147	143-163
5' 8"	126-139	136-150	146-167
5' 9"	129-142	139-153	149-170
5'10"	132-145	142-156	152-173
5'11"	135-148	145-159	155-176
6' 0"	138-151	148-162	158-179

proteins. Recently, the U.S. Department of Agriculture estimated that 3 ounces of sirloin steak contains 20 grams of protein and costs 94 cents. But the same amount of protein could come from canned tuna for 38 cents, beef liver at 23 cents, large eggs for 22 cents, or dry beans for 14 cents. A large lasagna with noodles, cottage, Swiss, and Parmesan cheeses, plus a pound of ground beef in tomato sauce, for instance, contains 263 grams of protein and costs *less than half* as much as the equivalent protein in round steak.

Labeling according to regulations tells what percentages of U.S. Recommended Daily Allowances (RDA) food contains. The labels also give number of calories per serving and percentages of protein, carbohydrates, vitamins A and C, thiamine, riboflavin, niacin, calcium, iron. To get the essential vitamins and minerals, add up the percentages of different foods so they total approximately 100 percent for each nutrient. Canned or packaged meals must list main ingredients by percentages (proportion of meat to potatoes, noodles, rice, vegetables, gravy), and complete meals must include three separate dishes listed in descending order in proportion to weight. Foods that need other ingredients (meats, and so on) to make a meal or main dish must state so. Read the labels, compare—and save!

What Vitamins Do We Need as We Grow Older?

We need the same vitamins and minerals we did when we were younger, except for less vitamin D. We also need calcium, potassium, iron, phosphorus, and iodine. The *best sources of such vitamins and minerals are the foods we eat*—including meats (especially liver), seafood, dairy products, enriched breads and cereals, dark yellow and green leafy vegetables, beans, peas, citrus fruits, vegetable oils, and iodized salt.

When you obtain nutrients from food, your body uses those vitamins and minerals necessary to maintain proper health, appetite, and resistance to infection, promptly eliminates excesses of vitamin C and B complex, and stores any excess of vitamins A and D in your liver and other body organs. There's usually a wide safety margin between the vitamins you need and a harmful excess. However, if you take concentrated amounts of vitamins A or D over a long period of time, they may eventually create a dependency similar to drug addiction and cause "withdrawal" symptoms when you stop.

Vitamin E has been heralded as a deterrent to aging, heart attacks, constipation, cirrhosis of the liver, and a myriad of other ailments. However, the National Academy of Science reports that there is no clinical evidence that vitamin E will "cure" cancer and heart disease, and Food and Drug Administration researchers insist that other "miraculous" claims are unproved. So, to save money and get the best possible health benefits, consult your doctor about the proper diet—including vitamins and minerals—for you. You can get the answers to questions concerning dietary supplements by sending $2 (includes postage and handling) to American Medical Association, Order Dept. OP-107, P.O. Box 821, Monroe, WI 53566. And for general information about nutrition, write Office of Consumer Affairs, FDA, 5600 Fishers Lane, Rockville, MD 20857.

How to Get the Best Buys on Essential Foods

I find I get the best buys by following these tips:

1. *I plan what I need.* For each meal I include at least one food from each of the Basic Four Food Groups. Starting with dinner, I decide which kinds of main protein dishes I want, then I choose foods from the other three groups to contrast with my main dish in shape, color, texture, taste. I resist impulse buying, but I'm flexible and knowledgeable enough to substitute "specials" such as seasonal bargains in meat or fresh produce.

2. *I shop for bargains.* I know I can save 10 percent by just "shopping the newspapers" and noting specials. And I've found that most stores have certain days for real bargains that save up to 20 percent off regular price.

3. *I know when to shop.* The best time to market is when your store has just restocked, you have plenty of time, and the store isn't packed. I've found that Wednesday and Thursday nights are best, and there are often good weekend and first-of-week specials. Experiment at your local stores.

4. *I compare prices.* Most stores now use unit pricing, which tells the cost per ounce or pound—regardless of the size or shape of the package. If the unit price isn't stated, do your own calculating by dividing weight into cost. You may be startled at the difference in cost of the same product packaged differently.

5. *I buy for use, not for looks.* As far as nutrition goes. there's no "best" grade of meat, eggs, canned fruits, and so on. Often the only difference in grades is mainly "cosmetic" (the higher grade might look better), yet a lower-grade product would give you the same food value if absorbed in a casserole, stew, or other mixture. "Private labels" (house brands) can offer substantial savings on products that don't vary in formula, such as salt, sugar, detergents, vinegar, vegetable oil, and so on. As one economist suggests: "Buy grade A for the table and grade B for the pot."

The Dangers in Nicotine and Caffeine

The New York Health Insurance Plan recently conducted studies that showed that *inactive men who smoke have a mortality rate five times higher than active nonsmokers of the same age.* Nicotine is thought to get into the system through membranes of the mouth and related areas, so the person who holds an unlighted cigar in his mouth may also absorb nicotine. While a little nicotine may not be harmful, most steady smokers absorb too much nicotine for their own good. Moreover, Dr. Harry Johnson of the Life Extension Institute suggests that few people actually enjoy more than 12 to 15 cigarettes daily—people who smoke more than that are jeopardizing their health needlessly.

Caffeine, like nicotine, can give you a "lift" if used moderately, but too much caffeine makes you headachy, irritable, and confused. Don't overlook the caffeine in beverages other than coffee: Tea leaves contain almost twice as much caffeine as an equal weight of coffee, although you use less tea than coffee to make a cup. Cola and chocolate also contain caffeine, and they, too, can make you physically dependent on them.

When Booze Is Bad

Your capacity to handle liquor diminishes after age 40. Also, because your liver, kidneys, and other organs can't tolerate or handle alcohol as efficiently as they once did, some people develop an "allergy" to alcohol. One doctor described an extra-dry martini as "a quick blow to the back of the neck."

Drinking too much and too fast jars the system—making you edgy instead of relaxed. Alcohol decreases your ability to concentrate, absorb, or produce thoughts or ideas. After drinking you're not as efficient at writing, drawing, handling objects, or driving. In fact, medical authorities feel that a stiff (two ounces of alcohol) drink or two bottles of beer makes most persons unfit to drive.

"The key to the real value of alcohol is intelligent drinking," says Dr. Johnson. He sometimes recommends a drink or two before dinner; however, he suggests a tall, well-diluted highball taken in a peaceful, quiet setting. Other doctors add that *moderate* drinking—no more than one and one-half ounces of whiskey, a half bottle of wine, or four bottles of beer per day—may have beneficial physical, social, or psychological effects.

HEALTH INSURANCE PAYS OFF

I've always had some form of health insurance, and although I don't now have an individual plan, I'm covered under my wife's plans (New York State public employee), which include hospital, medical, and major medical coverage. When she went to the hospital recently, we paid only $20 a day for a private room (the policy specified a semiprivate room). She was reimbursed for an examination connected with the operation, the doctor's and anesthetist's bills, and prescribed medications.

Almost all persons over age 65 are covered by Medicare Parts A and B (hospital and medical insurance), but Medicare at present pays less than 40 percent of the medical costs. While I've always believed in adequate health insurance, I've aimed first for broad coverage with few exclusions. Unfortunately, a policy with few exclusions but little depth (such as a quick cutoff date on hospital benefits) may sink you financially if major or long-term illness strikes—that's why I've always added *major medical* or *catastrophic* policies to my basic policy. If you're in the market for health insurance, here are some plans to consider:

1. *Basic hospital plans.* These plans, such as those offered through Blue Cross, should pay for all or most of your hospital bills for at least 60 days and sometimes 120 days or more. The policy should *pay the full prevailing daily rate* (many set "limits") of a semiprivate hospital room, including meals, routine nursing care, and minor medical supplies. If not covered in medical insurance (see below), the policy should also cover related services such as laboratory tests and X rays, anesthesia and its administration, use of operating room, drugs and medications, and local ambulance service.

2. *Basic medical expenses.* Offered by Blue Shield and many private insurance companies, these policies should pay the prevailing doctor rates when you're in the hospital, just as a hospital policy should pay prevailing room rates. The policy should also pay for surgery, doctor's visits, X rays, lab tests, and other related services not covered in the hospital plan. Often these policies pay only 80 percent (85 percent is tops) of these and related charges, and so, ideally, you should have a marriage between this plan and the above. An example would be a Blue Cross–Blue Shield policy in which the Blue Cross portion gives you hospital coverage for at least 120 days. The doctor-bill coverage usually can be added to a basic hospital policy at family group rates.

Blue Cross and Blue Shield benefits and rates vary around the country and in some cases are based on family income.

3. *Major medical insurance.* This policy usually takes over after a certain dollar amount—ranging from $50 to $1,000—and has a copayment clause, meaning that the insurance company pays only 75 to 80 percent of the expenses left after you pay the deductible. Benefits usually help pay for all types of care and treatment prescribed by a physician, both in and out of a

hospital, including hospital service; physician's treatment and specialist's consultation and care; X-ray and laboratory services; anesthesia and its administration; private-duty nursing; prescribed drugs and medicines. Some policies limit benefits for certain expenses, such as the cost of a hospital room or surgery. Experts recommend major medical policies with a $30,000 to $50,000 maximum.

4. *Catastrophic insurance.* Because of rising medical and hospital costs and the probability of national health insurance, a number of catastrophic policies are now being introduced on a group basis (also available to individual policy holders) with benefits as high as $250,000 and even $1 million. Another development in these "catastrophe" plans is the elimination of copayment by the insured person after an aggregate limit has been reached in the amount of covered medical expenses above the deductible. Beyond this cutoff point for copayment, the insurance company will pay 100 percent of covered expenses up to a maximum benefit.

I've found that if you have plans like Blue Cross and Blue Shield that cover you in and out of a hospital, you probably have adequate *basic* insurance. Beyond that, I advise that you get a major medical or catastrophic policy that will give you adequate protection in the case of major illness. You can then evaluate your other health-insurance needs along these lines:

1. *What risks can you take and how much can you afford to lose?* When I was the sole breadwinner, it would have been financial suicide if I had become disabled and couldn't earn money. But when my wife began to work, the pressure lessened. At one time I was offered disability insurance through a group employee plan, but I felt at that time the premium costs outweighed the risks.

2. *Insure the big losses rather than the small ones.* Deductibles lower premium costs because they lower the expenses on small claims, allowing you to buy major medical or catastrophe insurance with the savings in premium costs. However, in some policies, the deductible can start to apply again if the illness persists. The higher the deductible, the longer the benefit period should be. Benefit periods range from 1 to 10 years; 3 years is typical. Also note whether you reach the deductible limit by adding up bills. The more people and the more illnesses allowed to contribute, the sooner you reach your deductible limit.

3. *Compare costs before buying.* At one time I thought that you "get what you pay for" in insurance, and that costs of similar policies were about the same. But I've found that similar auto insurance policies can range from $350 to $550; annuities of the same amount may vary as much as 10 percent in costs; and some association insurance (in which members feel they are getting

a bargain group rate) is actually more expensive than similar individual policies. *Never assume any insurance—offered through an association or other organization—is a "bargain."* Not all illnesses or injuries qualify as disabilities; you've got to examine the fine print to detect differences. Even traditional life insurance policies vary, and health insurance policies probably vary the most of all. To be sure what you're buying, obtain a sample copy of each policy, examine the fine print, and ask questions about anything you don't understand. If you can't get answers from an insurance agent or broker—and if you want a list of companies offering similar policies (along with other information)—write to the Health Insurance Institute, 1850 K St. NW, Washington, DC 20006.

In reality, the best "health insurance" is proper diet, exercise, and rest, which improve your health and lower your insurance costs.

What We Should All Know About Medicare

Medicare is the hospital (Part A) insurance and the medical (Part B) insurance that is available to almost everyone over age 65 eligible for Social Security benefits, and also to those between ages 18 and 65 who are eligible for federal disability insurance and those with chronic kidney disease. A low-income elderly person who hasn't contributed to Social Security can buy Medicare coverage at nominal cost.

THE GOOD NEWS ABOUT MEDICARE: The hospital insurance is free (but you pay a deductible if you're admitted to a hospital) for the first 60 days, then there are nominal charges for the next 90 days. If you require continuous nursing or rehabilitation services as further treatment, you can enter an "extended care facility" in which you get free care up to 20 days and care up to 80 more days at a nominal charge. After discharge from a hospital or nursing home, you may qualify for unlimited home health visits for each benefit period, including part-time nursing and physical or speech therapy while you're confined at home.

Part B, the medical insurance, has deductibles and co-insurance features similar to Part A. For miscellaneous services prescribed by a doctor, Part B covers casts, splints, surgical dressings, braces, X-ray and radiation treatments, artificial eyes and limbs, and such items for home use as crutches or wheelchairs.

THE BAD NEWS ABOUT MEDICARE: Under Part A (hospital insurance), Medicare does *not* pay for what is essentially custodial care, private nursing care, convenience items (TV, telephone), or the cost of the first three pints of blood used but not replaced during a benefit period.

Under Part B (medical insurance), Medicare does *not* pay for dentures, regular dental care, glasses and eye examinations for glasses, hearing aids, immunizations, orthopedic shoes, patent medicines, prescription drugs, or routine physical checkups.

The widest—and most costly—gaps in Medicare coverage are *private nursing care* and *out-of-hospital drugs*. At present, Medicare pays less than 40 percent of the elderlys' medical bills, and health insurance experts advise that persons under Medicare get some sort of supplemental policy that includes private nursing care and out-of-hospital drugs, such as Blue Cross and Blue Shield, Aetna Life and Casualty, Bankers Life and Casualty, Benefit Trust, or Mutual of Omaha.

Before buying a supplemental policy consider these points:

■ *Don't be overinsured.* Health authorities estimate that 23 percent of those over age 65 who have private insurance have two or more policies that result in overlapping coverage. In areas of overlap, most policies state that *only one policy will pay for each gap.*

■ *Don't expect too much.* It's impossible to be 100 percent insured, and no one policy will give you complete coverage. Experts also cautioned against mail-order insurance, especially those policies that start to pay for coverage after 60 days in a hospital. The fact is that most Medicare patients remain in the hospital *less than two weeks*, and *only 0.3 percent have a hospital stay exceeding 60 days.* (If a patient needs more than 60 days care, he or she is usually moved to an extended-care facility.) You can get a free guide to choosing a continuing-care facility by writing American Association of Homes for the Aging, 1050 17th St. NW, Washington, DC 20036.

A good Medicare supplemental policy should:

■ Provide "service" (pay all or a percentage of actual unmet charges) rather than "indemnity" (set payment for each day) benefits.

■ Fill in as many of the gaps—large and small—as possible. When broader coverage is available, it should be offered as an extension of the basic coverage, not as a separate policy.

■ Limit any exclusion for preexisting illnesses to six months.

If you're in dire straits and need medical assistance, most states have Medicaid programs that provide medical assistance to the needy. You can get further information on health insurance and Medicare by sending for these publications: *Guide to Health Insurance for People with Medicare*, Dept. HHS, Health Care Financing Administration, Baltimore, MD 21235; *How to Shop for Health Insurance*, Consumer Information Center, Pueblo, CO 81009; *How to Use Private Insurance with Medicare*, Health Insurance Association of America, 1850 K St. NW, Washington, DC 20006. Most states are reforming their laws and regulations on the advertising and sale of Medicare supplemental policies to conform with new minimum standards mandated as of July 1, 1982. Your state insurance commissioner (located in your state capital) may also have some helpful booklets and advice on buying health insurance policies, both before and after Medicare. The federal government has a Medigap program that can give you free information on buying policies. Write Bureau of Program Operations, Dept. HHS, Rm. 500-East High Rise, 6325 Security Blvd., Baltimore, MD 21207. Also contact National Association of Insurance Commissioners, 350 Bishop Way, Brookfield, WI 53004, for Medigap information.

Is There Dental Insurance in Your Future?

The steep climb in dental fees (which have risen faster than the cost of living) is a main reason for prepaid dental insurance: the cost of having a tooth pulled has risen from about $10 in 1976 to over $25 today.

You can now get dental insurance policies through membership in a group plan or as a rider to a major medical policy. Present policies fall into three main categories: (1) *scheduled benefits* (fixed price for each dental procedure); (2) *combination* (co-insurance on the total bill); (3) *comprehensive* (co-insurance and deductibles on broad coverage). Dental insurance is expensive and not always economically feasible. I had *hundreds* of dollars of dental work up to and including age 35, but after that my dental condition "stabilized" until I reached age 45 and started to have some gum problems. I now go to the dentist at least once a year, and I usually require minor work. It *would* have paid for me to get dental insurance up to age 35; it wouldn't have been worth it from age 35 to 45; it may *now* be worth it (after age 45) if my gum problems persist. Ask your dentist if he thinks dental insurance would be worth it for you.

I've emphasized that the best "health insurance" is proper diet, exercise, and rest to improve your health and lower your health insurance costs. *But no matter how healthy you are, you need some form of health insurance—the basic hospital and medical plans, plus some form of major medical or catastrophic insurance.* Even those over age 65 who are covered by Medicare need some supplemental insurance to cover the "gaps"—mainly private nursing care and out-of-hospital drug costs. Meanwhile, a dollars-and-sense approach will save both your health and wealth. There are other ways you can save on health-care costs.

Are Annual Physical Exams Necessary?

Many specialists say an annual checkup isn't necessary for many people because the examinations rarely reveal presymptomatic illness where the start of early treatment actually makes a difference in the outcome. Other medical authorities say the frequency of examination should depend on the individual's age and likely health problems. Some guidelines:

■ If *you're 40 to 59 years old* many specialists say you may need a *complete* health examination only *once every five years.* This exam should include complete physical and medical history; tests for chronic conditions (high blood pressure, heart disease, diabetes, cancer, vision and hearing impairment); immunizations as needed; counseling in changing nutritional needs, physical activities, occupation, sex, adjustment to menopause, marital and parental problems, use of cigarettes, alcohol, and drugs. For those *over age 50,* annual tests are recommended for blood pressure, obesity, and certain cancers.

■ *If you're 60 to 74* you need a complete health examination *every two years.* This should include a complete physical and tests for chronic conditions (see above), counseling regarding changing life-style related to retirement, nutritional requirements, absence of children, possible loss of spouse, and probably reduction in income and physical resources. Annual flu shot and periodic podiatry treatments if needed.

■ *If you're 75 years and older* you should have a complete physical and medical examination *at least once a year.*

Are There Alternatives to Seeing a Doctor?

Researchers estimate that *routine self-care* accounts for 85 percent of all health care in the world—and that most often this care makes sense and is right. You can find guidelines for emergency self-care in first-aid manuals, and the American Red Cross offers first-aid classes. Local chapters of the ARC and the American Heart Association also offers courses in cardiopulmonary resuscitation (CPR), which has saved hundreds of victims of heart attacks, electrical shock, and drowning.

And some of the books listed below present checklists (called alogithms) that guide the reader through appropriate self-treatment and signal at what point you might need professional help.

You can also sign up for "activated patient" programs. This will help you and your family become involved in your health care. Activated patients attend classes on such topics as hypertension, common injuries, the proper use of drugs, yoga, foot care, and so forth. In addition, each participant gets a "black bag" and learns to use the tools it contains: a low-reading thermometer, a stethoscope for monitoring pulse and heartbeat, a sphygmomanometer for measuring blood pressure, a high-intensity penlight and an otoscope for examining ears. Courses are taught in 25 states and in Canada, and many are tailored especially for older persons. You can find out about them by checking with your doctor or local health resource agencies.

Also ask about *self-help groups* focusing on any particular health problem you or a family member might have. Such groups have been formed for those with ulcers, heart and stroke problems, arthritis, diabetes, and so on. Some are affiliated with national organizations like the American Heart Association or the Arthritis Foundation, but others are begun by patients themselves or their families who, often, can get federal, state, and local assistance. You can find out about such groups locally and through two national centers:

National Self-Help Clearing House
Graduate School and University Center
City University of New York
33 West 42nd St., Rm. 1227
New York, NY 10036

The Self-Help Center
1600 Dodge Center
Suite S-122
Evanston, Il 60201

Some good books on the subject (available at most public libraries):

- *How to Be Your Own Doctor (Sometimes)*, ed. Keith W. Sehnert, M.D., and Howard Eisenberg (New York: Grosset & Dunlap, 1981).

- *How to Choose and Use Your Doctor* by Marvin S. Belsky, M.D., and Leonard Gross (New York: Arbor House, 1979).

- *Talk Back to Your Doctor* by Arthur Levin, M.D. (New York: Doubleday, 1975).

- *Take Care of Yourself* by Donald M. Vickery, M.D., and James F. Fries, M.D. (Reading, Mass.: Addison-Wesley, 1981).

Also, write for the fact sheet "Mutual Health Groups," Consumer Information Center, Dept. 609K, Pueblo, CO 81009.

How Can I Save on Hospital Costs?

Health authorities estimate that up to 25 percent of all surgery may be unnecessary. So the first step (if you are told you need surgery) is to *get a second opinion.* The federal government, in cooperation with 44 private insurance carriers, have set up 162 referral centers where patients may get a second opinion. Anyone, including Medicare and Medicaid beneficiaries, may call the referral headquarters by dialing a toll-free number: 800/638-6833. In Maryland call 800/492-6603. Someone there will give you the number of the referral center nearest your home. The center, in turn, will provide you with the names of medical specialists whom you may call for a second opinion. You can also write for the booklet "Surgery," Dept. HHS, Washington, DC 20201.

Medicare pays 80 percent of the second-opinion medical fee after the annual deductible is met, and Medicaid pays for it in some states. And 96 percent of the health-insurance companies surveyed cover the cost of a second or third opinion, as do most Blue Cross–Blue Shield associations.

Realize, also, that many doctors prefer to treat problems with *drugs* rather than surgery. New drugs offer alternatives to surgery for patients with hemorrhoids, ulcers, back pain, and prostate enlargement, for example.

For most operations you can save from *30 to 60 percent* on the cost by getting them performed (if practical) at *same-day surgery centers.* Most of these are found in the Midwest and Southwest, but new centers are opening up in all parts of the country. They offer minor, elective surgery—for such procedures as dilatation and curettage (D&C), tonsillectomies, cataract removals, minor plastic surgery, orthopedic, and ear, nose, and throat procedures. Many insurance companies (and Medicare) now cover one-stop surgery, and you save on the overnight (or longer) stay in a hospital.

If you must enter a hospital, you can save costs in these ways:

■ Try to select a voluntary, nonprofit, teaching hospital accredited by the Joint Commission on Accreditation of Hospitals (JCAH). This assures you a hospital that conforms to basic standards in its operation and in the delivery of care and services and will give you the highest level of care at the lowest possible cost.

■ Don't be admitted to the hospital on a Friday, Saturday, Sunday, or holiday. Most routine testing services operate only from Monday morning to Friday afternoon, and so the best days to be admitted are Tuesday, Wednesday, and Thursday.

■ Try to get most preadmission testing done before checking in at the hospital. This can reduce your stay in the hospital and lower costs. As soon as you're up, try to get other tests and treatment performed on an outpatient basis in the clinic or doctor's office. Realize, also, that some X rays and laboratory tests done on you recently might still be usable by the hospital. And if you're scheduled for nonemergency surgery, ask your doctor about banking your own blood—which is the safest, least expensive, and best blood for your transfusions.

■ Be sure to understand what extra charges there are, especially if you want a private room, telephone, television set, even air conditioning. Check your hospital bill and question all charges. Hospitals can make mistakes that increase the bill.

■ Be sure you take all medical exemptions and tax deductions you're entitled to. This includes medical expenses for you, your spouse, and dependents, exceeding 5 percent of adjusted gross income.

How Can I Save on Nursing-Care Costs?

The American Public Health Association estimates that 10 to 25 percent of people in institutions could live at home if adequate services were available. And other health officials estimate that one in seven patients now cared for in hospitals could be treated as well or better at home.

This is particularly true for patients with illnesses like heart attacks, which involve a lengthy recovery period, for patients who are chronically ill (such as stroke victims), and for patients who are terminally ill (cancer). Home care is also preferable for those who have chronic bronchitis, emphysema, and arthritis.

Not only do these programs help patients recover better and faster, they save money. You can easily cut your hospital stay by 9 to 12 days, with a saving of over $1,000 just in the cost of the room.

The kinds of services available at home are expanding rapidly, and the number of home-care providers, both public and private, is growing as well. In many communities you can participate in home-care programs that provide nursing care; transportation to the doctor's office and/or hospital, and for rehabilitative services. And you can even get home-care services for shopping, cooking, and light housework.

Some 25 states now regulate home health agencies, and many insurance companies now cover them in their policies. Some states even mandate home-care services in public-health programs.

You can find out about services in your community through your doctor, local hospital, human resources agency, local or area offices on aging, information and referral services, and through these agencies:

■ National Council for Homemaker-Home Health Aide Services, 67 Irving Place, New York, NY 10003

■ National League for Nursing, 10 Columbus Circle, New York, NY 10019

■ National HomeCaring Council, 235 Park Ave. S., New York, NY 10003

■ Home Health Services and Staffing Association, Suite 205, 1101 15th St. NW, Washington, DC 20005

Some helpful pamphlets on the subject:

■ *Home Health Care*, a Public Affairs Pamphlet (50¢ from PAP, 381 Park Ave. S., New York, NY 10016)

■ *A Guide to Home Health Care*, available free from Upjohn Health Care Services, 3651 Van Rick Dr., Kalamazoo, MI 49002

Are There Any Alternatives to Home Care?

There are over 600 *adult day-care centers* throughout the United States that provide such services as one-stop medical and nursing care, rehabilitation, social services, recreational activities, and hot meals, as well as transportation between home and center. Participants attend from three to six hours daily, one to five days a week, depending on individual needs. All programs share similar goals: preventing physical and mental decline and teaching self-care skills to promote continued independent living.

Day-care costs vary widely. For individuals not covered by public or private insurance, the costs may run from $25 to $40 a day. But in some states, such as California and Massachusetts, day-care costs can be covered by Medicaid. Medicare Part B (medical insurance) pays part of the bill for physician services, therapy, and other skilled care provided to patients in need of active rehabilitation. And some insurance companies may reimburse certain outpatient medical services (check individual policies).

A major advantage of day care is that it provides a respite for families. The centers offer "humane cost effectiveness" because participants can return home in the evenings and remain a part of the family and of the community.

For further information, check with the local resources listed above or contact your nearest senior or geriatric center.

How Can I Save on Prescription Drugs?

If your doctor prescribes a drug, here are ways to hold down costs:

■ *Ask you doctor to prescribe the drug by its generic (family) name.* In most instances, brand-name prescriptions cost 5 to 30 percent more than their generic counterparts. Most states now have made it easier for prescriptions to be filled with generic drugs. If not, ask your doctor for the cheapest equivalent to the brand name.

■ *Shop around for prescriptions.* Many states and drug companies now post the names and prices of the most frequently prescribed drugs. One survey of drug prices showed a range from $3.50 to $6.71 for drugs that cost the pharmacies $1.51 to $3.31. And another survey of drugstores in New York City showed that the same prescription for 15 capsules of *Achromycin* (a frequently prescribed antibiotic with the generic name of "tetracycline") ranged in price from $1.50 to $6. Generally, prices are lowest in pharmacies of discount, department, and chain stores as well as mail-order outlets like Getz Pharmacy, 916 Walnut St., Kansas City, MO 64199 and Prescription Delivery Systems, 136 S. York Rd., Hatboro, PA 19040.

■ *Get the largest quantity advisable.* Large quantities are usually cheaper and save trips to the pharmacy. However, make sure the drugs won't deteriorate (drugs in dark bottles or which must be refrigerated usually deteriorate rapidly). Ask your doctor about expiration dates (they are now mandated).

■ *Ask your doctor for "starter" samples.* If your doctor isn't sure about the suitability of a long-term drug, he may be able to provide you with free office samples. Then, if undesirable side effects show up, you won't be stuck with the cost of a useless drug. However, if the doctor starts you out with a small supply of a drug, then wants to double the dosage, it's cheaper if he writes a new prescription for the larger amounts than if he renews the old prescription.

■ *Keep track of all expenses.* You'll be able to deduct for the cost of all *prescription drugs* and *insulin* you might need during the year, assuming your medical costs exceed 5 percent of adjusted gross income.

Where Can I Get Further Information on Health Care?

You can contact these *organizations:*

■ Office of Public Affairs, Public Health Service, Dept. HEW, 200 Independence Ave., Washington, DC 20201

■ National Institute on Aging, Bldg. 31, Rm. 5C36, Bethesda, MD 20205

■ National Information Center on Health for the Aging, American Health Care Association, 1200 15th St. NW, Washington, DC 20005

■ Consumer Communications, Food & Drug Administration, Dept. HEW, 5600 Fishers Lane, Rockville, MD 20857

You can also get these *books* (available at most libararies):

■ *Feeling Alive After 65* by Robert B. Taylor, M.D. (Westport, Conn.: Arlington House, 1973).

■ *Your Health After 60* by Sanders-Brown Research Center on Aging, ed. M. M. Blacker and D. R. Wekstein (New York: E. P. Dutton, 1979).

■ *Secrets of Staying Young and Living Longer* by Norman D. Ford (by mail-order only; $4.95 plus 50¢ postage from Harian Press, 1 Vernon Ave., Floral Park, NY 11001).

■ *Sixty-Plus and Fit Again* by Magda Rosenberg (New York: M. Evans, 1977).

■ *The Fitness Challenge in the Later Years: An Exercise Program for Older Americans* (75¢ from Supt. of Documents, Gov. Printing Office, Washington, DC 20402).

■ *A Diet for Living* by Jean Mayer (New York: Pocket Books, 1976).

■ *Help Your Doctor Help You* by Walter Alvarez, M.D. (Millbrae, Calif.: Celestial Arts paperback, 1976).

For further information on *mental health*, contact these organizations:

■ National Clearinghouse for Mental Health Information, Dept. HEW, 5600 Fishers Lane, Rockville, MD 20852. (Contact, especially, the Center for Studies of the Mental Health of the Aging.)

■ American Psychiatric Association, 1700 18th St. NW, Washington, DC 20009.

■ American Psychological Association, 1200 17th St. NW, Washington, DC 20036.

PROFILE ANALYSIS: HEALTH MEANS WEALTH

You can pinpoint your health needs and wants by taking the test below. First, place a check by the answer that most nearly fits your situation:

1. LONGEVITY. The *average* age at death of my parents and grandparents:

A. over *70* and death came from natural causes_____

B. over *50* and death came from internal illness_____

C. *under 50* and death came from illnesses or accidents_____

2. HEALTH EXAMINATION. I see my doctor under the following circumstances:

A. at *regular intervals* for a checkup._____

B. only *on occasion* when I'm not feeling up to par_____

C. only in *an emergency* or when I can't get help elsewhere_____

3. DOCTOR-PATIENT RELATIONSHIP. When I talk with my doctor I:

A. ask and answer *all questions* pertaining to my health condition_____

B. answer *only those questions* he asks me_____

C. tell him only what I think he should know_____

4. EXTERNAL HEALTH. As to my skin, eyes, ears, feet, teeth, I:

A. understand *what changes are normal* but report any abnormalities_____

B. see my doctor only when *changes are painful or embarrassing*_____

C. *ignore most symptoms* because they are just part of aging_____

5. INTERNAL HEALTH. As to arthritis, cancer, diabetes, heart disease, I:

A. know how to *prevent or forestall them;* know dangerous symptoms_____

B. feel I *can't do much myself;* would see my doctor if I "felt bad"_____

C. feel that *"something will get me"* so just ignore aches, pains_____

6. SEXUAL ACTIVITY. My attitude toward sex in the later years is:

A. do what I *feel like doing* when I feel like doing it_____

B. feel that I should *slow down* because I'm getting older_____

C. feel that I don't need or want sex anymore because I'm "over the hill"_____

7. MIND OVER MATTER. As far as my mental attitudes are concerned:

A. I *accept and adapt to change* and still want to learn "new" tricks_____

B. I feel *that your mind slows down* like your body_____

C. I can't and don't want to "learn new tricks" because I'm too old_____

8. ACTIVITIES. For "exercise" I generally do the following:

A. walking, swimming, cycling, dancing for enjoyment as well as fitness_____

B. tennis, golf, bowling, skiing, other sports and game "for fun" only_____

C. no exercise because I don't feel up to it_____

9. NUTRITION. My eating habits are best described as:

A. I know what's good for me and *eat to live*—not live to eat_____

B. don't worry too much about food; *eat what I want*_____

C. I eat what I want, when I want, and as much as I want_____

10. HEALTH INSURANCE. My health isurance coverage includes:

A. basic coverage plus *major medical; Medicare supplements* if over age 65_____

B. just basic protection; figure Medicare is enough if over age 65_____

C. no protection to speak of; figure state or county will take care of me_____

Add up the score by giving yourself *10 points* for every A checked; *5 points* for every B checked; *0 points* for every C checked. Here are what the scores mean:

1. If you have *90 to 100 points*, your health care and knowledge are excellent and you should just review the new developments and techniques in this section.

2. If you have *75 to 90* points, you could use some improvement where you checked B and C answers. Review and study the appropriate sections in "Health Means Wealth."

3. If you score *less than 75 points*, don't wait: review "Health Means Wealth" section thoroughly and take immediate steps to correct any poor health habits and to protect your future.

PART III.

HOW TO

HATCH YOUR NEST EGG

NOW

No matter at what age you retire—or how much or how little money you have now—you *must adjust* to changing conditions. Your income and expenses will change; interest rates and investment returns will change.

To be financially free during retirement, you'll need enough *savings* for emergencies, *guaranteed income* to meet current expenses, and *investment income* to keep ahead of inflation.

You can start reaching these goals now by finding answers to these questions:

HOW MUCH MONEY DO I NEED?

If you want to live in retirement the way you do now, you'll need only about two thirds to three quarters of the income you have now. Why? Because a lot of your current expenses are business related: transportation, clothes, business lunches, gifts, entertainment. You'll also have increased *tax advantages* in retirement: double federal tax exemptions; a tax exemption on the profit from selling your home, if any; Retirement Income Credit (15 percent of retirement income for those eligible); medical tax exemptions; and many personal and property tax exemptions (see tax section, pages 159 to 161 and 205 and 206).

Also, much of your retirement income will be *tax exempt:* Social Security and Railroad Retirement benefits are, and so are pension and annuity income to the extent of your contributions.

Of course, your personal life-style enters into this picture, but assuming you want to maintain your present life-style in retirement, the President's Commission on Pension Policy estimates that these are the replacement ratios you'll need:

RETIREMENT INCOME NEEDED

GROSS PRERETIREMENT INCOME	DOLLARS (SINGLE)	RATIO	DOLLARS (MARRIED)	RATIO
$10,000	$ 7,272	73%	$ 7,786	78%
$15,000	9,941	66	10,684	71
$20,000	12,282	61	13,185	66
$30,000	17,391	58	18,062	60
$50,000	25,675	51	27,384	55

Does It Depend on Where I Live?

Yes. Generally, the cost of living and taxes are highest in the northeastern part of the United States. Costs and taxes are generally lower in the South and West. Part of this is due to the relatively mild weather in the Sunbelt region. Homes don't need central heating or air conditioning (in some instances); you don't need as much shelter or insulation; you don't need garages or basements. Property taxes are lower because you need fewer public services—such as snow removal.

Here is how the various regions rate in the cost of living. Using 100 as the average cost-of-living index for a retired couple in the United States (which for 1984–1985 = $16,700 for a reasonably comfortable life-style), here is how the Bureau of Labor Statistics rates these areas. The figures include *total consumption costs* for housing, food, transportation, medical care, clothing, personal items, but not personal taxes. (Note: index numbers indicate percentages above or below average, which is 100. At 122, Boston is 22% above average; at 96, Lancaster is 4% below average.)

REGIONAL RATING OF COST OF LIVING

AREA	CITY	TOTAL BUDGET CONSUMPTION
NORTHEAST	Boston	122
	Buffalo	107
	Hartford	107
	Lancaster	96
	New York	117
	Philadelphia	104
	Pittsburgh	102
	Portland	102
	Nonmetropolitan areas	96

AREA	CITY	TOTAL BUDGET CONSUMPTION
NORTH-CENTRAL	Cedar Rapids	100
	Champaign-Urbana	104
	Chicago	100
	Cincinnati	96
	Cleveland	103
	Dayton	98
	Detroit	106
	Green Bay	100
	Indianapolis	99
	Kansas City	102
	Milwaukee	103
	Minneapolis	100
	St. Louis	98
	Wichita	99
	Nonmetropolitan areas	89
SOUTH	Atlanta	91
	Austin	96
	Baltimore	98
	Baton Rouge	91
	Dallas	98
	Durham	93
SOUTH	Nashville	94
	Orlando	91
	Washington, D.C.	107
	Nonmetropolitan areas	85
WEST	Anchorage	134
	Honolulu	113
	San Diego	96
	San Francisco-Oakland	106
	Seattle-Everett	106
	Nonmetropolitan areas	89

URBAN U.S. = 100
Metropolitan areas = 104
Nonmetropolitan areas = 88

How Will Spending Patterns Change in Retirement?

The Bureau of Labor Statistics estimates that these are how average spending ratios differ before and after retirement:

SPENDING CATEGORY	BEFORE RETIREMENT (%)	AFTER RETIREMENT (%)
HOUSING	45.0	32.9
FOOD	18.1	29.4
TRANSPORTATION	18.6	10.1
MEDICAL CARE	4.8	10.1
CLOTHING & PERSONAL CARE	5.1	7.1
ENTERTAINMENT & OTHER	7.8	10.5

Where Is the Money Coming From?

The Social Security Administration estimates that these are the sources of retirement income:

SOURCE OF INCOME	PERCENTAGE (%)
EARNED INCOME, people still working full or part time	23
SOCIAL SECURITY	38
PUBLIC PENSIONS	7
PRIVATE PENSIONS	7
ASSETS (investments, houses, accumulated capital)	19
PUBLIC ASSISTANCE	2
CONTRIBUTIONS from others	1
ALL OTHER	3

In general, most retirees get their major income from *Social Security*. This ranges from 30 to 55 percent of a person's earnings in the year prior to retirement. Another way to estimate the amount is to take *30 percent* of average of the last five (or highest five) years of salary.

The Social Security Administration estimates that the median percentage of preretirement income it will replace is:

COUPLE'S INCOME BEFORE RETIREMENT	PERCENTAGE SOCIAL SECURITY WILL REPLACE
$8,700 to $13,100	52
$13,100 to $17,500	48
$17,500 to $21,900	45
$21,900 to $27,300	37
$27,300 to $32,800	32
$32,800 and up	25

For *company benefits*, figure that the annual pension equals 1.66 percent of the average salary over your last five years of work (or your highest five years) plus 0.5 percent for every year over 30. The company would probably subtract 50 percent of your Social Security from a 30-year pension. This would still add up to about 16 percent of your salary if you worked 20 years; 31 percent if you worked 25 years; 50 percent for 30 years.

All told, figure that *your combined pension and Social Security should average between 50 and 70 percent* of preretirement pay. Social Security rises with inflation (even if your pension doesn't).

How Does Inflation Affect Your Planning?

Realize that inflation is cumulative—prices tend to rise each year from their previous base. So 10 years from now many items may cost almost twice what they cost today. Also, some items will rise faster in price than others; seniors tend to spend a greater proportion of their budgets for goods and services—housing, maintenance, and repairs, property insurance, taxes, medical care—which have risen in price more than most commodities.

Here are the *inflation factor* standard multipliers (multiply the amount by the amount you need today to find out your needs tomorrow) for various years:

NUMBER OF YEARS	6% INFLATION	8% INFLATION	10% INFLATION
5	1.338	1.469	1.611
7	1.594	1.851	2.144
9	1.791	2.159	2.594
11	1.898	2.332	2.853
16	2.540	3.426	4.595
18	2.854	3.996	5.560
20	3.207	4.661	6.727
24	4.049	6.341	9.850
28	5.112	8.627	14.421
30	5.743	10.063	17.449

Coping with inflation requires balancing means with necessities. If you want to continue eating steak when the price of beef goes up, you must make more money, start eating hamburger, or cut down someplace else. The longer you live, the more you must take inflation into account (see table on page 8).

How Can I Figure My Retirement Income Needs?

Throughout this book you'll find the information you need to complete the steps below. And just a few minutes figuring will give you a good idea of how much you'll need in any retirement year. No matter how big your retirement needs, if you start *now* to accumulate the money, chances are that you'll have more than enough to meet your needs and wants in retirement.

Step 1: Subtract work-related expenses from present expenses   _____

Step 2: Subtract any tax advantages from current taxes (see pages 160 and 161)   _____

TOTAL REDUCED RETIREMENT EXPENSES   ==========

Step 3: Find life expectancy from table on page 8. Put number here   _____

Step 4: Find inflation factor that corresponds to life expectancy (or in any retirement year you want to figure for). Put number here   _____

Step 5: Multiply number (step 4) by reduced retirement expenses to give you:

RETIREMENT MONEY NEEDS   ==========

Step 6: Estimated Social Security benefits (40% of average annual earnings. Figure anticipated salary increases between now and retirement to get average. You can also use 30% of the average pay for the five years preceding retirement to get an estimated benefit).   _____

Step 7: Figure company pension at 1.66% of average salary over last five years of work (or highest five years) plus 0.5% for every year over 30. Subtract 50% of Social Security benefit (above)   _____

ANTICIPATED RETIREMENT INCOME   ==========

Step 8: To find any gap between anticipated retirement income and retirement money needs, subtract Step 5 (retirement money needs) from Step 7 (anticipated retirement income). This should give you an idea of your *Retirement Gap.* However, this gap might be reduced by income from investments and other sources, and any work you may do in retirement.

ANY RETIREMENT GAP   ==========

Another way to figure your retirement income needs and any "Retirement Gap" or "X-Factor" is to use the worksheet below. If there is a gap, rest assured that you can fill it in by either (or both) making and/or saving money. Develop a *game plan* rather than a grim battle plan. Keep it *simple* and *flexible* and don't be afraid to make adjustments as you go along. In the next few pages we'll explore ways to *make* as well as *save* money in retirement.

FINANCIAL PLANNING WORKSHEET

ESTIMATED MONTHLY INCOME FORM

	NOW	AT RETIREMENT
Company pension	_____	_____
Social Security	_____	_____
Savings accounts	_____	_____
Bonds and preferred stocks	_____	_____
Life insurance (endowment or annuity)	_____	_____
Real estate	_____	_____
All other sources	_____	_____
TOTAL A		TOTAL C

ESTIMATED MONTHLY EXPENSES

	NOW	AT RETIREMENT
Housing (includes rent or payments, utilities, furnishings, maintenance and operation)	_____	_____
Food and beverages	_____	_____
Clothing (include cleaning, etc.)	_____	_____
Medical care (include cost of any health insurance or service)	_____	_____
Transportation (all types)	_____	_____
Taxes	_____	_____
For savings, insurance, investments	_____	_____
Personal and miscellaneous	_____	_____
TOTAL B		TOTAL D

Your X-Factor (subtract **Total D from Total C**)   _____

Use your X-Factor figure to establish realistic financial planning goals. Now is the time to start reducing this X-Factor (difference between D and C) on your own terms. Don't trust to luck!

How Can I Save on Expenses?

Time is money; money is time. The more you have of the one, the less you need of the other. If you have *less money*, then you should spend *more time* planning how to spend, make, or save money. Included is the time you spend reading this book . . . making a master plan, shopping list . . . contacting consumer specialists or agencies *before* making a major purchase.

You'll get more and spend less if you follow these general rules and guidelines:

1. *Plan what to buy.* If you go into a store with a list or plan, you'll know what you really want and can afford. You'll avoid the *impulse shopping* that wastes time and money. Supermarket managers are aware that every minute you linger beyond the normal half-hour shopping trip adds at least 50 cents to your bill.

2. *Know what you really need and want.* By knowing the correct sizes, colors, fabrics of clothes; the nutrients and other values of foods; the service and life-expectancy of household appliances you'll save time and money.

3. *Read the ads and time your purchases.* Reading ads can help you determine what is and what isn't a "special." A Stanford University study shows that shoppers can save 10 percent and more by "shopping the newspapers." Stores often have certain days, weeks, or months for specials that save up to 20 percent off regular prices. Don't overlook food-buying co-ops and discount stores that sell items from one to two cents lower than other stores.

For household appliances, furnishings, TV sets, cameras, and other equipment, you might find best buys at factory outlets, warehouse sales, garage sales, flea markets, wholesale mail-order houses, catalog showrooms, wholesale warehouse outlets.

In some instances you can select your item from a catalog and either phone in your order or go to a showroom to inspect a sample (as in a catalog showroom). Many discounters don't advertise their services, you must seek them out. One of the largest such services is Unity Buying Service, 810 S. Broadway, Hicksville, NY 11802. Unity also has outlets in Schaumburg, Ill.; Camarillo, Calif.; and Atlanta, Ga. It sells everything from apparel to woodenware and lets you charge on credit cards. Write to them for details.

You can also write for these *national directories* for best buys in your area:

■ *Save on Shopping Directory* by Iris Ellis, $8.95 plus $1 postage from S.O.S. Directory, Box 10482, Jacksonville, FL 32207.

■ *The Underground Shopper Discount Mail Order Catalog* with over 500 listings of where to shop by mail at discount prices. $3.95 plus $1 postage from SusAnn Publications, 3110 North Fitzhugh, Dallas, TX 75204.

■ *Directory of Shop-By-Mail Bargain Sources.* $3.50 from Pilot Books, 103 Coopers St., Babylon, New York, NY 11702.

MONTH-BY-MONTH BEST BUYS CALENDAR

This calendar of best buys was compiled from national retail sources. Most local stores feature these best buys of each month:

JANUARY: Most clothing and accessories, coats, underwear, cosmetics, jewelry, lingerie, sweaters, yarn and notions, winter sports equipment, stationery, furniture, white sale items, home accents, books.

FEBRUARY: Active sportswear, boots, gloves, hosiery, small appliances, audio equipment, china, gloves, clocks, housewares, spring fabrics, air conditioners.

MARCH: China and glassware, calculators, luggage, umbrellas, home improvement equipment, washers/dryers.

APRIL: Dresses, suits (after Easter), rainwear, sleepwear, summer fabrics.

MAY: White sale items, lingerie.

JUNE: Hosiery, swimsuits (late June).

JULY: Most clothing and accessories, underwear, cosmetics, toiletries, handbags, lingerie, shoes, swimsuits, bedspreads, blankets, furniture, garden equipment, white sale items.

AUGUST: Coats, accessories, furs, typewriters, summer sporting equipment.

SEPTEMBER: Small electrical appliances, china and glassware, clocks, cutlery, household items, adult games.

OCTOBER: Coats, outerwear, handbags, small leather goods, sweaters, audio equipment, televisions, draperies, curtains, silverware, luggage.

NOVEMBER: Coats, outerwear, china and glassware, tablecloths, silverware, fabrics.

DECEMBER: After December 25: Sales in most departments of large retailers, especially on toys, cards, and other holiday items.

■ *The Barter Project*, 111 N. 19th St., Suite 500, Rosslyn, VA 22209. Lists neighborhood projects near you.

When shopping, *don't be afraid to ask for a discount.* The repeal of "fair trade" legislation makes it easier to bargain. And retailers are exempt from certain provisions of the truth-in-lending law when they grant discounts of no more than 5 percent to buyers who *pay in cash.* If you're willing to settle for a 5 percent discount, ask whether the store offers a discount for paying cash.

Finally, add in all costs. This includes time, energy, and expense of getting to and from the store—doing without one item so you can buy another—the value to your health, morale, general pleasure, and satisfaction—in the long as well as the short run.

HOW CAN I MAKE MORE MONEY IN RETIREMENT?

Besides income from second careers, part-time jobs, at-home or small businesses (which we'll discuss later) most retirees earn money through *investing.* However, before considering investing, you should get answers to this question: *What financial risk can I take?* Generally, the younger you are and/or the more money you have, the more risks you can take and the easier you can replace lost money. The older you are and/or the less money you have, the more you should stress *safety* and *income* to meet current needs. Compare the investment objectives of three persons: (1) age 45, (2) age 55, (3) age 65. Each has $10,000 to invest:

TYPES OF INVESTMENTS	AGE:	45	55	65
		Amount of Money		
Emergency Money—insured savings		$ 2,000	$ 2,500	$ 3,000
Guaranteed Money—bonds, preferred stocks, government issues, annuities, floating rate notes, money-market		1,000	2,500	5,000
Investment Money—common stocks, mutual funds, investment trusts, real estate, precious metals, collectibles		7,000	5,000	2,000
		$10,000	$10,000	$10,000

To help you determine what financial risks you can take, complete the Profile Analysis: What Investment Categories Should *You* Emphasize? on the next page. Once you determine what risks you can take, then you can decide what investments would be most suitable for you.

Now That I've Added Up My Score and Divided by 9, What Does the Median Number Mean? The median number indicates your *financial objectives,* which correlates with the *Investment Strategies* that follow. The Investment Strategies indicate financial objectives ranging from *emergency savings* to *chaos hedges.* By matching the median score with the financial objectives, you'll know what investment categories to emphasize. If you have a fraction (between numbers), then consider investments from Investment

PROFILE ANALYSIS: WHAT INVESTMENT CATEGORIES SHOULD *YOU* EMPHASIZE?

Directions: Circle the answer that most nearly applies to you. Write that number in the space at right. Then add up the numbers and divide by 9 to get a median score.

AGE—My age is closest to:

(9) 45   (7) 50   (5) 55   (3) 60   (1) 70   _____

INCOME—My annual income from all sources is nearest to (in thousands):

(2) 15   (4) 25   (5) 35   (6) 45   (8) 55   _____

ANNUAL EXPENSES—In relation to income, my annual expenses approximate:

(1) 100%   (3) 90%   (5) 80%   (7) 70%   (9) 50%   _____

NUMBER OF DEPENDENTS—I currently have these dependents (without self):

(9) 0   (8) 1   (6) 2–3   (4) 4–5   (1) 6 or more   _____

ESTIMATED VALUE OF ASSETS—My house, insurance, savings, and investments to (in thousands):

(1) 50   (3) 100   (5) 250   (7) 350   (9) 500 or more   _____

LIABILITIES—My bills, mortgages, installment payments, and debts in relation to my assets approximate (in percentage):

(9) 30%   (7) 50%   (5) 75%   (3) 90%   (1) 100%   _____

SAVINGS—I have cash on hand in savings or other liquid assets to equal expenses for:

(1) 2 months   (3) 3 months   (5) 4 months   (7) 5 months   (9) 6+ months   _____

LIFE INSURANCE—My life insurance coverage equals (in thousands):

(9) 250   (7) 150   (5) 100   (3) 50   (1) 25 or less   _____

HEALTH INSURANCE—My health insurance coverage (including Medicare) includes:

(1) Basic   (5) Major Medical plus Basic   (9) Basic, Major Medical, Catastrophic   _____

Strategies both above and below the whole number. You shouldn't put *all* your investments in these categories, but these are the ones you should emphasize the most.

FINANCIAL OBJECTIVE NUMBER (the median number from Profile Analysis Score)	INVESTMENT STRATEGIES
1	Insured savings, money-market funds, "insurance" gold and silver, cash value of life insurance
2	High-grade Treasury, government securities
3	High-grade corporate and municipal bonds, preferred stocks, investment trusts, annuities
4	Lower-rated (higher yielding) corporate and municipal bonds, preferred stocks, investment trusts, convertible bonds, and preferred stocks, variable annuities
5	Higher-grade common stocks and investment trusts
6	Lower-rated (more speculative) common stocks and investment trusts
7	Speculative stocks, bonds, investment trusts
8	Rare and exotic investments: stamps, rare coins, art, antiques, gems and jewelry, rare books, autographs, prints and lithographs
9	"Chaos" gold- and silver-related investments, foreign-currency investments

Because of rapidly changing interest rates, prices, and stock and bond returns, keep your investment plans *flexible*. The following table describes five *investment climates*, one of which is prevailing at any given time. I then describe how to shift investment emphasis to adjust to changing conditions, for both *income* and *growth*. And on page 96 I describe how the various retirement investments compare.

INVESTING IN VARYING ECONOMIC CLIMATES

You must change investment strategies to meet changing economic conditions. Interest and inflation rates will vary; income and expenses will change. Below are five economic climates—one of which is prevailing at any given time. But as conditions change, you must be prepared to shift with the changing winds. Here are suggestions for both the *growth-* and *income*-oriented investor.

ECONOMIC CLIMATE	GROWTH STRATEGY	INCOME STRATEGY
1. *Calm and steady.* Inflation rate stabilizing at 5%; short-term rates stabilizing at 7% or less; economy gradually rising.	Take more risks in long-term investments. Liquidity can be low.	Invest in quality bonds with a maturity date of 10 years or more.
2. *Cool and overcast.* Inflation is down, short-term rates stabilizing above lows; business recovery gradual but uneven.	Invest in quality securities that should do well in up and down markets; have 10% insurance in gold.	Keep fixed-income investments under 10 years. Consider floating-rate issues.
3. *Barometer falling; cloudy.* Inflation and interest rates up; economic growth rising; environment becoming less stable.	Take profits and upgrade stock portfolio. Add to gold/silver reserves. Put spare cash in money-market funds.	Keep fixed-income investments under 5 years, and stick with AA-rated or better. Consider convertible bonds.
4. *Storm clouds gathering; winds increasing.* Inflation and interest rates rising fast; economic growth accelerating; instability increasing.	Take profits in weaker issues and put money in money-market funds. Gold and silver mutual funds for hedge.	Buy only T-bills under 1 year and roll over if interest rates remain high.
5. *Stormy and windy with little letup in sight.* Inflation and interest rates at new highs with no relief in sight.	Gold and silver should form 20% of portfolio. Keep only high-yielding stocks. Invest only in money-market funds.	Buy deep-discount bonds of Bell Systems and leading utilities. Keep T-bills to 3 months.

HOW VARIOUS RETIREMENT INVESTMENTS COMPARE
(A = excellent, B = good, C = fair)

EMERGENCY MONEY

INVESTMENT	AVERAGE YIELD	SAFETY	LIQUIDITY	INCOME
Commercial banks, savings accounts	C−	A	A	C−
Savings and loan, savings banks	C	B	A	C
Time contracts (under $10,000)	C+	A−	C	C+
Certificates ($10,000+)	B+	A−	C	B+
Credit unions	C+	A−	A−	C+
Money-market funds & accounts	B+	B	B	B+
"Insurance" gold/silver	B	B	C	B

GUARANTEED MONEY

	AVERAGE YIELD	SAFETY	LIQUIDITY	INCOME
U.S. Treasury issues	B+	A	A−	B+
High-grade corporate bonds	B	B	B	B
Municipal bonds (tax-free)	B	B	B	B+ (high tax bracket)
High-grade preferred stocks	B−	B−	B	B−
U.S. savings bonds	B−	A	B	B−
Annuities (interest and principal)	C+	A−	C	C+

INVESTMENT MONEY

	AVERAGE YIELD	SAFETY	LIQUIDITY	INCOME
Common stocks for income	B−	B	B	B
Common stocks for growth	B+	B	B	B−
Open-end (mutual) funds	B−	B	B	B−
Closed-end funds	B	B	B	B
Investment gold/silver	B+	B	B	B
Stamps (quality issues)	A	B	C	A
Rare coins	A	B	B	A
Real estate (REITs, land, bldgs., morts.)	B	B−	C	B
Art & antiques	B−	B	C	B
Diamonds	B−	B	C	B−
Foreign currency	B−	B−	B	B−

After you've determined what risks you can take and what investment goals you should emphasize, you can now start putting your money to work to earn more. Assuming that you know the basics of most investments, I will give you the best overall investments in each of the major categories, including how and when to buy (or perhaps sell) to get the most for your money, and some general sources for further information. And, of course, my monthly *Retirement Letter* keeps you up to date on all making and saving money aspects. (Note: To have money to invest for retirement, the International Society of Preretirement Planners suggests a goal of saving 5 percent of pretax income between ages 30 and 40 and then increasing the amount by one percentage point each year until you level off at 10 percent at age 45.)

Where Should I Put Emergency Money?

You should have from three to six months' expenses to cover emergencies and to protect your other investments. Generally, you'll get highest rates of interest from credit unions, savings banks, and savings and loan associations. Ideally, your savings should be in an *insured* savings institution that's convenient (near home or office), one that offers all the services you need, pays interest from day-of-deposit to day-of-withdrawal, features monthly grace days, compounds interest daily, pays quarterly, and has the highest basic rate of interest.

In times of high interest rates, you may get your best yields by "parking" your money in *money-market funds*. These funds invest in highly liquid, short-term securities like U.S. Treasury and agency issues, bank certificates of deposit, and commercial paper. Their yields may lag the prime rate by two to three months, but in times of high short-term rates, they pay much more than savings accounts. And they don't come down as fast as the prime rate. You can write checks against your account (usually for $250 or more); as it takes several days for checks to clear, you can get extra income and still pay big bills. And you can usually get your money out in a day or two by telephone redemption.

If you invest in money-market funds, stick with the *biggest* (they have enough funds to meet heavy investor withdrawals), those with *short maturities* (under 30 days so they can take advantage of higher interest rates faster), and those that provide a *family of funds* (so you can transfer freely as economic conditions change).

Among some recommended funds (which have a family of funds):

- Dreyfus Liquid Assets, 767 Fifth Ave., New York, NY 10022.

- Fidelity Daily Income, 82 Devonshire St., Boston, MA 02109.

- Kemper Money Market Fund, 120 S. LaSalle St., Chicago, IL 60603.

- Merrill Lynch Ready Assets, 165 Broadway, New York, NY 10080.

- Oppenheimer Monetary Bridge, 1 New York Plaza, New York, NY 10004.

- Rowe Price Prime Reserve, 100 E. Pratt St., Baltimore, MD 21202.

You can find out more about money-market funds by subscribing to *Donoghue's Moneyletter*, P.O. Box 411, Holliston, MA 01746. This organization also sells a *Money Fund Directory*. Write to them for details. Also write *Money Fund Safety Ratings*, 3471 N. Federal Highway, Ft. Lauderdale, FL 33306, and ask about their guide to money-market funds.

Central Assets Account for One-Stop Savings, Investing

You can get a money-market fund *and* checking services, brokerage services, credit or debit card, and monthly statements through a *central assets account* available at many brokerage houses and credit card companies. Generally, you must have $10,000 to $25,000 in cash or securities to open such an account, and it would be helpful if you were an active investor and buyer so you would get full use of the services (annual fee runs from about $25 to $100).

Here's how the account could work for you: Let's say you want to make a $15,000 purchase but you only have $10,000 in your money-market fund or checking account. However, you have *borrowing power* because of your securities holdings. The computer would first tap money in your least costly reserve—perhaps idle cash waiting to be put into the money-market fund or in your checking account. It would then withdraw the money in your money-market fund. And whatever additional amount was needed would be authorized by a loan with your securities as collateral.

Here is a sampling of central assets accounts with toll-free (800) numbers. If toll-free number won't connect you, look up local number in directory.

- Advest "Reserve Cash Account" 800/441-7786

- A. G. Edwards & Sons "Total Asset Account" 800/825-9310

- Dean Witter Reynolds "Active Assets Account" 800/221-3778

- Edward D. Jones & Co. "Daily Passport Cash Trust" 314/576-0001 (not toll-free)

- Fidelity "Ultra Service Account" 800/225-6190

- Kidder Peabody "Premium Account" 212/635-5081 (not toll-free)

- Merrill Lynch "Cash Management Account" 800/221-4146

- Prudential-Bache "Command Account" 800/222-4321

- Reserve "CPA Account" 800/223-2213

- Shearson/American Express "Financial Management Account" 800/522-5429

- Smith Barney "Vantage Account" 800/221/3434

Central assets accounts shouldn't be confused with *financial supermarkets* that have sprung up in major cities throughout the country. Sponsored by national retailers such as Sears, J. C. Penney, Kroger, Commercial Credit, the Scott Group, and Investors Diversified Services, the financial supermarkets offer many of the services above as well as insurance, real estate, or whatever other products the retailer specializes in.

Where Should I Invest for Guaranteed Income?

If you have *under* $10,000 and can tie up your money for two-and-one-half years, you could get *market rate certificates* at savings and loan associations or savings banks. These require a minimum of $100 and are based on the yield of U.S. Treasury notes. If you have $10,000 or more, you can get top interest in *U.S. Treasury bills.* As these are sold at a *discount* from face value (you pay less for the high yield) and they are *exempt from state and local taxes*, they usually yield more than savings certificates based on the T-bill yields.

U.S. Treasury bills are auctioned each Monday (except holidays) to mature in 91 or 182 days. One-year (52-week) bills are auctioned every four weeks. And you can buy them *without charge* if you buy them directly from a Federal Reserve Bank. The Federal Reserve has branches in many major cities, but here are the main branches:

- *Boston*—600 Atlantic Ave., Boston, MA 02106.

- *New York*—33 Liberty St., New York, NY 10045.

- *Philadelphia*—100 N. 6th, Philadelphia, PA 19101.

- *Cleveland*—1455 East 6th St., Cleveland, OH 44101.

- *Richmond*—100 North 9th St., Richmond, VA 23213.

- *Atlanta*—104 Marietta St. NW, Atlanta, GA 30303.

- *Chicago*—230 LaSalle St., Chicago, IL 60690.

- *St. Louis*—411 Locust St., P.O. Box 422, St. Louis, MO 63166.

- *Minneapolis*—250 Marquette Ave., Minneapolis, MN 55440.

- *Kansas City*—925 Grand Ave., Kansas City, MO 64198.

- *Dallas*—400 South Akard St., Dallas, TX 75222.

- *San Francisco*—400 Sansome St., San Francisco, CA 94120.

DOUBLING YOUR MONEY: HOW LONG DOES IT TAKE

Below is a table that shows you how many years it takes for $1,000 to double at various rates of interest and compounding schedules, starting with the 5.5 percent passbook savings rate. The yearly values have been carried out to three decimal places to give you fractions of years.

As you'll see, *daily compounding* doubles your money the fastest. Monthly compounding doubles your money about 11 days later than daily compounding. Quarterly compounding will double your money about 31 days later than if your money was compounded on a daily basis. Finally, monthly compounding doubles your money about 21 days sooner than quarterly compounding.

RATE OF INTEREST	YEARS TO DOUBLE		
	WITH DAILY COMPOUNDING	WITH MONTHLY COMPOUNDING	WITH QUARTERLY COMPOUNDING
5.5%	12.603	12.632	12.689
6.0	11.553	11.581	11.640
7.0	9.903	9.931	9.981
8.0	8.665	8.693	8.751
9.0	7.703	7.731	7.788
10.0	6.932	6.960	7.018
11.0	6.302	6.330	6.388
12.0	5.777	5.805	5.862
13.0	5.333	5.361	5.418
14.0	4.952	4.980	5.307
15.0	4.622	4.650	4.707
16.0	4.333	4.361	4.418
17.0	4.078	4.106	4.163
18.0	3.852	3.880	3.937

Write or call for information about submitting bids. You can also write to the Bureau of Public Debt, Securities Transaction Branch, Rm. 2134, U.S. Treasury Bldg., Washington, DC 20226, and ask for the booklet, "U.S. Securities Available to Investors" (PD-800-A). Most major brokerage houses also have booklets on buying Treasury securities (bills, notes, bonds) as well as *Federal Agency Issues* (Federal Land Banks, Federal Home Banks,

Federal National Mortgage Association) that sell for as little as $1,000 and *yield a bit more* than Treasury issues because they lack the specific backing of the government. And for as little as $1,000 you can buy shares in mutual funds that have portfolios of U.S. Treasury and Federal Agency issues. Among these:

- Capital Preservation Fund, 459 Hamilton Ave., Palo Alto, CA 94301.

- Fund of U.S. Government Securities, 421 7th Ave., Pittsburgh, PA 15219.

In times of high yields, also consider buying *deep discount bonds* issued by the Bell System or leading utilities. Discount bonds sell for less than face value for two reasons: (1) they were issued when interest rates were lower, so their price has dropped to bring their current yield into line with prevailing rates; (2) the bonds are (or have become) more speculative and their ratings are lower (or have been lowered).

However, these bonds can be good buys if they mature in a year when you have little or no income (such as a retirement year). You'd get full face value when the bonds matured, and you'd pay taxes at favorable capital gains rates. Meanwhile, you could be collecting some high current income.

While it doesn't pay to buy less than five ($5,000 worth) bonds, for as little as $1,000 you can buy shares in these discount bond funds. Write for prospectuses from:

- Federated High Income Securities, 421 7th Ave., Pittsburgh, PA 15219.

- Fidelity Aggressive Income, 82 Devonshire St., Boston, MA 02109.

- High-Yield Securities, 1080 Deesser Tower, Houston, TX 77002.

- Kemper High Yield, 120 S. La Salle St., Chicago, IL 60603.

- Keystone B-4, 99 High St., Boston, MA 02110.

- Oppenheimer High Yield Fund, 1 New York Plaza, New York, NY 10004.

Also, you could buy *U.S. Savings Bonds* to build a retirement nest egg. Yields are now more attractive, based on 85 percent of the average return on five-year marketable Treasury securities. The Treasury sets new savings bonds rates twice a year, in November and in May. Each change reflects market activity during the previous six months. The rate is guaranteed never to go below 7.5 percent. However, you must hold a bond five years from date of issue to receive the variable rate.

You can defer taxes on Series E or EE bonds by converting them into Series HH bonds that mature in 10 years. The HH bonds pay interest twice a year, and the interest is taxable in the year it is paid. Accumulated interest from EE bonds is deferred until HH bonds are cashed in.

And interest on U.S. Savings Bonds is exempt from state and local taxes. For further information on U.S. Savings Bonds, contact the nearest Federal Reserve Bank or write Bureau of the Public Debt, Washington, DC 20226.

If you are a single person with a taxable income of $20,000 or a married couple with a joint taxable income of $30,000 or more, often you can make more money by investing in tax-exempt (municipal) bonds. The bonds are exempt from federal taxes and, usually, from taxes of the state and city of issue. (New York City residents would have a triple tax exemption.) And District of Columbia, Guam, Virgin Island, and Puerto Rico bonds are exempt from *all* taxes no matter where the investor lives.

To find out what taxable equivalent you'd have to get to match *tax-exempt yield*, use the formula below. Check your federal, state, and local tax returns for the highest percentage rate at which your taxable income is taxed.

$$\text{Equivalent taxable yield} = \frac{\text{Tax-exempt yield}}{1 - (\text{federal} + \text{state} + \text{local tax rate})}$$

For example, if you are in the 36 percent federal tax bracket and the issue is exempt from 5 percent state income tax (with no local tax) here is what taxable yield you'd have to get to match a 6 percent tax-exempt yield:

$$\text{Equivalent taxable yield} = \frac{6\%}{1 - (.36 + .05 + 0)} = \frac{6\%}{.59} = 10.17\%$$

If you buy tax-exempt bonds, stick to those rated A or better, and, preferably, *general obligation* bonds backed by unlimited taxing power. You can spread the risk by buying (for as little as $1,000) shares of *unit trusts* sponsored by Merrill Lynch, Shearson Hayden Stone, E. F. Hutton, John Nuveen, Paine Webber, and so on. These unit trusts are usually self-liquidating and operate like closed-end funds (additional bonds are not added to the portfolio). However, you can buy *municipal bond mutual funds*, which offer continuous management of an ever-changing portfolio. Some of the leading funds are:

■ Dreyfus Tax Exempt Bond Fund, 767 5th Ave., New York, NY 10022.

- Federated Tax-Free Income, 421 7th Ave., Pittsburgh, PA 15219.

- Fidelity Municipal Bond Fund, 82 Devonshire St., Boston, MA 02109.

- Nuveen Municipal Bond Fund, 61 Broadway, New York, NY 10006.

- Rowe Price Tax-Exempt Income, 100 E. Pratt St., Baltimore, MD 02109.

- Scudder Managed Municipal Bonds, 175 Federal St., Boston, MA 02110.

In times of stable interest rates, the unit trusts offered by brokerage firms usually offer highest yields. But in rapidly changing times, the better-managed mutual funds above could be a better bet. And in uncertain markets, *convertible bonds* give you the downside protection of a bond with the capital gains potential of a stock. You would have a good buy in a convertible if the interest rate is within 1 percent of the interest paid on the nonconvertible and if the conversion price is within 15 percent of the current stock price.

In *weak* markets concentrate on convertibles in utilities, food processors, dairy products, and finances. In *strong* markets concentrate on convertibles in machinery, steel, aerospace, and construction.

You've got to watch convertibles closely. If the stock splits or pays a dividend with additional shares, the shares you convert to should be increased accordingly. If the conversion rate is subject to change or if the issue is callable, you may lose money. To protect yourself you might want to consider *convertible bond funds* like those below, some selling at discounts:

- American General Convertible Securities, 3910 Keswick Rd., Baltimore, MD 21211.

- Bancroft Convertible Fund, 660 Madison Ave., New York, NY 10021.

- Putnam Convertible Fund, 1 Post Office Sq., Boston, MA 02109

HOW CAN I KEEP AHEAD OF INFLATION?

Traditionally, the more "aggressive" investments—selected common stocks, open-end (mutual) and closed-end funds, real estate, precious metals, collectibles, stamps, coins—have kept ahead of (or at least paced) inflation. But as these investments become riskier, they are better suited to those who can afford to risk money and who need to provide for more years of financial security. However, *at any age*, we all must take inflation into account. Here are some ways to invest in inflation hedges:

COMMON STOCKS. During the last 40 years, common stocks have proven *fair* inflation hedges in periods of *moderate* inflation. But in times of double-digit inflation, tight money and high interest rates drive stocks down to historic lows. When the stock market rises, about one third of the stocks pull up the rest; the others mark time or decline. So you must find that one third of the stocks that lead the others. Generally, the basic demand for the company's product should be steady or expanding. The company's labor costs should be low and return on equity high, so profit margins can narrow without disappearing.

You can invest in two types of common stocks: (1) *growth:* electronics, aerospace, machinery, mining, manufacturing, textiles, and crude oil followed in lesser degree by chemicals, paper, petroleum products, and retail trade; (2) *income:* stocks that represent the necessities of life and will always be in demand like food, water, gas, electric power, telephone, and banking. Price fluctuations aren't violent and rate of return remains fairly constant.

As I pointed out, *timing* is most important in buying stocks. That's why it's important to follow a broad index of stock movement like the *New York Stock Exchange (Composite) Index.* This index can help you: (1) spot the general direction in which prices are moving; (2) determine whether or not your own investments are doing as well as the overall market; and (3) find bargains.

Also, check the *most actively traded issues* each day, as these can give you a clue to market trends. If the issues on this list *rose* when the stock market declined, particularly if the decline has continued for some time, then it's most likely that the market has "bottomed out" and will start going back up. On the other hand, if the stocks on the most active list *declined* while the Dow Jones Average went up, then there's a possibility of a "top" having been reached, and the market will decline. And its a *bullish* sign if the stocks on the most active list rise and include many higher-priced issues; it is *bearish* (declining market) if the most active stocks rise but include only low-priced stocks.

Here are further tips on *buying* stocks.

1. Buy only *quality stocks* when they are undervalued, have bright prospects, and are becoming popular. *Don't go against a trend* and buy when the stock is falling; wait for a floor price to set, then buy *when the stock is moving up.* But buy only when total returns can be expected to be *35 percent or more in the next 24 months.* This assures you of at least 15 percent annual return on your money.

2. *Time your purchases.* Generally, good stocks rise *before the end of quarters* (March 31, June 30, September 30, December 31) when they will be

purchased by investment trusts seeking to add to their reported gains, and *before holidays* (markets rose almost 70 percent of the time over a 42-year period). If you seek a *low market* for good buying opportunities, look for a period of between *12:00 and 2:00 p.m.* on a *Monday* during the *middle of the months* of February, April, June, and October. Historically, these have been low points of stock markets.

If you want to *sell* a stock, here are some of the best times:

Toward the *end of the day* of an upward market on a *Friday* toward the *end of the month* in December, August, and July. Historically, these have been high points of stock markets.

Also, *sell* a stock when its price/earnings ratio rises above its historic levels, or when the dividend is threatened.

And at all times, it's best to *buy* quality stocks for the long haul and sell only when you need the money, can take needed profits, or can establish a favorable tax loss. When buying stocks, consider *total returns: income plus appreciation.* Interest is taxed at your highest rate, but capital gains are taxed at only 40 percent of the profit. Out of every $1 you get from a stock you keep:

TAX BRACKET	INTEREST/DIVIDENDS	CAPITAL GAINS
32%	.68¢	.87¢
36	.64	.856
39	.61	.844
45	.55	.82
50	.50	.80

Good investment goals should be:

■ *Industrial/service corporations* = 25 percent from dividends and 75 percent from capital gains.

■ *Utilities and financial corporations* = 75 percent from dividends and 25 percent from capital gains.

If you select your own stocks, you can save from 10 to 60 percent by buying through *discount brokers.* The discounters can do this because they merely execute orders, often pooling investors' money to buy at a certain time of day. Here is a partial list of discounters:

■ Baker & Co., 1801 E. 9th St., Cleveland, OH 44114.

■ W. T. Cabe & Co., 1270 Ave. of the Americas, New York, NY 10020.

OPTIONS—ANOTHER "OPTION" FOR INVESTORS

Options give you the right to buy (call) or sell (put) a set number of shares of a specific common stock at a predetermined price for a limited period of time (usually 9 months maximum). The price at which you have the option to buy or sell a stock is called the *exercise* or *striking* price; the premium is what you pay for the option itself (generally around 10% of the exercise price).

Here's how you might make money in buying (calling) a stock option:

Let's say you think that Stock A will climb from its present price of, say, $50 to $70 in 6 months. If you are right and if you had bought the stock outright, you would have made $2,000 on 100 shares costing $5,000 or a 40 percent return (before commissions). If you had bought the stock on 50 percent margin, the return on your $2,500 investment would have been 80 percent (before commissions and interest on the margin loan).

However, if you bought an option call at $7 (entitling you to buy 100 shares prior to the expiration date), you would have had to put up only $700 premium (plus commission which might run 10 to 15 percent of the price of the option). Had you exercised the call at $70, your gross profit would have been $2,000 less the $700 cost of the option, or $1,300—a 185 percent return.

And here's how a *put* (sell) can make money for you:

Let's say you feel the same stock is overvalued at $70. You might buy a put option on the stock for, say, $4, which for $400 gives you the right to sell 100 shares of the stock for $70 regardless of what happens to the market price during the exercise period. If Stock A drops to $64, your option to sell it at $70 becomes more valuable and climbs, say, to $10 or a total of $1,000—a 150 percent profit.

You could also sell (or *write*) call options against stock you already own. This method of using options reduces the risk of owning stock by the amount of money you receive from the sale of the calls. The premium you receive from the calls also can produce a good return on the stocks even if they don't appreciate.

Before getting into options, get some basic booklets from your broker, such as "Understanding Options" and "Option Writing Strategies." These booklets are also available from the Chicago Board Options Exchange, 141 W. Jackson Blvd., Chicago, IL 60604.

- Dis-Com Securities, 1725 E. Hallandale Beach Blvd., Hallandale, FL 33009.

- Fidelity/Source, 70 Pine St., New York, NY 10005.

- Letterman Transaction Services, 19742 Blvd., Irvine, Calif. 92715 (offices also in San Francisco, Los Angeles, Houston, San Diego, Dallas, Phoenix).

- Marquette de Bary, 30 Broad St., New York, NY 10004.

- Odd Lot Securities, 60 East 42nd St., New York, NY 10017 (offices also in Rochester; Washington, D.C.; New Port Richey, Fla.).

- Quick & Reilly, 120 Wall St., New York, NY 10005 (offices in many major cities).

- Charles Schwab & Co., the Schwab Bldg., 1 Second St., San Francisco, CA 94105 (offices in many major cities).

- Springer Investment & Securities Co., 6060 North College, Indianapolis, IN 46220.

- Thrift Trading, 223 Northstar Center, Minneapolis, MN 55402 (also St. Paul).

Note that over 600 *banks* also offer discount brokerage services.

Mutual (Open-) and Closed-End Funds

Rather than try to pick individual securities, you can spread the risk and diversify by buying shares in a portfolio of common stocks (and some bonds) through open-end (mutual) or closed-end funds. A mutual (open-end) fund is an investment company that issues new shares at any time and redeems them at any time. A *closed-end* fund issues only a certain number of shares of its own stocks, sells these, and uses the money to invest in securities of other companies.

In buying mutual funds, your best bet is to stick with established funds that have a good track record in good times as well as bad. Here are some funds with varying objectives (in parentheses) that have done well over the years. Most have toll-free telephone numbers you can get from the toll-free (800) operator:

- Oppenheimer Target, 2 Broadway, New York, NY 10004 (maximum capital gains).

- Fidelity Select Portfolio, 82 Devonshire St., Boston, MA 02109 (long-term growth).

- Twentieth Century Select, P.O. Box 200, Kansas City, MO 64141 (growth & income).

- United Services Gold Shares, P.O. Box 29467, San Antonio, TX 78229 (gold-precious metals).

■ T. Rowe Price New Income, 100 E. Pratt St., Baltimore, MD 21202 (income).

As *families* of funds (several funds under one management; you can switch as objectives change) these have done the best over the past five years:

■ Value Line, 711 3rd Ave., New York, NY 10017.

■ Kemper, 120 S. La Salle St., Chicago, IL 60603.

■ Oppenheimer, 2 Broadway, New York, NY 10004.

■ Security, 700 Harrison St., Topeka, KS 66636.

■ Sigma, 3801 Kennett Pike, Wilmington, DE 19807.

Note: For those who want to switch in and out of individual mutual funds (especially those in different families) you can use "switch services" like *Telephone Switch Newsletter*, 16872 Bolsa Chica Ave., P.O. Box 2538, Huntington Beach, CA 92647. Write to these funds for prospectuses. You can get a list of additional funds by writing:

■ Investment Co. Institute, 1775 K St. NW, Washington, DC 20006.

■ No-Load Mutual Fund Association, 11 Penn Plaza, Suite 2204, New York, NY 10001. Send $2 for directory.

■ Association of Publicly-Traded Funds, 767 5th Ave., New York, NY 10022 (closed-end funds are now called "publicly traded funds").

■ National Association of Investment Clubs, P.O. Box 220, Royal Oak, MI 48068.

The Precious Metals—Gold and Silver

Mature, conservative investors should have 10 to 15 percent of their investments in gold- and silver-related investments to protect against losses in stocks and bonds and losses in the purchasing power of the dollar.

Gold and silver prices generally rise on "bad news" and drop on "good news." This is particularly true of gold, which is valued as a *monetary metal*, rather than silver, which is viewed as an *industrial metal*. Gold forecasts trends in the money markets; silver, which usually moves in tandem with gold, has not always paced these moves. But the long-term outlook for silver may be as favorable as for gold. Thus, if you invest in both metals for the long term, your patience will be rewarded. Let's examine each of these metals:

GOLD. Generally, gold has *not* been a good *short-term* inflation hedge because it usually lags behind rises in the wholesale price level. But *over the long term* gold usually closes the gap with the price index. And in terms of *purchasing power* of the U.S. dollar, gold has more than held its own.

So if you buy gold at a low point and *hold for the long term*, you'll have a good inflation hedge.

Gold's price is "fixed" (determined) twice daily (10:30 A.M. and 3:00 P.M. London time), when representatives of the five internationally respected member firms of the London Gold Market gather at the Rothschild Bank. They match their buy and sell orders until they arrive at a *balance* between the two. The price is then *fixed* at this point and communicated by wire service to all parts of the world for use in commercial and investment transactions.

Here are factors that *contribute to price rises:*

1. *Drying up of supplies.* When the U.S. Treasury and the International Monetary Fund suspended sales of gold, this dried up a lot of supplies coming onto the market. The greater the demand (especially from investors and speculators), and the scarcer the supplies, the higher the price.

2. *Political events at home and abroad.* When international tensions rise, investors—particularly those with insecure governments and currencies—tend to put their assets in a currency accepted everywhere: gold. And any domestic political uncertainties or upheavals also push up the price.

3. *Inflation expectations.* In the long run, inflation will push up the price of everything—including gold. And if just 1 percent more of the American people start buying gold as an "inflation hedge," this could mean an additional 2 million buyers creating a demand—and higher prices—for the yellow metal.

4. *Role in monetary transactions.* More and more countries are revaluing their gold reserves to market-related prices. Also, gold is being used for transactions as well as a store of value. The more countries, businesses, and persons demanding payment in gold, the higher the price.

5. *Seasonal trends.* Gold prices are highest during the winter months, as *production rates* are lower (immigrant workers in the mines return to their farming communities to work the fields). Also, *demand is highest* during the holiday season for gold jewelry and other gifts. While an *announcement* of a gold auction sends down the price, the price often goes up after the auction, especially if the demand was particularly heavy. And gold prices usually rise

when other investments (stocks and bonds and real estate) are out of favor with investors. Gold usually "mirrors" the dollar and moves in the opposite direction (that is, a weak dollar will strengthen gold prices). Also, when interest rates bottom out, gold prices firm and start moving up.

6. *New uses*. Gold is practically indestructible. It won't tarnish, rust, or corrode. It can easily be hammered, molded, shaped into an infinite number of forms. One ounce can be drawn into a wire 50 miles long. And new uses are being found for gold every day: from computer circuits to energy-saving gold glass for office buildings.

Factors contributing to *price declines* include:

1. *Lessening political crises*. There's an old saying about buying and selling gold: "Buy when the cannons are booming; sell when the violins are playing." Repeated and sustained crises will boost the price, but once investors get used to a crisis, they don't react as violently as they did at first, and the price drops.

2. *Reduced inflation*. If investors feel that the government is using a recession to lick inflationary problems and that a healthy, noninflationary recovery will follow, then the price of gold will tend to decline.

3. *Increased sales*. Even the "threat" of sales by a government or the International Monetary Fund can cause the price of gold to plunge. The day to buy gold is when the government announces a sale, because after the announcement of a sale, the actual auction will have little effect on the metal, since the market has already discounted the effect of the sale.

4. *Seasonal trends*. Generally, gold prices are *lowest* during *summer months* when production is greatest, fabricators are closed for vacations, and Islamic religious observances restrict commercial activity.

Given the factors above that cause the price to rise and fall, it's best to buy gold when it is at a *low level*, has set a firm floor price, and is starting to move back up. One of the easiest ways to invest is through the shares of gold-mining companies. As the price of mining ore is fixed (around $200 an ounce for many South African firms), any rise or fall in the price of bullion is magnified in the price of the shares of these companies. Thus, they often rise in price faster (and before) bullion prices, and fall steeper and sooner than bullion prices. So you could have huge capital gains (or losses) and good income, too, as some South African mines yield 15 percent or more (partly because prices are depressed due to political and racial uncertainties). But you can spread your risks and improve your chances by investing in *mutual funds* that have portfolios of both gold- and silver-mining shares from both

South African and North American companies. Minimum investment is usually $1,000; write for prospectuses from:

■ ASA Ltd., P.O. Box 1724, FDR Station, New York, NY 10022 (holding company traded on stock exchanges).

■ Golconda Investors, 11 Hanover Sq., New York, NY 10005.

■ Fidelity Select Metals, 82 Devonshire St., Boston, MA 02109.

■ International Investors, 122 East 42nd St., New York, NY 10017.

■ Precious Metals Holdings, 60 State St., Boston, MA 02109 (closed-end, sold on stock exchanges).

■ Research Equity Fund, 155 Bovet Rd., San Diego, CA 94402.

■ U.S. Gold Fund, P.O. Box 29467, San Antonio, TX 78229.

You could also invest in *gold coins.* If you do, stick to the *bullion* coins that sell for a small premium (5 to 8 percent) over gold or silver content. The most popular gold coins are the Krugerrand, the Mexican gold peso, the Austrian Corona, and the Canadian Maple Leaf. You can buy these through major brokerage houses, some commercial banks, through the office of Deak-Perera (toll-free 800/424-1186. Washington, D.C., residents call 202/872-1233) or Investment Rarities (toll-free 800/328-1860).

SILVER. Historically, the ratio of gold prices to silver has been about 27 to 1. So if gold is selling around $500 an ounce, silver should be selling around $18. This isn't always the case, as silver is basically an *industrial* metal and its price is determined largely by supply and demand. Major industrial uses (in order of importance) include photography, coinage, electrical and electronic contacts and conductors, sterling ware, brazing alloys and solders, catalysts, and silver art. In addition, new uses are being found for silver every day, and demand has been rising, especially in the United States and Japan.

As with gold, buy silver on *price dips* and wait for a firm floor price to be reached. One of the best ways to own silver is through shares of silver-mining companies like Callahan Mining, Hecla Mining, and Sunshine Mining. You can also buy shares of companies like ASARCO and AMAX, which mine a variety of metals, including silver. And through the mutual funds like International Investors and U.S. Gold Fund (above) you can buy a portfolio of both gold- and silver-mining companies.

You can also buy *silver bullion coins* that were minted before 1965 and contain 90 percent silver. They are usually sold in bags containing $1,000 in face-value coins. Each bag contains 720 ounces of silver that, at $10 an ounce, would be worth about $7,200. Add about 5 percent premium to buy these bags. You can buy these through dealers like Deak-Perera and Investment Rarities. You can also buy small gold bars and certificates representing gold and silver bullion through most major brokerage houses and Deak-Perera.

Real Estate

You can make money in real estate by: (1) investing in mortgages; (2) buying improved property (land with buildings); and (3) buying unimproved land that will increase in value. You could also invest in real estate investment trusts (REITs), which are mutual funds of property investments (real estate and mortgages). The best of these are invested in property in growing areas of the Sunbelt. But don't invest in real estate unless you know the *property and people involved.* Perhaps the safest way to invest in mortgages is by investing in the Federal National Mortgage Association (Fannie Mae) or the Government National Mortgage Association (Ginnie Mae), which insures home mortgages, including those insured by the FHA and VA. These packages are put together by mortgage brokers who keep ½ percent for their efforts, then pass along the proceeds to investors. You can check with your broker for further details, or you can write to this no-load mutual fund, which specializes in mortgages:

■ Lexington GNMA Income Fund, 580 Sylvan Ave., P.O. Box 1515, Englewood Cliffs, NJ 07632.

You can also invest in real estate through the many public and private *real estate partnerships* on the market. The safest bet would be the public offerings made by major brokerage houses like Merrill Lynch, Dean Witter, and so on. For $5,000 you can get tax sheltering as well as the possibility of capital gains.

Don't overlook the inflation value of your home. Many older homes have greatly increased in value, but this doesn't do you any good unless you sell the house or refinance the mortgage. In some cases this pays—even at rates of 13 percent on a first mortgage and 17 percent on a second mortgage—because you substantially increase your tax deductions for interest. You would then have thousands of dollars to invest, set up a business, travel. If you *sell* your house and one of the owners is age 55 or older, you can avoid the tax on profit up to $125,000.

Collectibles

When the rate of inflation outstrips the rate of return on many conventional investments, you can make more money in art; antiques; rare stamps, books, coins; and other investments that are pleasing to behold and profitable to possess. But you must know what you are doing, how to buy and sell, and what profits and pitfalls you might encounter. Here are some tips.

1. *Know what you're doing.* Through books, magazines, auctions, exhibits, clubs, museums, and appraisers you can get a good idea of what to look for. Some helpful books:

■ *Investments You Can Live With and Enjoy* by Richard H. Rush (New York: Simon & Schuster, 1974).

■ *The Insiders Guide to Antiques, Art, & Collectibles* by Sylvia O'Neil Dorn (New York: Cornerstone, 1977).

■ *Investing for Pleasure and Profit* by John Peterson (Princeton, N.J.: Dow Jones Books, 1977).

■ *The Time-Life Encyclopedia of Collectibles* (Alexandria, Va.: Time-Life Books, 1978).

2. *Buy what you know and like.* If you buy something you like, it will probably be worth whatever price you pay for it, and you can enjoy it as well as profit from it. And it pays to base your collection on previous interests or professions (a pharmacist collects old apothecary equipment; a publisher, rare books; a photographer, old cameras and prints).

3. *Get to know your dealer.* A good dealer can steer you to reading materials and exhibits that will expand your knowledge. Ideally, the dealer will post prices and be a member of a professional society and a member of the Better Business Bureau or Chamber of Commerce. You can check this out by calling the local organizations to see if the dealer is registered and if there have been any problems or complaints.

4. *Get independent appraisals.* Often, you can get independent appraisals from professional societies, museums, and through auction houses. You can also contact the American Society of Appraisers, P.O. Box 17265, Washington, DC 20041, or the Appraisers Association of America, 60 E. 42nd St., New York, NY 10165, for members near you. Either through the professional society, testing laboratory, appraiser, or dealer you should get some written assurance of authenticity.

5. *Set up a budget and stick to quality.* Determine how much you can

afford to invest and put limits on any one purchase. But stick to quality; one $1,000 investment in the work of a famous artist is worth more than $100 each in 10 obscure works. If you can't afford a master's top-quality paintings, specialize in his less expensive drawings and prints. Also, *have enough cash reserves.* You might find it hard to sell an object on short notice. In fact, most experts advise that you might have to wait *10 years or more* to realize a worthwhile gain on your collectible.

6. *Know the tax angles.* If you collect as an *investor* you can write off expenses to the amount of income produced by a sale. And you can write off losses from sales. But you may have to limit the personal use of your purchases. If in doubt, check with your local office of the Internal Revenue Service.

Here are some of the more pleasurable and profitable collectibles:

■ Seventeenth-century old master painting and prints.

■ Victorian furniture, paintings, drawings, porcelain, silver and antiques of all kinds.

■ Japanese pottery and porcelain, ivory and enamels.

■ Italian Baroque paintings and Renaissance statuary.

■ American primitives.

■ Egyptian, Greek, and Roman antiquities.

■ American Indian artifacts.

■ Antique gold watches.

■ Rare manuscripts, books, and autographs.

■ Victorian and Edwardian jewelry.

■ Art Deco furniture.

You can pick up some of the above at antiques or secondhand stores, garage sales, flea markets, estate sales, and auctions. And you can get prices of antiques through *The Kovels' Complete Antiques Price List* by Ralph and Terry Kovel (13th ed., New York: Crown, 1981) and *Price Guide to Antiques and Collectibles* (published quarterly and available at some newsstands, or write Babka Publishing Co., 100 Bryant St., Dubuque, IA 52001).

Foreign Currencies

When interest rates ease, the value of the dollar moves down, and other currencies usually rise in value. To "hedge" your U.S. dollar investments, you might want to have some dollars invested in foreign-currency-related investments.

You can buy foreign currencies outright through the foreign currency departments of major banks or through major foreign exchange dealers like Deak-Perera (main office is 29 Broadway, New York, NY 10006, with offices in major cities throughout the world); Manfra, Tordella & Brookes, 1 World Trade Center, New York, NY 10048; and Texas Foreign Exchange, P.O. Box 1400, Houston, TX 77081. You would probably pay at the interbank middle rate that, with commissions, might be around 3 percent over the spot market. But if you were dealing in large amounts, you might buy *traveler's checks* for only around 1 to 1½ percent above the interbank middle rate. Foreign currency traveler's checks are sold by some large commercial banks and by offices of American Express and Thomas Cook. And Rusech International, 1140 19th St. NW, Washington, DC 20036, is now offering "Foreign Currencies Certificates" in 15 different currencies. These certificates entail commissions ranging from ¼ to 1 percent to both buy and sell, and are warehouse receipts for physical currency stored in a trustee account with a Swiss bank. The certificate holder receives no interest and makes money only on market fluctuations.

A more conservative approach would be to open an *interest-bearing savings account* in the foreign currency. You may not get as much interest on the savings account as you would in the United States, and you may have to pay taxes in the foreign country (which can be taken as either a deduction from or credit against your federal return—if you itemize). But your real gain could be in the gain of the foreign currency against the U.S. dollar. You can open these accounts by mail. For further information, contact these U.S. offices of foreign banks:

Swiss

- Swiss Bank Corp., 4 World Trade Center, New York, NY 10048.

- Swiss Credit Bank, 100 Wall St., New York, NY 10005.

- Union Bank of Switzerland, 14 Wall St., New York, NY 10005.

German

- Deutsche Genossenschaftsbank, 630 5th Ave., New York, NY 10020.

■ Westdeutsche Landesbank, 450 Park Ave., New York, NY 10022.

Japan

■ Fuji Bank, Ltd., 1 World Trade Center, New York, NY 10048.

■ Nippon Credit Bank, 2 Wall St., New York, NY 10005.

French

■ French American Banking Corp., 120 Broadway, New York, NY 10005.

■ Banque Française du Commerce Extérieur, 645 5th Ave., New York, NY 10022.

Dutch

■ Algemene Bank Nederland, 84 William St., New York, NY 10038.

■ European-American Banking Corp., 10 Hanover Sq., New York, NY 10005.

Canada

■ Canadian Imperial Bank of Commerce, 22 William St., New York, NY 10005.

■ Canadian Bank of Commerce, 20 Exchange Place, New York, NY 10005.

Mexico

■ Banco Nacional de México, S.A., 375 Park Ave., New York, NY 10022.

■ Banco Mexicano, S.A., 44 Wall St., New York, NY 10005.

You can also hedge your bets by investing in *foreign stock markets*. These have different cycles from U.S. markets, and when the U.S. market is sliding, chances are that one or more of the important foreign markets is rising. International growth stocks are dynamic, fast moving, easy to buy, and simple to follow. Some 400 foreign stocks trade actively as ADRs— American Depositary Receipts—while another 200 securities are listed daily in such papers as *The Wall Street Journal*.

An American Depositary Receipt (ADR) is a negotiable receipt issued by an American bank for an international security held in safekeeping abroad. About 10 major banks issue ADRs, the largest being Morgan Guaranty Trust.

The bank issuing the certificates collects dividends on the underlying foreign common stocks, converts these funds to dollars, and remits them to the registered owner. The bank also acts as transfer agent, canceling old receipts and issuing new ones as transactions are made in the ADR. Any broker can get price quotations on a security in ADRs through the NASD (National Association of Securities Dealers) system. When a foreign corporation has a large capitalization so that its shares sell for only a few dollars, each ADR may represent more than one share. However, your broker should be able to "translate" this price into U.S. dollars.

You can buy foreign securities through most major brokers, and the larger brokerage firms like Merrill Lynch, Drexel Burnham Lambert, E.F. Hutton, and Bache Halsey Stuart have foreign securities departments. While most brokers prefer dealing in ADRs instead of buying stock directly on the foreign exchange, buying direct is more private (no records of dividend payments). You don't save any money buying direct, and share certificates might take five or six months to arrive, compared to a couple of weeks when buying with ADRs. But if you're interested in buying direct (especially South African gold shares) contact these firms.

Richard G. Johnson & Co.   Bruce Greene
Petroleum Tower Lobby   Bear Stearns Inc.
419 Edwards St.   230 W. Monroe
Shreveport, LA 71101   Chicago, IL 60606

Here are some foreign securities that have proven profitable for American investors:

■ *Australia*
Broken Hill Proprietary   Santos
Commonwealth Industrial   Western Mining
  Gases

■ *France*
ELF-Aquitaine   Matra   Thomson CFS

■ *Canada*
Aquitaine-Canada   Brascan   Dome-Petroleum

■ *Germany*
Altana   Deutsche Bank   Siemens

■ *Hong Kong*

| China Light & Power | Hongkong & Shanghai Banking | Hongkong Land |

■ *Japan*

Ajinomoto	Mitsubishi Chemical
Fujisawa Pharmaceutical	Nihon Kohden Kogyo
Fujitsu Fanuc	Olympus Optical
Hitachi	TDK Electronics

■ *Mexico*

Aurrera

| Cervicia-Montezuma | El Puerto de Liverpool | Kimberly de Mexico |
| | | Tubos de Acero |

■ *Singapore and Malaysia*

| Development Bank of Singapore | Pan Electric |
| Genting Berhad | Sime Darby Holdings |

■ *South Africa*

| Anglo American | Drufonteine Consolidated |

■ *Switzerland*

| Bank Leu | Hoffmann-La Roche | Oerlikon-Buhrie |

You can also buy shares of investment companies that buy and sell a foreign company's shares on the company's national exchanges. Write for prospectuses from:

■ Canadian Fund, 1 Wall St., New York, NY 10005.

■ The Japan Fund, 1 Rockefeller Plaza, New York, NY 10020.

■ Kemper International Fund, 120 South La Salle St., Chicago, IL 60603.

■ Merrill Lynch Pacific Fund, 165 Broadway, New York, NY 10080.

■ Rowe Price International Fund, 100 East Pratt St., Baltimore, MD 21202.

■ Scudder International Fund, 175 Federal St., Boston, MA 02110.

■ Templeton World Fund, 41 Beach Drive SE, St. Petersburg, FL 33701.

Remember that exchange rates fluctuate daily, and there may be a time when the U.S. dollar is stronger than the Swiss franc, German mark, or

Japanese yen. So if you invest in any foreign-currency-denominated stock or bond, do so with only 10 percent or less of your investment money, and then only as a hedge against further erosion of the dollar.

Although some *foreign bonds* have been yielding only 3 to 6 percent, the real rate of return has been in capital gains against the U.S. dollar. Adding the capital gains, the real rate of return of some Swiss-denominated bonds has been as high as 16 percent and those of Germany and Japan (which also have strong currencies) 12 to 14 percent. Some bonds, such as Japanese and Swiss, may be hard to buy directly, but a secondary market exists for them as well as for German and Dutch bonds. You can find out about these through the foreign bond departments of major brokerage houses like Merrill Lynch.

You may have to pay a tax on these bonds (although you can deduct the amount on your U.S. tax return), and you usually have to buy a minimum of $5,000 worth, although many corporate, World Bank, or European investment bank bonds are available in smaller denominations.

You can also buy foreign bonds hinged to oil, gold, and foreign currencies. *Mexican petrobonds* yield 10 percent and more, and their 3-year redemption value rises with any increase in the price of Mexican oil. The bonds are guaranteed by the Mexican government and must be purchased in Mexico in pesos. Remember, though, the Mexican peso has been devalued several times.

French gold bonds contain gold payment formulas that relate the interest to the market price of gold. These bonds are exempt from French taxes and are available in units of $1,000 or less; they can be bought through most French or European banks. However, as with the bonds above, you can probably arrange to buy them through the foreign bond department of major brokerage houses.

You can also buy *Eurobonds*, medium- and long-term bonds issued by corporations (U.S. and foreign), governments, and government agencies. Floated in third-country capital markets out of the issuers' national boundaries, they may or may not be denominated in the issuers' currency. Some are traded on stock exchanges, such as those of Luxemburg, Frankfurt, or London, and some on secondary exchanges. These bonds are usually sold in denominations of $1,000 (U.S.) and mature in 15 years or less. You can find out about Eurobonds from major brokers like Merrill Lynch. And for information on bonds payable in Swiss francs and issued by companies and governments from Austria to Denmark, France, Finland, Mexico, New Zealand, Norway, Sweden, and the United States, write to Bankhaus Deak, Rathausstrasse 20, A-1010, Vienna, Austria.

You can also buy *international certificates of deposit* through major brokers like Merrill Lynch, and Dreyfus, among others. These are six-month

unit trusts consisting of portfolios of certificates of deposit issued by foreign
and domestic banks. These unit trusts generally pay 1 to 2 percent higher
than domestic unit trusts, and the banks issuing them have enough major
assets to make them sound investments. Minimum investment is usually
$1,000 with about a 6 percent sales charge.

For $5,000 or more you can buy international certificates of deposit
directly from the foreign bank. This could give you both a yield in a strong
currency like the Swiss franc or German mark and the possibility of capital
appreciation against the U.S. dollar. For further information, contact the
foreign banks listed in the beginning of this section, or contact local consul-
ates or embassies located in Washington, D.C.

Another possibility would be to buy foreign-currency-denominated *annuities*. You can buy these either with a single premium or by annual
premiums, and the income can start immediately or be deferred. You can find
out about these annuities by writing to:

International Insurance Specialists, S.A.   or   ASSUREX, S.A.
Case Postale 949-G, CH-1211   Volkmarstrasse 10
Geneva 3, Switzerland   Box 209-16, CH-8033
                                                Zurich, Switzerland

Good Books for Winning on Wall Street

■ *Understanding Wall Street* by Jeffrey B. Little and Lucien Rhodes, $6.95,
Liberty Publishing Co., 50 Adam Rd., Cockeysville, Md. 21030.

■ *The Only Investment Guide You'll Ever Need* by Andrew Tobias (New
York: Bantam Books, 1981).

■ *The Paine Webber Handbook of Stock and Bond Analysis*, ed. Kiril
Sokoloff (New York: McGraw-Hill, 1979).

■ *The Inflation Beater's Investment Guide—Winning Strategies for the
1980s* by Burton Malkiel (New York: W. W. Norton, 1980).

■ *How the Experts Beat the Market* by Thomas C. Noddings (Homewood,
Ill.: Dow-Jones Irwin, 1976).

■ *How to Invest Your Money & Profit from Inflation* by Morton Shulman
(New York: Random House, 1980).

■ *Penny Stocks Book* by R. Max Bowser, $5.95 from Books for Business-
men, P.O. Box 7777, Dept. 1080, New York, N.Y. 10001.

■ *Your Guide to a Financially Secure Retirement* by C. Colburn Hardy (New York: Harper & Row, 1983).

■ *The Retirement Money Book* by Ferd Nauheim (Washington, D.C.: Acropolis Books, 1982).

■ *The Omega Strategy* by William Montapert (Santa Barbara, Calif.: Capra Press, 1982).

You can get a *Financial Planning Bibliography* by writing to College for Financial Planning, 9725 E. Hampden Ave., Denver, CO 80231. And for a list of investment books, periodicals, and advisory services, send a self-addressed, stamped envelope to the Business Library, 280 Cadman Plaza W., Brooklyn, NY 11201.

MODEL PORTFOLIOS FOR RETIREMENT PLANNING AND LIVING

Earlier in this section I offered the following advice about determining your financial objectives: Generally, the younger you are and/or the more money you have, the more you should emphasize *growth* and *inflation protection*. The older you are and/or the less money you have, the more you should stress *safety* and *income* to meet current needs. Also, all of us need these four basic investment objectives: *savings* for emergencies, *guaranteed income* to meet expenses, *investment income* to keep ahead of inflation, and *survival insurance* to protect against economic and political disasters.

I compared the various retirement investments and gave you a *Profile Analysis* that should help you pinpoint the types of investment you should be mainly concerned with. However, I tempered this with the suggestion that you *keep financial plans flexible* in the face of *changing economic conditions*.

Keeping these strategies in mind, let's develop three model portfolios for those (1) approaching retirement; (2) living in retirement; (3) who are widowed.

A Portfolio for Approaching Retirement

This is the "nailing down" decade when you are winding up past goals and are settling down for the future. Your earnings may be at a peak, but so are expenses for college educations, marriages, and so forth. This should also be the nest-egg-building stage before retirement.

INVESTMENT GOAL	PERCENTAGE	BEST PLACES TO MEET INVESTMENT GOALS
Emergency	15%	*Insured savings* in savings & loan, savings banks, credit unions, money-market funds.
Guaranteed	15%	High-quality corporate and utility *discount* bonds like those of the Bell Systems, banks, oil companies. Some state and local municipal bonds rated A or better. Perhaps bonds hinged to oil, gold, foreign.
Survival Insurance	20%	*Gold- and silver-related* investments like South African gold-mining stocks, North American silver mines; precious stones.
Inflation Protection	50%	*High-quality stocks* with above-average yields: Carolina Power & Light, Exxon, Irving Bank, Reynolds (R.J.), Tenneco, United Telecomm., Woolworth. *High-quality mutual funds* like 44 Wall Street, 20th Century Growth, Evergreen, Value Line, Mathers. *Closed-end* funds like General American, Lehmann, Niagara. *Real estate* (second or vacation home rented when not in use). *Collectibles* like rare books, stamps, coins.

A Portfolio for Living in Retirement

This is the true "settling in" decade when people make final plans for the rest of their lives. You hope that family responsibilities and expenses are behind, and a lifetime of leisure is ahead. Income may be lower but so are expenses. However, the emphasis is now on *income* and *safety* and less on growth and inflation protection. Here are some investment suggestions for retirees:

INVESTMENT GOAL	PERCENTAGE	BEST PLACES TO MEET INVESTMENT GOALS
Savings	20%	*Insured savings* in commercial banks of highest quality; time deposits; U.S. Treasury bills.
Guaranteed	40%	U.S. Treasury notes with 2–4 year maturities. High-quality-yielding corporate bonds with 5-year maturities issued by utilities, oil companies, AA corporations. *Annuity* income from investment annuities. *Municipal bond unit trusts* or AA-rated bonds of local and state governments. *Mortgage unit* trusts and mutual funds.

INVESTMENT GOAL	PERCENTAGE	BEST PLACES TO MEET INVESTMENT GOALS
Survival Insurance	15%	*Gold- and silver*-mining holding companies like ASA Ltd., Anglo-American South African, Anglo American Gold Investment; semi-precious stones.
Inflation Protection	25%	*Highest quality common stocks* like AT&T, Central & So. West, Florida Power & Light, New England Electric, Royal Dutch Petroleum, Texaco, Union Carbide. *Balanced funds* like Kemper Total Return or Vance Sanders. *Collectibles* like art and antiques.

A Portfolio for Older Widows and Widowers

At this age and stage of life, *one can't take chances*. All investments should be made to *generate income with maximum safety*. Here's how such a portfolio might look:

INVESTMENT GOAL	PERCENTAGE	BEST PLACES TO MEET INVESTMENT GOALS
Emergency	30%	Only *insured savings* accounts of highest quality. Passbook accounts or time deposits of one year or less.
Guaranteed	50%	*Straight life or charitable annuities. U.S. Treasury notes or bonds.* Withdrawal plans from U.S. Fund for Government Securities or American Fund of Government Securities. Perhaps Federal Agency Issues that are implied or direct obligations of the U.S. government like Federal National Mortgage Assn., Government National Mortgage Assn., or Federal Land Bank. Perhaps AAA-rated *municipal bonds* of home state.
Survival Insurance	10%	*Gold-and-silver* mutual funds like International Investors or United Services Gold Fund.
Inflation Protection	10%	*Highest-rated-and-yielding* common stocks that have paid dividends for 40 or more years: American Electric Power, Arizona Public Service, Baltimore Gas & Electric, Boston, Edison, Cincinnati Gas & Electric, Commonwealth Edison, Cleveland Electric Illuminating, Dayton Power & Light, Duquesne Light, Kansas City P & L, Orange & Rockland Util., Pacific Gas & Elec., Ohio Edison, Philadelphia Electric, San Diego Gas & Elec., United Illum., Virginia Electric & Power. Perhaps *balanced* funds like Kemper Total Return or Union Income.

WHAT ARE SOME OFTEN-OVERLOOKED SOURCES OF INCOME?

Here are some sources you might investigate:

Cash Values of Life Insurance

If you have a straight life or endowment insurance, it usually has built up a cash value equal to about one-half to three-quarters face value. Since you probably won't need as much life-insurance protection in retirement, consider these options:

1. Take the cash value of your policy or apply it to a smaller amount of paid-up insurance.
2. Elect to receive the cash value proceeds in regular installment payments on an annual, semiannual, quarterly, or monthly basis.
3. Choose a life annuity income settlement. Under this option you and your spouse will receive a guaranteed income as long as either of you live.
4. Use the cash value to continue protection on an extended-term basis.
5. Take out a loan on your insurance (usually at a rate lower than bank or credit union loans) and use it to finance your retirement.

Free the Inflation Value of Your Home

Many older homes have greatly increased in value; however, this doesn't do you any good unless you sell the house or refinance the mortgage. But you have other options including a *reverse annuity mortgage*. In this arrangement, a mortgage lender gives you up to 80 percent of the value of the home in a new mortgage. With the proceeds, you buy an annuity that not only guarantees mortgage payments but provides you with a monthly income (surplus after mortgage payment).

In Buffalo, New York, a nonprofit organization offers a plan called HELP (Home Equity Living Plan). Under this plan, elderly homeowners receive a monthly stipend based on the appraised value of their house, and according to their age. The organization pays property taxes, insurance, and repairs, and allows owners to remain in the house until death. After that HELP takes title to the house.

Under "Lifetime Income Plan," American Homestead Inc., of Moorestown, New Jersey, offers the following plan: homeowners age 65 or over receive a guarantee of a lifetime flow of income, but principal and interest on the loan are paid by their estate out of proceeds from their house. American Homestead shares in the appreciation of the value of the house. For further details write American Homestead, 724 Signal Light Road, Moorestown, NJ 08057.

Some states such as California and Oregon have tax deferral plans that allow property taxes to accrue and to be paid from house sale proceeds after death. Wisconsin has a similar plan for home improvements. In New Jersey, another approach to home equity conversion is a plan begun in Plainfield and now being implemented by the Bergen County Housing Authority. It gives elderly homeowners long-term financing on funds to add a rental unit (for other elderly) to their homes. Check with your local housing authority, office on aging, information and referral service to find what plans may be available. And for further information on freeing the equity in your home:

■ Equity Access, Merrill Lynch, P.O. Box 1212, Stamford, CT 06901.

■ Equity Line, Crocker National Bank, P.O. Box 38001, San Francisco, CA 94138.

■ Home Equity Conversion Project, 100 East Main, Rm. 1020, Madison, WI 53703.

■ Triple-A Checking, Beneficial Corp. (see telephone directory—available in 30 states).

Consider a Part-Time or Temporary Job

More than 1,000 U.S. companies have adopted a four-day workweek, and at least 10 percent of U.S. workers are now on some sort of flexible-time schedule that allows for part-time work opportunities. There are other sources of part-time (some full-time) jobs, through state employment offices (many of which have older-worker specialists), professional or trade associations, labor unions, churches, YMCAs or YMHAs, Forty-Plus Clubs, chambers of commerce, and nonprofit volunteer employment agencies (available in many cities through local information and referral sources).

Many retirees find part-time jobs through temporary-help agencies. Temporary-help firms don't consider themselves to be employment agencies, but they do provide a link between businesses and a job-seeker by doing the hiring and placement, paying salaries, and testing and upgrading skills. You can find temporary-help firms in your area by looking under "Employment Agencies" in your local Yellow Pages. Among the larger firms are Olsten, Kelly, Manpower, Mature Temps, and Western.

Most part-time or temporary-help jobs are found in the service fields or those classed as "managerial" or "proprietary," including schools, churches, stores, gas stations, hotels, restaurants, refreshment stands, hospitals, movie theaters, amusement parks, and construction firms. Grocery stores and fast-food chains have advertised for retirees to work their checkout lines and counters.

You can even apply to U.S.-based organizations for jobs overseas. Write for details from:

■ International Executive Service Corps., 622 3rd Ave., New York, NY 10067.

■ Peace Corps, ACTION, Washington, DC 20525 (offices in many cities and job opportunities available in other branches of ACTION).

■ National Council of Churches, Overseas Personnel Office, Rm. 668, 475 Riverside Dr., New York, NY 10115.

■ United Nations Development Program, 1 United Nations Plaza, New York, NY 10017.

■ United States State Department, Washington, DC 20525; The Agency for International Development, Washington, DC 20533; the Central Intelligence Agency, Washington, DC 20525.

The outlook for older workers is becoming brighter: The Census Bureau predicts that the number of new workers aged 18 to 24 will drop by 16 percent over the next two decades. Meanwhile, the over-65 segment of the population will grow by 28 percent between now and the year 2000. Thus, more and more companies are going to have to hire or retain more and more older workers.

Some helpful books on the subject:

Second Career Opportunities for Older People, available free from Institute of Lifetime Learning, 1909 K St. NW, Washington, DC 20049.

Part-Time Employment After Retirement by Harold L. Sheppard and Richard E. Mantovani, $3.50 from National Council on the Aging, 600 Maryland Ave. NW, Washington, DC 20024.

Part-Time Work: A Bibliography. A complete resource book for employers, researchers, counseling centers, and part-time employees. Published by the Association of Part-Time Professions, $4.95 from APTP, P.O. Box 3419, Alexandria, VA 22302.

Consider an At-Home or Small Business

Many retirees are working out of their homes as salesmen, real estate dealers, insurance brokers. Others are teaching bridge, piano, and languages to at-home groups; still others have set up repair shops in which they fix appliances, bicycles, dolls, toys, and typewriters. Many have set up small businesses, including franchises, near their homes.

But wherever your business is located, you should make sure you have the background, knowledge, and equipment for the business. Each year in the United States over 400,000 small businesses fail—one quarter in their first year. The failure of most small businesses is caused by (in order): (1) lack of business records; (2) lack of business experience; (3) insufficient stock turnover; (4) poor collection of money; (5) inventory shrinkage; (6) poor inventory control; (7) lack of finances; (8) improper markup; (9) and lack of sales. The odds are six out of ten that a new small business won't last five years.

Test yourself and your qualifications for starting a small business by asking these questions:

Do you know how much money you will need to get started properly?

Can you borrow money at reasonable rates if you need it?

Have you enough money for initial costs, including advertising and promotion, inventories, extending credit?

Do you know the business you are starting, and do you have the right experience?

Are you prepared for the strain of long hours on you and your family?

Do you know your competition?

Have you a competent accountant and a sympathetic banker?

To help determine your qualifications, you can get a list of helpful booklets from field offices of the Small Business Administration (in major cities) or from SBA's publications center, P.O. Box 15434, Ft. Worth, TX 76119. Phone toll-free 800/433-7212 (Texas only, call 800/792-8901). You can also arrange for loans through the SBA, which can put you in touch with Small Business Investment Companies (SBICs), which is privately owned but federally licensed, and which offers financial aid. And you can get free business advice through SCORE (Service Crops of Retired Executives), which provides counseling to small businesses. Contact SCORE through ACTION, Washington, DC 20525 (SCORE also has local offices in major cities). And you can call the SBA "Answer Desk" for help in setting up a small business by telephoning 800/368-5855; in Washington, DC, 202/653-7561.

Through the Bank of America you can get small-business profiles that can help you set up various enterprises. You can get information on these booklets through local branches of Bank of America, or write Corporate Communications, Bank of America, 6 E. 43rd St., New York, NY 10017, or Special Services, P.O. Box 37000, San Francisco, CA 94137.

Helpful booklets are also available through:

American Management Association, 135 W. 50th St., New York, NY 10020. Among their titles: "Profit from Your Money-Making Ideas" and "Business Information Guide." Write for other titles, prices, and shipping costs.

Pilot Books, 103 Cooper St., Babylon, NY 11702. This company will send you postpaid copies of the following: "How to Start a Profitable Retirement Business" ($2); "Starting a Business After 50", "Profitable Part-Time, Home-Based Business" ($2.50 each); "Small Business Ideas for Women—And How to Get Started" ($2); "Turning Your Ideas into Dollars" ($3.50). Also ask for a list of other helpful booklets.

Other books available through bookstores or libraries:

How to Run a Small Business by the J. K. Lasser Tax Institute (5th ed., New York: McGraw-Hill, 1982).

Professional Service Management by William Joseph (New York: McGraw-Hill, 1982).

The Insider's Guide to Small Business Resources by Jeffrey Timmons and David Gumpert (New York: Doubleday, 1982).

How to Start and Operate a Mail-Order Business by Julian L. Simon (3rd ed., New York: McGraw-Hill, 1980).

You can also contact these *trade associations* for help in setting up an at-home or small business:

■ National Alliance of Homebased Businesswomen, P.O. Box 95, Norwood, NJ 07648.

■ National Association for the Cottage Industry, P.O. Box 14460, Chicago, IL 60614.

■ National Federation of Independent Business, 150 W. 20th Ave., San Mateo, CA 94403.

■ National Small Business Association, 1604 K St. NW, Washington, DC 20006.

Franchises

And then there are franchises. If you buy a franchise, you receive the right to sell or distribute goods or services under the parent company's banner. Franchises exist for virtually all types of businesses (motels, fast foods, services), and many big companies like General Electric, Western Union and Pillsbury are in the market.

With a franchise you become part of an established and growing chain, profiting directly from your own efforts and investment while benefiting from the parent company's advertising, large-scale purchases, and expert management consultation. However, there have been fraudulent schemes in the industry and there are these drawbacks:

■ *Franchises aren't cheap.* In some cases it might cost $50,000 or more just for the franchise fee and perhaps another $25,000 before you open the door. This doesn't include operating capital and long-term debt.

■ *You have to work long hours* and probably involve other family members. A recent survey of fast-food franchises found that workers average a 60-hour week, with the spouse working additionally 35 hours, and the children, 25.65 hours.

■ *You pay royalities and advertising assessments* ranging from 4 to 8 percent.

■ *You may net only a modest profit.* Most franchises probably net under $50,000 a year.

Before you invest in a franchise—investigate. The Franchise and Business Opportunities Rule requires a franchise and business-opportunity seller to give you a disclosure document at least 10 business days before you pay any money or legally commit yourself to purchase a business. You can get the details of this law and what to look (out) for by writing for "Franchise Business Risks," Federal Trade Commission, Public Reference Branch, Rm. 130, 6th St. and Pennsylvania Ave. NW, Washington, DC 20580. You can also get helpful information from these sources:

Franchise Opportunities Handbook, $10 postpaid from Supt. of Documents, Government Printing Office, Washington, DC 20402.

International Franchise Association Membership Director, 1025 Connecticut Ave. NW, Suite 1005, Washington, DC 20036.

Hobbies

Those associated with the arts and crafts are big business. More than 400,000 Americans are now associated with more than 1,200 crafts organizations. And 16 percent of these hobbyists are earning over $1,000 a year; 9 percent over $5,000 a year from that source. There are now about 6,000 arts-and-crafts shows staged each year, with sales ranging from a few thousand dollars to as much as $2,500,000. In fact, four particular shows—the ones sponsored by American Craft Enterprises, a subsidiary of the American Craft Council (see below)—are generating annual sales of nearly $10 million.

Not only can you earn money, you can learn new skills, broaden your interests, and make new friends in the process. Some of the most profitable hobbies include gardening, photography, writing, picture framing, catering, dog breeding, raising birds and fish, growing mushrooms, making jewelry out of mosaics and semiprecious stones, painting, leathercraft, woodworking, bookbinding, rug and needlework, knitting, glasswork, plastics, candle making, doll making and repairing, and providing music for social occasions.

Hobbyists not only *make* money but they *save* money by writing off (on taxes) the space they use in their home exclusively as a workshop or office. And they can write off *all expenses* associated with their products (cost of materials, traveling, training and education, selling expenses) *as long as they make an effort to sell the items.*

You can market your wares by:

1. *Holding a sale.* Pick a location, usually a vacant store, preferably in a popular shopping center, keep it a "one person show," and display your wares prominently, marking them for sale. Invite every potential customer you can think of (using Christmas mailing lists, and so on) and personalize the invitations. When people drop in, have them sign a visitors' log, offer a door prize, and serve refreshments so buyers will stay longer.

2. *Selling wares to sales outlets.* Some specific crafts have their own organizations and offer tips on selling wares, and some communities also sponsor "craft fairs" where you can market items. You can get a list of helpful publications (on making crafts as well as selling them) from the American Craft Council, 401 Park Ave. S., New York, NY 10016 (attn. Publications Dept.). This organization sponsors craft museums at 44 W. 53rd Street and 77 West 45th Street in New York City, operates a nationwide audio-visual service, and has a subsidiary, American Craft Enterprises, that covers crafts markets in various parts of the United States.

3. *Selling to retail outlets or selling on consignment.* You can sell crafts and other wares to department stores, but it may take as long as 60 days to 6

months for you to get paid. You can also sell on consignment through retail shops, but an item can languish for months, and consigned goods are sometimes returned in shopworn or damaged condition. Many communities have Women's Exchanges, Junior League Shops, Co-Op Crafts Shops, and Elder Craftsmen Shops that take items on consignment, and you can find these through your telephone directory, city recreation department, church, office on aging, and so forth.

4. *Selling through direct-mail or advertisements in newspapers and magazines.* Many mail-order houses specialize in unique or unusual merchandise. If you offer a unique and salable item, write to these mail-order houses and ask if they'd be interested and on what basis. Many specialized publications have classified and display ads for crafts and wares. Among them are (write for information):

■ *The Crafts Fair Guide*, P.O. Box 262, Mill Valley, CA. 94941.

■ *The Crafts Report*, P.O. Box 1992, Wilmington, DE 19899.

■ *Goodfellow Review of Crafts*, P.O. Box 4520, Berkeley, CA 94704.

■ *National Calendar of Indoor/Outdoor Art Fairs*, 5423 New Haven Ave., Ft. Wayne, IN 46803.

■ *The Quality Crafts Market*, 521 5th Ave., Suite 1700, New York, NY 10017.

And for an outstanding book on the subject, send $6.95 ($1 off retail price) to Merle E. Dowd, 7438 S.E. 40th St., Mercer Island, WA 98040, and ask for *How to Earn More Money from Your Crafts.*

Some other books on crafts (available at libraries or bookstores):

■ *Career Opportunities in Crafts—The First Complete Guide for Success as a Crafts Professional* by Elyse Sommer (New York: Crown, 1977).

■ *The Crafts Business Encyclopedia* by Michael Scott (New York: Harcourt Brace Jovanovich, 1979).

■ *Craftsmen in Business—A Guide to Financial Management and Taxes,* rev. ed. by Howard Connaughton (New York: American Craft Council, 1979).

■ *Craftworker's Market* (Cincinnati: Writer's Digest, 1980).

■ *Creative Cash—How to Sell Your Crafts, Needlework, Designs, and Know-How* by Barbara Brabec (Tucson: H. P. Books, 1981).

■ *The Auction Companion* by Daniel J. and Katherine Kyes Leab (New York: Harper & Row, 1981).

■ *An Insider's Guide to Auctions* by Sylvia Auerbach (Reading, Mass.: Addison-Wesley, 1981).

Some other books on businesses, jobs, and crafts:

Time Is Money—A Guide to Selling Your Professional Services by Richard Creedy (New York: E. P. Dutton, 1980).
How to Start and Operate a Mail-Order Business by Julian L. Simon (3rd ed., New York: McGraw-Hill, 1980).
How You Too Can Make at Least One Million in the Mail-Order Business by Gerardo Joffee (New York: Harper & Row, 1979).
The Entrepreneurial Woman by Sandra Winston (New York: Newsweek Books, 1979).
A Woman's Guide to Her Own Franchised Business, rev. ed. Anne Small and Robert S. Levy; Pilot Books, 103 Cooper St., Babylon, NY 11702, ($2).

These books are also available from Pilot Books for the mail order price as shown:

Starting and Operating a Clipping Service by Demaris C. Smith ($2.50).
Profitable Part-Time, Home-Based Businesses ($2).
How to Start a Profitable Retirement Business ($2).
Starting a Business After 50 ($2.50)
Annual Directory of Franchise Organizations ($3.95)

You can get further *help* from these organizations:

Federal Trade Commission, Bureau of Consumer Protection, Washington, DC 20036.
Industry and Trade Administration (ITA) of the Dept. of Commerce (on franchising), Washington, DC 20230.
Pension Benefit Guaranty Corp., 2020 K St. NW, Washington, DC 20006.
Social Security Administration, Dept. of Public Inquiries, Baltimore, MD 21235.

Securities & Exchange Commission, 500 N. Capital St. NW, Washington, DC
    20549.
SCORE (Service Corps of Retired Executives), 1441 L St. NW, Washington,
    DC 20416.

The chart below is a hypothetical illustration of the interest earnings accumulated on $25,000 at 7.5 percent interest* compounded in a tax-deferred annuity
versus the earnings accumulated on the same amount in a vehicle bearing 7.5
percent interest that is taxed annually before compounding.

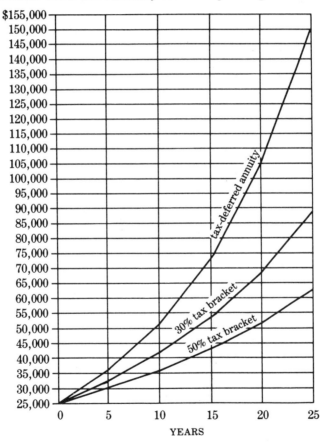

*The 7.5% rate is for illustrative purposes only and is not a representation of the
interest rate to be credited under the contract.

And you can get further *information* from these books:

Step-by-Step Guide to Your Retirement Security by Jack Melnick (New York: Times Books, 1978).
How to Finance Your Retirement by Martin R. Dunetz (Reston, Va.: Reston, 1979).
Become Financially Independent by Richard C. Vreeland (Englewood Cliffs, N.J.: Prentice-Hall, 1979).

For further information on *pension plans*, send for these booklets:

Know Your Pension Plan and *Often-Asked Questions About the Employee Retirement Security Act* (ERISA), free from Pension and Welfare Benefit Program, U.S. Dept. of Labor, Washington, DC 20216.
Pension Facts I and *Pension Facts II* are available for 25 cents each, and *Retirement Income*, a news magazine containing articles by knowledgeable sources in the field, is available for $2 from Pension Rights Center, 1346 Connecticut Ave. NW, Rm. 1019, Washington, DC 20036.
Federal Benefits for Veterans and Dependents, $2 from Consumer Information Center, Pueblo, CO 81009.
Plain Talk About IRA's, $1.50 from Consumer Information Center, Pueblo, CO 81009.

For information on pension benefits for federal employees, write National Association of Retired Federal Employees (NARFE), 1533 New Hampshire Ave. NW, Washington, DC 20036.

KEOGH vs. NON-KEOGH INVESTMENTS

Assume two investors, "A" with a Keogh plan and "B" without. Both are in the 40 percent tax bracket, and both invest $5,000 annually. As "B" (non-Keogh) doesn't have a plan, he must first give IRS $2,000 of his $5,000, leaving $3,000 to invest at 8 percent. "A" (Keogh) doesn't have to pay taxes on his $5,000, although he will at a later date when his tax bracket is lower. Here's how they make out, assuming "A" takes his money back in a qualified lump-sum payout.

"A"-KEOGH INVESTOR	5 YRS.	10 YRS.	15 YRS.	20 YRS.
Amount accumulated before tax on withdrawal	$ 29,000	$ 72,000	$137,760	$229,000
Special averaging tax	3,300	13,870	30,870	63,500
Net after tax	$ 25,700	$ 58,130	$106,890	$165,500

"B"-NON-KEOGH INVESTOR	5 YRS.	10 YRS.	15 YRS.	20 YRS.
After-tax accumulation	$ 17,000	$ 37,000	$ 65,000	$ 99,000
Net added after-tax amount by use of Keogh	$ 8,700	$ 21,130	$ 41,890	$ 66,500

IRA TAX ADVANTAGES

Individual Retirement Accounts are tax deductible, and the income earned is tax-sheltered until withdrawal. Here are the advantages of such a program, assuming that $1,500 is invested each year, and the funds earn 6 percent a year, compounded:

"A"-25 PERCENT TAX BRACKET	5YRS.	10 YRS.	15 YRS.	20 YRS.
IRA Total	$ 8,456	$ 19,771	$ 34,914	$ 55,178
Taxable Fund Total	$ 6,155	$ 13,824	$ 23,382	$ 35,293
Advantage with IRA	$ 2,301	$ 5,947	$ 11,532	$ 19,885
"B" -50 PERCENT TAX BRACKET				
IRA Total	$ 8,456	$ 19,771	$ 34,914	$ 55,178
Taxable Fund Total	$ 3,982	$ 8,598	$ 13,949	$ 20,153
Advantage with IRA	$ 4,474	$ 11,173	$ 20,965	$ 35,025

The table below compares the results of putting $25,000 into a taxable instrument and into a tax-deferred annuity. The first three columns show the same facts that are graphically illustrated in the chart above.

The last two columns show what you would net after taxes if you withdrew the annuity in a lump sum after 5, 10, 15, 20, or 25 years. Of course, in reality, if you elect to take monthly payments over a number of years or your lifetime, you would probably be in a lower tax bracket and you could actually collect a larger amount after taxes than what is shown here.

End of Year	VALUE OF TAXABLE INVESTMENT 50% Tax Bracket	30% Tax Bracket	Value of Tax Deferred Annuity	AFTER-TAX ANNUITY TERMINATION VALUE 50% Tax Bracket	30% Tax Bracket
5	$ 30,053	$ 32,288	$ 35,890	$ 30,445	$ 32,623
10	36,125	41,703	51,525	38,263	43,568
15	43,428	53,860	73,973	49,488	59,280
20	52,205	69,563	106,198	65,600	81,838
25	62,755	89,845	152,458	88,730	114,220

SPECIAL REPORT: THE SOCIAL SECURITY PAYOFF

Social Security benefits will supply a major portion of your retirement income. The average benefit replaces about 40 percent of a person's earnings in the year prior to retirement, ranging from 30 percent for a high-wage earner to 55 percent for a low-wage earner. Fully 90 percent of retirees receive some Social Security, most of them *under* age 65. In 1984 the maximum individual benefit is around $750 a month; the average around $500 a month. Dependent spouses draw reduced benefits, according to age.

Before you can get retirement checks, you must have credit for a certain amount of work that is covered by Social Security. For those who reached 62 in 1983, you needed 8 years of coverage; this rises to 9 years for those who reach 62 in 1987 and to 10 years for those who reach 62 in 1991 or later.

You get full retirement benefits if you wait until age 65. If you apply earlier, these benefits are reduced by 20 percent at age 62; 13½ percent at age 63; 6⅔ percent age 64. However, because you would be drawing benefits over a longer period of time, generally you would be ahead for about 15 years. But after that you would make more money if you had waited until age 65. Widows are eligible for reduced benefits at age 60 and full benefits at age 65. Spouses get 50 percent of the retiree's benefit at age 65, but if your spouse is 62 and wants benefits at that age, he or she will get 37¼ percent of your full benefit. At age 63, your spouse can get 41⅔ percent; at 64 he or she will get 45⅚ percent of your full benefit—providing he or she doesn't draw a pension from municipal, state, or federal government.

All benefits are increased in any year in which the Consumer Price Index rises 3 percent or more. However, for 1985 through 1988, if reserves in the old-age and disability funds ever fall below 15 percent of the money needed to provide payments for a year, automatic cost-of-living increases will be based on the rise in the CPI *or* the average gain in wages, whichever is lower. In 1989, this trigger will rise to 20 percent.

What If You Decide to Work After Retirement?

Currently, you will gain an extra 3 percent in Social Security benefits for each year of delay from age 65 through 71. Beginning in 1990, you'll get an additional ¼ of 1 percent for each year of delay. This rises until it reaches 8 percent in 2009. You can earn up to a ceiling amount (around $7,000 in 1984) and not have your benefits reduced; over that you lose $1 in benefits for every $2 you earn working. This stretches to $1 lost in benefits for every $3 earned, starting in 1990. But even under present rules, you could earn almost $25,000 and still receive some Social Security benefits. And after age 70, you can earn any amount without losing benefits.

There is a special rule that applies to people only in the year they retire. Under this rule, even if earnings exceed the *annual* exempt amount, a benefit can be paid for any month the person's wages do not exceed the *monthly* limit and the person does not perform substantial services (more than 45 hours a month) in self-employment.

How and When to Apply for Benefits

Once you decide to retire, you should apply two or three months before your retirement month. Your checks will then start for the month you retire. You should telephone for the best time to come in (in some cases you can do the paperwork over the telephone). According to Social Security officials, it's best to call or visit a local office on the last three days of the week and during the second half of the month. Offices are busiest on Mondays and Tuesdays and during the first two weeks of the month. These are the documents you will need:

■ Your *Social Security card* or a record of the number.

■ *Proof of age.* This should be an official record of your birth or a religious record of your birth or baptism recorded before you were age 5. Only original records or copies certified by the issuing agency can be used. If this is not possible, submit the best (oldest) evidence you have. If in doubt, check with the Social Security office.

■ Your *Wage and Tax Statement* (W-2) forms for the last two years. If you are self-employed, copies of your self-employment tax returns and proof of filing (a canceled check, for example) for the last 2 years, since reports may not be in your records. If your spouse is age 62 he or she may be eligible for benefits on your record. They will need the same documents. It would also be a good idea to have your marriage certificate available; if either of you were married before, you'll need information about the duration of the previous marriage.

At the time you sign up for Social Security benefits you should ask about Medicare protection as well, which starts at age 65. You don't have to be drawing Social Security benefits to get this protection.

When your claim is approved, you'll receive a "certificate of award" and a copy of the booklet *Your Social Security Rights and Responsibilities*. This booklet lists the events that might affect your benefit checks. It tells you how to report them and what you should know about your rights and responsibilities. Your Social Security office also has booklets covering other aspects of the program that might affect you, including disability payments, how to estimate your benefits according to your current age and age of retirement, your right to appeal Social Security and Medicare decisions, and survivor and death benefits.

Note that, beginning in the year 2003, the retirement age will advance by two months each year until it reaches 66 in 2009. In 2020, it will begin rising again until it reaches 67 in 2027. Thus, persons born in the years 1943 through 1959 will have to wait until age 66 to get full benefits; those born in 1960 or later must wait until age 67. For further information, contact your local Social Security office.

SPECIAL REPORT: PENSION PLANS FOR EVERYONE!

Almost everyone with earned income (money from working rather than from investments) can set up an *Individual Retirement Account* or a *Keogh* plan (see below). The main stipulation: you can't withdraw before age 59½ and you *must* start withdrawing (and you can't put any more in) after age 70½. Here are basics of the plans:

■ *Individual Retirement Accounts* (IRAs)—You can contribute up to $2,000 of earned income (total of $2,250 with a nonworking spouse) in any number of accounts as long as it doesn't exceed the maximum limits (which may expand). Any excess is subject to a 6 percent penalty tax, and any funds withdrawn before you reach age 59½ are subject to a 10 percent penalty (waived if disabled). Funds in your IRA in the year you reach 70½ must be withdrawn according to life expectancy; a single man has to use up his account within 12.1 years of the year he reaches 70½, while a woman has 15 years to deplete the funds. Married IRA owners have longer times allowed, depending upon the age of the spouse. All funds withdrawn are taxed as ordinary income (in a retirement year your tax brackets are lower). As the money accumulates tax-free, most investors are best off having some sort of savings plan that compounds at a regular rate (like money-market funds).

■ *Keogh plans*—the limit on *defined contribution* (the amount you put in) Keogh plans is $30,000 or 25 percent of compensation. But the maximum annual benefit of a *defined benefit* (the amount you get) Keogh (also called a maxi Keogh) is $90,000 or 100 percent of compensation from $136,425.

Owner-employees are allowed to make voluntary aftertax contributions to Keoghs as long as the plan's total funding does not exceed the yearly ceilings—which may expand. Note, however, that those with earned income can have *both* Keogh and IRA plans if they are not covered by corporate pension plans.

Self Directed Plans—Some trustees allow you to set up IRA or Keogh plans using stamps, diamonds, and other "hard" assets as investments. You can get further information from:

First Citizens Bank & Trust Co.
P.O. Box 3028
Greenville, SC 29602

Lafayette Bank & Trust Co.
345 State St.
Bridgeport, CT 06604

First State Bank of Oregon
1212 S.W. 6th Ave.
P.O. Box 1191
Portland, OR 97207

Lincoln Trust Co.
5600 Syracuse Cir.
P.O. Box 5831
Denver, CO 80217

SPECIAL REPORT: HOW TO GET THE MOST FROM YOUR LIFE INSURANCE

Hundreds of life insurance companies offer policies under a host of puzzling names like "Value Guard" and "The Solution." How do you choose among them? For the most part these policies are variations of a few basic and relatively easy-to-understand terms. Once you understand the basic plans as described below, you'll be able to decide which type of insurance is best for you and your family at any given stage of life.

■ *Term Insurance.* This insurance covers you for a cerain period—a term of 5, 10, or 20 years—usually until age 65. After each term you must renew the policy, usually at a higher rate. If you have *Renewable Term* you must pay a higher rate when you renew, but you don't have to undergo an insurance company physical examination. Similarly, if you buy *Convertible Term*, you can exchange it for a more expensive permanent protection without taking another physical. You can also buy *Decreasing Term*, which has constant premiums as you grow older, but the face value gradually decreases to zero. Some insurance experts recommend you buy decreasing term to age 65 (or retirement age) and that you use the savings in premiums over cash-value insurance to invest.

■ *Whole (Straight) Life Policies.* This insurance protects you for your whole life, but the premiums never go up. The cost of whole life is higher than term, because part of the premium goes to build up a cash reserve. You can also buy whole life policies with *limited payment* (the policy is paid up within a certain period of time) or *graded premium* (in the beginning years cash reserves are low, but after 10 years or so, the policy levels off in premiums at whole-life rates, and builds cash value quickly). Graded premium could be inexpensive for even a 50-year-old.

■ *Retired Life Reserves.* The cash generated from premiums is invested in certificates of deposit, money-market funds, or mortgages. You make the selection and the ultimate payoff is geared to the investment.

■ *Variable Life.* Reserves are invested in common stocks, and cash values and benefits vary with the fund's performance. This type of insurance is often sold through brokerage houses and by insurance companies like Equitable Life, John Hancock, and Monarch of Mass.

■ *Adjustable Life.* This permits you to switch between term and cash-life policies as your needs and budget permit.

■ *Universal Life.* This plan consists of a flexible, do-it-yourself combination of life insurance and a high-interest accumulation account. You can arrange these elements to match your changing requirements and ability to pay premiums. The amount of protection can be adjusted up and down, accumulation in cash value can be used to pay premiums, and direct withdrawals are also available.

■ *Joint Life.* This policy covers two people (some policies may allow more), but pays only on the death of the first to die. Some companies will pay twice the policy amount if both parties die at the same time. You can buy joint life in various forms: whole life, term, decreasing term, and mortgage policies (which are decreasing-term policies designed to pay off the balance of a mortgage when the insured dies).

■ *Annuities.* An annuity is a contract sold by an insurance company that guarantees you a fixed payment for life (and sometimes to a beneficiary after you die) of a fixed number of dollars each month. You can buy several types of annuities, either in a lump sum or in installments. Annuities have some tax advantages because taxes are deferred on accumulated interest until you actually collect the interest. That payout often represents return of capital, which is then usually tax exempt.

If you need maximum income and have no dependents, or have provided for them in other ways, some experts say you should sign up for a *straight life annuity* that offers you maximum income. If you want to guarantee payments for a certain number of years for yourself and/or a dependent, a *life annuity with installments certain* might be best. You could also buy a *cash refund annuity* that pays your beneficiary a lump sum if you die before collecting the original investment.

But if you have little or no life insurance and want annuity income to support yourself and wife, you might consider a *joint and survivor annuity*. This works best only if you and your wife are around the same age or state of health. If your wife is younger than you, the payments may be too low for your needs.

How Much Insurance Do You Need at Various Ages and Stages of Your Life?

Life insurance should provide enough money to pay your debts and allow survivors to maintain their standard of living. The amount of coverage varies with obligations. A single person with no responsibilities or debts doesn't need any insurance; a sole breadwinner with growing children may need hundreds of thousands of dollars of protection.

You can determine your insurance needs by:

1. *Estimating the income* your survivors would need to maintain their living standards and to settle your estate (debts, taxes, funeral expenses).

2. *Subtracting the income* survivors could expect from Social Security, pension, annuities, wages, interest, dividends, and other sources.

Your needs may fit into these categories:

If you're in your forties, you need enough insurance to pay off the mortgage and any installment credit, to provide for college educations and other family obligations, to cover 5 years' expenses for a nonworking spouse. If your spouse works, you would need less individual coverage but you should both have protection in proportion to income. *Best insurance possibilities:* convertible term, universal life, adjustable life, joint life (if spouse works and provides needed income).

If you're in your fifties, your insurance should be building up cash reserves or investment income for remaining family obligations and for retirement planning. If you have term insurance, you could convert some of it into universal or whole life. If you have decreasing term, consider investing whatever your saving over the whole life. You should also be looking into Retired Life Reserves, Graded Premium, and other low-cost policies. If you have an older policy, consider cashing in this policy to buy a newer one at lower cost, or take a loan on the cash value to make it produce more income for you.

If you're in your sixties, stop paying insurance premiums. Cash in the policy and use the money to finance your retirement, or convert to a paid-up policy of lower face value (enough to settle your estate and provide survivor protection) or convert to some form of annuity that will provide retirement income and needed survivor benefits.

For more information on insurance needs before and during retirement, you can write:

■ American Council of Life Insurance, 1850 K St. NW, Washington, DC 20006.

You can also check your library for these helpful books:

■ *Life Insurance: A Consumer's Handbook* by Joseph M. Belth (Bloomington: Indiana University Press, 1973).

■ *Your Insurance Adviser* by Saul Sokol (New York: Barnes & Noble, 1977).

■ *Live Smart—Die Smarter* by DeWitt M. Shy (Huntsville, Ala.: Strode Publishers, 1978).

You can check out the reliability of insurance companies by asking your reference library for ratings by *Best's Insurance Reports*. Below are some companies to consider for particular types of policies (listing does not constitute recommendation):

LOW-COST TERM INSURANCE

American Health and Life
300 St. Paul Place
Baltimore, MD 21202

Philadelphia Life
111 N. Broad St
Philadelphia, PA 19107

Federal Kemper Life
Kemper Insurance Bldg.
Long Grove, IL 60049

Security-Connecticut Life
Security Dr.
Avon, CT 06001

UNIVERSAL LIFE POLICIES

Life of Virginia
6610 W. Broad St.
Richmond, VA 23230

United Fidelity Life
1025 Elm St.
Dallas, TX 75202

ADJUSTABLE LIFE POLICIES

Minnesota Mutual Life
345 Cedar St.
St. Paul, MN 55101

Bankers Life of Iowa
711 High St.
Des Moines, IA 50307

SINGLE-PREMIUM ANNUITIES

John Alden Life
5100 Gamble Dr.
St. Louis Park, MN 55416

Anchor National Life
2202 E. Camelback Rd.
Phoenix, AZ 85016

LIFE INSURANCE LINKED TO GOLD

Gold Services Inc.
94 Main St.
Howard Bank Bldg., Box 1278
Montpelier, VT 05602

PART IV.

YOUR

CHANGING LEGAL

NEEDS

Let's take a typical day. You wake up, eat breakfast with your spouse, walk your dog, drive to the golf course for 18 holes, return home, order something from the store, go into the basement to make gifts for friends and relatives.

While these activities are routine, they do have legal implications: your marriage contract covers many legal rights and obligations. If your dog bites someone, you could be held liable. If you hit someone on the golf course, you could be sued. When you drive, you must obey traffic laws. When you order something from the store, you make a contract. If the delivery man falls down the stairs, you could be liable for damages. If you sell your handmade gifts, you could run into legal knots.

In short, there's a law governing just about everything you do. And as you go from pre- to postretirement, you'll be faced with an *entirely new set* of legal rights and responsibilities, and your options will narrow as you'll have less time and money to recover any losses.

The law varies from city to city and state to state, and there will be times when you aren't sure of the law or how it aplies in a particular situation or activity. In the next several pages we'll discuss legal aspects of everyday living and some special situations of retirement: making a contract, Social Security and Medicare benefits, federal and state tax laws, buying retirement housing, starting a retirement business, a late or second marriage, taking care of an ill or incompetent relative or friend, types of ownership, making a will, estate planning. We'll also examine when you need a lawyer, how to choose one, and where you can get help and advice from other special advisers whose services are inexpensive or free. The more you know about the law, the more you'll save on legal fees.

In each case we'll explore the *general* law covering the situation or activity. But it's up to each of us to find out how the *specific* law applies to your particular situation. When in doubt, check with your lawyer.

CONTRACTS—FINE PRINT TRAPS OR WEBS OF SECURITY?

You probably enter into more contracts than you realize. When you take a job, you make a contract—written, spoken (oral agreement), or implied. Are you buying a car or TV on time? Do you have insurance? Do you order from a store? All involve contracts. Do you realize that you make a contract whenever you make an *offer*, and someone *accepts*, or there's some form of *consideration* (the "I do" of a marriage ceremony; money, work, or goods). Most contracts are oral (you order something over the telephone) and sealed with a handshake or a verbal agreement.

The majority of contracts are oral, but some contracts must be in writing and signed to be valid. Generally, any agreement that is not to be honored within one year or consummated before the end of a lifetime should be in writing.

Thus, an apartment lease for more than one year should be in writing, and an agreement to support someone during his lifetime must be in writing. Also in writing should be agreements of promises made in consideration of marriage; to answer for another's debt; to transfer personal property; to provide for someone in a will; to set up a trust; to assign or name someone a beneficiary of an insurance policy; to buy, sell, or transfer stock; to change an interest in real or personal property; to assign a contract.

Before signing a contract, know what you're signing. Watch out for words or clauses like: "waiver or statutes of limitations," "confessions of judgement," "waiver of exemption," "homestead right." In some cases you might be protected by "cooling-off" periods under the Truth-in-Lending Law and Federal Trade Commission rules. Also, laws in most states permit courts to throw out contracts that, if enforced, would cause injustice: those you were forced to sign or those that are for illegal purposes. But in many cases, when you sign, you're set.

Never sign a contract with blanks in it (it's illegal in some states) and realize that *you can always change a printed contract.* If the salesman says, "This is the form everyone signs," don't take his word. Most people are awed by printed contracts and probably do sign them. But *you can change a printed contract*—strike out or add anything you wish, provided the other party agrees to the change and signs the contract. *A written contract is only as good and reliable* as the person or firm you're dealing with. If the other party breaks the contract, or if any breach occurs, you might have to take the person to court.

When the Head Should Rule the Heart

There's an old saying that a "widow with money isn't a widow for long." In some cases, a "smooth-talking Charley" has turned into a snarling ape once he's got his hands on a widow's money. Or perhaps the children object to the new marriage—not for sentimental reasons but for practical ones. After all, who will get the money when Dad (or Mom) dies?

To resolve these and other legal questions, it's wise to draw up an *antenuptial agreement* (sometimes called a prenuptial agreement) that specifies who owns what after the marriage. This agreement should be drawn up in *contemplation* of marriage and signed *before* the ceremony. If not possible, see a lawyer about doing so after the marriage.

This agreement would be vital if you wanted to make sure that you retained control of your personal property and that you could will it to whomever you wished. This control could extend to the family home, stocks, or proceeds from a deceased spouse's insurance. An antenuptial agreement settles property rights, but it can't be used to alter or eliminate personal rights or obligations of the marriage relationship. For instance, it can't be used to eliminate sexual relations from marriage.

REAL ESTATE—"LET THE BUYER BEWARE"

Buying and selling housing involves much of your time and most of your money, yet you don't get the same protection as you do when you buy aspirin or have your hair done.

"Let the buyer beware" still holds true when you buy real estate. The seller has the legal duty not to hide dangerous wiring or holes in the floor, but the law imposes few other obligations, and you must be on guard. In *selling* real estate, you'll want answers to these questions:

■ *Who gets the sales commission?* In some states you may have to pay a real estate agent even after the listing period expires. According to the law in some states, the real estate agent might earn his commission when he produces a buyer who's "ready, willing, and able" to enter into a contract on terms acceptable to you—even when the deal falls through or when it's concluded after the listing period runs out.

■ *What about capital gains tax?* In the chapter on Retirement Housing, we discuss the special tax advantages if you sell your house after age 55. Learn all aspects of this, including whether you'd be better off selling the house for cash or taking a mortgage. By taking a mortgage you may save on income taxes if the payment schedule complies with income tax rules.

■ *Buying a home.* In buying a home you should know who gets the deposit if the deal falls through. Can you get your down payment back if you can't get a loan? Can you pay early to save on interest? Must the seller turn the place over to you by a set time (what happens if he doesn't)? Have you checked and insured yourself against boundary disputes, liens, easements, restrictions? Do you need a termite inspector, and who pays for it? What guarantees do you have with the contractor if you're building or improving a home?

Any agreement should set out all terms of the sale. Know, also, if your escrow papers contain terms that are binding upon you.

■ *Condominiums and co-ops.* Condominiums and co-ops often have elaborate contracts that affect your pocketbook and personal freedom (in some cases affecting whether you can will or sell your units; in other cases restricting your activities). That's why it's so important to understand—or have your lawyer look over—any condominium or co-op contracts. Check out these conditions:

1.   What services are included and what are the charges? Are charges subject to change? If so, under what conditions?

2.   Are there restrictions on your personal life or in selling, renting, or willing your property? In some cases, a board of directors or the management might have a "private" set of conditions as to who they will allow you to rent to or sell to (often based on racial or religious grounds). This is an illegal action, of course, but you should be aware that it does happen.

3.   What rights and responsibilities do you have for the common grounds (including recreational areas)? Are charges subject to change if the management turns over the facilities to residents?

4.   If you rent for a trial period, can you get your money back if you decide not to buy? If you do decide to buy, will the rent be applied to the purchase price?

■ *Retirement hotels, residence clubs, and life-care housing.* These housing units, in which you sign up for long-term leases (sometimes for life), usually offer a trial period before they accept you (and vice versa). If you do sign up for a trial period, know what refund arrangements you get. Then, before signing any long-term commitment, understand *all* the terms (including those above). If in doubt, check it out with a lawyer. It's better to pay his fees than to get into housing that could tie you down or leave you broke.

■ *Living with someone—or having someone live with you.* If you enter into any formal agreement to live with someone or have someone live with you, you'll probably need the advice of a counselor in a social service agency or perhaps a lawyer. If any specific time period or money is involved—or if you deed (or receive) property in return for support—get a written agreement; preferably drawn up by a lawyer.

WHEN DOES YOUR HOBBY BECOME YOUR BUSINESS?

Suppose you make the best cherry pies in the neighborhood—for your friends, your church, your parties. Baking pies is your hobby, and you give them away as gifts. But if the store down the street hears about your wonderful pies and wants to buy some for resale, then you're in business. Going into the pie-making business involves several legal considerations, many of which apply to other businesses.

1. *Home food laws.* If you sell a food product, you may have to follow strict food and drug laws involving ingredients, labeling, sanitation, and inspection. You should check with your local health department or field agent of the Department of Agriculture.

2. *Labeling laws.* If you want to sell pies (or other products containing ingredients), check label laws with the State Department of Agriculture; if you want to sell to other states, check your nearest field agent of the Department of Commerce.

3. *Licenses.* You may need city, county, or state licenses to operate your at-home business, and you may need a sales tax permit to collect and report tax. Check with city, county, or state tax offices.

4. *Zoning laws.* Your city or state may have certain laws regarding operating a business out of your home, especially if customers come to your door. You can determine these regulations by checking with your city clerk.

5. *Tax deductions.* While you may be able to deduct most legitimate business expenses, the government will require you to put forth a "business-like and diligent effort" to make money. If you do and can prove it, the government will even allow you to show a loss and deduct it. Be sure you know what tax records to keep; check with your local tax board or accountant.

6. *Business arrangements.* If two or more persons get together to carry on a business for profit, the law will probably consider them *partners*, and they may be liable for claims against the business. You must determine if you are an independent contractor, an employee, a partner, or an agent. If

you're not sure, talk it over with a lawyer. He'll tell you what position you occupy and if you need a formal contract.

7. *Buying a business.* Suppose you buy into Brown's business, and he helps you get started. When things are really prospering, he leaves—and opens a similar business around the corner, competing with you and taking back his former customers. Before buying, you should have insisted that the purchase agreement prohibited Brown from opening a similar business in the area. Or suppose you buy Jones's business and his inventory and equipment. Things look fine—until the bills start coming in. "These don't belong to me," you say. "They belong to Jones." Do they? To protect creditors who send merchandise or perform services before the sale, some state laws say that creditors must be informed of the sale—such as by recording and publication of a legal notice. This gives "constructive notice" to creditors whether or not they see it. And if you are buying a business that is being operated on rented premises, be sure to find out if you need the consent of the landlord and if the landlord has the right to terminate your tenancy at any time; if there's a lease, be sure to know the expiration date and understand all other legal aspects. Also, know legal aspects of any contract you sign for a franchise, dance lessons, or introductory services; before you publish a book through a "vanity press," and before you buy equipment or "instructions" for an at-home business.

PERILS AND PITFALLS OF TYPES OF OWNERSHIP

Most couples own property in some form of joint ownership with "right of survivorship." They do so for these advantages: the transfer doesn't go through probate—the other person gets the property quickly, and there may be no probate cost; in some states, the rights of survivors may come ahead of those of creditors.

However, there are certain *disadvantages* of jointly owned property: Such property generally goes to the surviving co-owner(s) without the possibility of distributing the property among several heirs or placing the property in a trust; joint ownership often increases tax liabilities. We'll examine these drawbacks after this listing of joint ownership arrangements. The first two are *without* right of survivorship:

1. *Community property.* In Arizona, California, Idaho, Louisiana, Nevada, New Mexico, Texas, and Washington, each spouse is presumed to be the owner of one half of their combined property, and in some cases this presumption may apply regardless of which spouse purchased or inherited it

or in whose name it appears. Generally, community property retains community status even when it is removed to a common law state. But this can vary among the community property states, so it might be best to set up a revocable trust in the common law state if you want to segregate the property. If you die without a will, *all* your property may go to your surviving spouse (and *none* to your children) if the judge decides that all of your property was community. But if the judge decides all your property was separate, your children may be entitled to a substantial share.

2. *Tenancy in common.* Two or more persons own undivided shares in real or personal property; co-owners' shares pass to heirs or beneficiaries, not to surviving co-owners.

These next two are *with* rights of survivorship:

3. *Tenancy by the entirety.* This form of joint ownership is limited primarily to husbands and wives and usually restricted to real estate. Generally, neither spouse can act alone in disposing of the property, and upon the death of one, the other automatically becomes sole owner. It is not recognized in certain states.

4. *Joint tenancy.* Two or more persons own property as joint tenants. Generally, an attempted conveyance (transfer) by one spouse can destroy the joint tenancy and may have a bad effect on the rights of the other. Joint tenancy isn't recognized in some states except under special circumstances, and even where recognized, rules differ from state to state. However, under the Economic Recovery Tax Act of 1981, starting in 1982, property owned jointly by spouses will automatically be divided equally in value when the first spouse dies—and one half the property's value will be included in his or her estate.

In most states, joint tenancy with suvivorship rights on a safety deposit box applies only to the box, not the contents. In this case, it's best to indicate clearly who owns what in a joint safety deposit box. Unless you do, tax officials usually assume that everything in a box belongs to the first joint tenant to die and tax it accordingly.

Often joint tenancy is used as a means of enabling one spouse to continue managing the joint-tenancy asset (whether cash or real property or otherwise) in case the other becomes ill or incompetent or dies. But in some cases a guardianship or conservatorship is advisable or essential in order to avoid legal attacks from relatives of the ill or incompetent spouse. Worse, joint tenancy can be particularly bad if one spouse is an alcoholic or compulsive gambler: Sober, competent spouses may find they have suddenly become a kind of "partner" to an unknown moneylender to whom the spouse has made an assignment. This can be disastrous.

Generally, lawyers say you should avoid tenancy if:

1.   You want to will property to someone besides the surviving joint tenant(s).

2.   You don't want to end up owning property with a stranger. One joint tenant can break a joint tenancy without the knowledge or consent of the other.

3.   The property has greatly increased in value.

4.   The estate is valued at over the federal estate tax exemption.

5.   You want to sell the property at any time without someone else's signature.

Adding it up, it might make sense to have the *home* and *checking account* in joint names so the surviving spouse would have shelter and money until the estate is settled, but it might be best to *divide all other property equally* (including stocks, bonds, other assets) or to change the joint tenancy to *tenancy in common*. In this way, each spouse can dispose of his/her property via will, and any gift tax would be far less than an estate tax. However, it may not be as simple as just changing the ownerships; you should check with your lawyer and coordinate any changes with changes in your will.

HOW VARIOUS JOINT OWNERSHIPS DIFFER

In his book *Joint Property* ($9.70 postpaid from Fireside Books, 1230 Ave. of the Americas, New York, NY 10020), Alexander A. Bove, Jr., a practicing attorney and financial columnist for the *Boston Globe*, compares the various joint ownerships:

CHARACTERISTIC	JOINT PROP.	TENANCY BY ENTIRETY	TENANCY IN COMMON
Survivorship rights	Yes	Yes	No
Right to sell share	Yes	No	Yes
Right to divide	Yes	No	Yes
Can creditors reach share	Yes	Maybe	Yes
Included in estate	Yes (unless owned with spouse then 1/2)	Yes (1/2)	Only your share

JOINT PROPERTY VERSUS TRUST

CHARACTERISTIC	JOINT PROPERTY	TRUST
Avoids probate	Probably	Yes
Saves on estate taxes	No	Yes
Helps avoid creditors' attack	No	Yes
Provides for unexpected	No	Yes
Affected by simultaneous death	Yes	No
Affected by disability of owners	Yes	No
Affected by divorce	Yes	No
Easy to obstruct	Yes	No
Can provide for spouse, children, grandchildren	No	Yes
Can protect from creditors of beneficiaries	No	Yes
Reduces overall costs and expenses	No	Yes
Can predict outcome	No	Yes

A WILL SHOWS YOU CARE—SAVES YOU MONEY

With a will, you can distribute property in whatever portions you want and to whomever you want. *In many cases a will saves you money.*

For instance, if you die without a will (intestate), the court will appoint an *administrator* who will have to be bonded, with the cost of the bond charged to your estate. He may then have to spend much time (and money) getting court orders to carry out duties you could have specified in your will. In your will you can choose an *executor* who can serve without bond, and you can prevent your estate from being carved into ungainly or unmanageable proportions that may fail to take advantage of some estate tax exemptions.

Without a will, the state may: Give your spouse one third of the property and your children two thirds; give your spouse half and your children half; in community-property states, give all community property to your spouse and divide only separate property among your children. In some cases they would have to sell property in order to divide the proceeds.

The only way you can divide assets as you wish is by making a will. What constitutes a will? Generally, a will is a document—which must meet every single legal requirement of your state—that specifies how you wish to distribute your assets after you die. To be valid, a will must contain: precise legal language (who gets what); proper signatures (usually at the end); proper number of witnesses (in some states two; other states three), and meet other legal requirements (show a testamentary intent in the correct language; show that both witnesses were present at the time; show that the testator declared to the witnesses that the document was a will; show that the witnesses were not themselves beneficiaries, and other requirements).

A WILL ISN'T A DO-IT-YOURSELF DOCUMENT. Some people think they can write their own wills, but *only about half the states* recognize homemade (holographic) wills. And unless they contain *precise legal language* and follow the *precise legal requirements* of your state, they may not be valid. The same goes for "blank-form" (printed) wills that you fill in. (*Note:* Even California's famous $1 "fill-in-the-blanks" will carries a suggestion that users consult with a lawyer for assistance in filling in the form.)

In one instance a man made out his own will specifying that one third of his estate should go to one son. But he didn't mention his daughter and another son (illegitimate). Also, he didn't have his homemade will witnessed. But a week before he died, he went to his neighbors and asked them to witness this will. When it was probated, the court was shocked to find that the will had been witnessed only a week before his death, and it didn't mention the other heirs. The illegitimate son and daughter contested the will, and it ended up intestate (as though no will had been drawn).

For as little as $50 a lawyer can draw up a simple will that will meet your state's requirements, suit your family's needs, and save you money. Both husband and wife should make wills because it's possible that both may die in a common accident. Single persons should also make wills.

What Should Go Into a Will?

A will is like a tuxedo—it must be tailored to fit. When planning your will, here are points to consider:

1. *What are your assets?* Besides assets held in joint tenancy (which aren't ordinarily affected by a will as long as there's a surviving joint tenant), your assets (including half of community property) include such items as cash, real estate, securities (stocks, bonds, mortgages), business or partnership interest, automobile, household and personal effects. Don't overlook certain prized possessions (like stamp or china collections, jewelry, documents) that have personal as well as practical value.

Now, *subtract your debts* and make allowances for funeral expenses, costs of administering your estate, estate and inheritance taxes, and so forth.

WHO NEEDS A WILL?

Answer these questions with a "Yes" or "No":

1. Do you want to take care of the possibility that your heir may not live long?

2. Do you want to make sure your executor will be free to act with the minimum number of court orders and red tape and to serve without a bond?

3. Do you wish to leave a share of your community property to your children?

4. Do you want to leave more to one heir than another—perhaps because one is independently wealthy, or because you've provided for him in another way?

5. Do you want to leave something to charity, church, or school?

6. Do you wish to forgive a debt someone owes you when you die?

7. Do you want to set up a trust fund to provide income for your wife or children?

If you answered "Yes" to any *one* of these questions, you need a will.

2. *How do you want to distribute your assets?* In the case of a home or other real estate, you can leave it outright to one or more beneficiaries or place it in trust along with other property. Also, you could direct that the property be sold and the proceeds added to your estate or let one beneficiary have the use of it for life, with outright ownership passing to another beneficiary. In the case of an unincorporated business, it will probably have to be sold. If it's incorporated, you may be able to specify who could continue running it.

If you want to make cash gifts (legacies) to individuals or institutions, it's probably best to leave the money in fractions or percentages of totals. You won't know how much money you'll have to distribute until all debts and taxes are paid.

In most cases you'll want to make outright bequests, but in other cases you may want to let the heirs divide the possessions as they see fit. Any item not bequeathed in some way then becomes part of your "residuary estate"— that which is left after payment of debts and other expenses. You could also set up a trust in your will to manage property, save on taxes, make provision for charity, provide income for heirs.

Be sure to at least mention an heir who's entitled to a share of your estate. You don't have to leave him much of anything, but if you fail to mention any heirs, they might still be able to claim a share of your estate. In some states, only certain specified heirs need be mentioned. A child or grandchild not mentioned may be allowed to inherit just as though the will did not exist. A spouse not mentioned may be allowed to inherit just as though the will did not exist.

Who Should Be Your Executor?

You don't necessarily do a friend or relative a favor by naming him (or her) an executor. Someone once said that the ideal executor should combine the business acuity of a Lady Bird Johnson with the humanity of an Abraham Lincoln.

Generally, your executor must see that funeral arrangements are made, have a lawyer start probate proceedings, inventory assets and documents of the estate, and liquidate investments or a business if the will gives no specific instructions, hire accountants or investment advisers if needed, approve payment of valid debts, arrange distribution of cash legacies, make a final accounting to the court.

Because your executor may die, move away, not be available or have the necessary special knowledge, it might be best to choose a bank or trust company as executor. The institution continues to run regardless of what happens to the individuals.

Changes That Could Affect Your Will

Once you've made a will, keep it in a safe place (preferably in your or your lawyer's deposit box or safe) and let your executor and other family members know where it is.

However, you should review your will often, as certain changes could alter it. These changes include:

1. *Heirs.* Have there been deaths, marriages, births, or changes in their financial status? Have you changed your mind about any of them?

2. *Cash demands.* Would your estate have enough marketable securities on hand to pay debts, death taxes, and make cash bequests? Have there been any major changes in the value of your assets?

3. *Residence.* Have you moved from the state in which you made your will? If so, *be sure your will conforms to your new state's law.* And be sure to

establish residency in your new state; if you don't, both your old and new state could claim a share of your estate in the form of death taxes.

4. *Federal and state tax laws.* Have there been changes in the federal or state tax laws that could change conditions of your will?

5. *Executor.* Has he or she died, moved away, will he or she outlive you?

If you've experienced any of these changes, perhaps your will needs updating. In most cases your lawyer can write a codicil (a supplement to your will) to take care of any necessary changes; in other cases you may have to draw up a new will. In any event, keeping your will up to date protects your beneficiaries, your estate, and your peace of mind, and you avoid later conflict and confusion.

Can You Beat Probate?

When a person dies, the will must go through probate court (sometimes called "orphan's" or "surrogate" court) to settle the estate. The process is not only time-consuming but often costly (up to 10 percent of the estate's assets, up to a year or more of time). However, many states have adopted a Uniform Probate Code that may save time and money and distributes property even if there isn't a will. In this case, the spouse receives 100 percent of the estate up to $50,000 and one half of the remainder. The code also may simplify procedures for handling assets located in more than one state and give funds immediately to the surviving spouse.

Wisconsin was the first state to adopt "do-it-yourself probate." In this informal administration of an estate the assets are distributed, bills paid, and tax returns filed with a minimum of delay and expense. However, if you don't live in Wisconsin or a state with Uniform Probate Code, you may find that except for jointly owned property passing to the survivors, life insurance proceeds payable to named beneficiaries, U.S. savings bonds with a designated beneficiary, and certain trusts, your estate would have to go through probate and may be required to pay estate taxes.

HOW TO MINIMIZE ESTATE TAXES

The Economic Recovery Act of 1981 increased the amount of lifetime and testamentary transfers that can pass free of tax. Under the act the unified credits and corrresponding amounts exempt from tax are:

YEAR OF DEATH OR GIFT	UNIFIED CREDIT	EXEMPTION EQUIVALENT
1984	$ 96,300	$325,000
1985	$121,800	$400,000
1986	$155,800	$500,000
1987	$192,800	$600,000

Also, by 1985 no portion of your estate will be taxed at rates higher than 50 percent. Other changes of the act will save you money through:

■ *Unlimited marital deduction.* Anything you leave to your spouse will reduce the size of your estate for tax purposes. However, you should review your will if it was made on or before September 12, 1981—*especially if it has a formula clause* leaving a certain percentage to your spouse. Unless you amend your will, the unlimited marital deduction may not apply. Also, the act says that you can leave your spouse what is called "qualifying terminable interest property" and still claim the full marital deduction. *Qualifying terminable interest property* is property in which a surviving spouse has a qualifying income interest for life.

■ *Increase in the amount of gift tax exclusion.* You can give up to $10,000 a year ($20,000 if you are married) to as many people as you like and pay no gift tax using none of your estate and gift tax credit).

■ *Simplification of joint tenancy.* As noted earlier, under the act property owned jointly by spouses will automatically be divided equally in value when the first spouse dies—and one half of the property's value will be included in his or her estate. This change will not only simplify matters, but it will probably result in the reduction of the taxable estate of many people who, at least until recently, have paid for most of the property they own jointly with their spouses.

For other ways to reduce estate taxes, including assigning insurance policies, making gifts of appreciated assets, setting up custodian accounts, and establishing trusts, get a free copy of "A Guide to Federal Estate and Gift Taxation" (publication #448) from your local IRS office.

OTHER TAX BENEFITS FOR OLDER AMERICANS

Much retirement income, including most Social Security and Railroad Retirement benefits, is not taxable. Neither are workmen's compensation payments, veterans benefits, some pension and annuity payments, money or property received as a gift or inheritance, disability payments, life insurance proceeds, and unemployment benefits. These exceptions are spelled out in "Taxable and Nontaxable Income" (publication #525) from your local IRS office. Also, most states, counties, and cities have personal and property tax exemptions for seniors, some starting at age 60. Check with your local Office on Aging (listed in local telephone directories) to find out what tax exemptions you may be eligible for.

Besides the special capital gains exemption for selling your house after age 55 (see page 192), seniors have these other tax exemptions:

■ *Double exemption for age.* If you or your spouse is age 65 or older, you may claim an extra tax exemption. This tax exemption applies to those who have turned age 65 by January 1 of any year (you are considered age 65 on December 31 of the previous year). You may also claim an extra exemption if you are blind.

■ *Tax credit for the elderly.* If you are over age 65, you may claim the tax credit for the elderly. The amount of the credit may be as high as $375 if you are single or $562.50 on a joint return, but the base on which the credit is computed is reduced by Social Security and other tax-free pension benefits and one half of adjusted gross income exceeding $7,500 if you are single, or $10,000 on a joint return. A credit is also available to retirees under age 65 who receive a pension from a public retirement system.

■ *Pension and annuity income.* Basically, *if you did not* contribute to a pension plan, all the benefits you receive from that plan are taxable. *If you did* contribute to the plan and will collect an amount equal to your contribution within three years, you may exclude the benefits from your income until they equal the amount you contributed. From that point, all benefits are subject to taxation.

■ *For self-employed persons,* or those not covered by an employee pension plan, a tax deduction is available in the year a contribution is made to an IRA or Keogh plan. Also, tax deferral on income earned under the plan and special tax treatment, such as special 10-year averaging, also exist.

For further information on pensions and annuities, send for the free IRS publication #575, "Tax Information on Pension and Annuity Income."

And for information on tax benefits for seniors, ask for publication #554, "Tax Benefits for Older Americans."

HELP IN MANAGING YOUR MONEY AND LEGAL AFFAIRS

There might be a time when you, a relative, or a friend might be too old or ill to manage money and legal affairs. If so, you have many sources of help:

BANKING SERVICES. The trust department of commercial banks offers various services to help manage money. Included are *custodian accounts;* in which you appoint the bank the custodian, and the bank holds stocks, bonds, collects dividends and interest, and any other income. The bank pays utility and other bills, income and property taxes, and handles almost any other financial detail. A variation is the *investment management account* in which the bank is responsible for investment advice and distributes assets over various securities, collects dividends, and even provides cash income. In a custodian or investment management account, you give the bank limited power of attorney (see below) to sign your name (or that of your relative or friend) under certain circumstances.

TRUSTS. Your lawyer could draw up a trust arrangement in which a bank would invest the money and pay bills. Under a typical plan, $50,000 might be invested in a common stock account and for an annual fee of a few hundred dollars yield around $200 monthly out of earnings. The principal would be left intact for emergencies. For a somewhat higher fee, the trustee could arrange for automatic payment of some bills and even make arrangements for emergency health care, and so on.

SOCIAL SECURITY PAYMENTS. If people are unable to manage their own affairs, the Social Security Administration will mail the check to a qualified individual. You can get further information from local Social Security offices.

RAILROAD RETIREMENT. If an annuitant has been declared incompetent, the regular check will be sent to the court-appointed representative or one selected by the Railroad Retirement Board. To initiate such proceedings, check with a Railroad Retirement Board district office.

FEDERAL EMPLOYEES RETIREMENT PROGRAM. The Civil Service Commission will conduct an investigation to judge whether or not a payee is capable of handling his or her own affairs. For further information, write to the Bureau of Retirement, Insurance, and Occupational Health, CCSC, Washington, DC 20415.

PRIVATE PENSION PLANS. Practices vary, but most plans have an arrangement for some qualified person to receive the check of someone who is too old or ill to manage his or her affairs. Check the personnel office.

Care for an Ill or Incompetent Relative or Friend

If you have relatives or friends who are too old or ill to take care of themselves, you have these options to provide care:

APPOINTING A "REPRESENTATIVE PAYEE." This is a pact prepared by a lawyer and signed by those concerned that provides that the income of the elderly person (Social Security, stock dividends, and so forth) goes to the representative payee who sets up a special fund. From this fund, he or she pays the older person's bills. This arrangement doesn't have to be approved by the court and can be canceled if it doesn't work out.

APPOINTING A "CONSERVATOR" OR "GUARDIAN." In about one third of the states you can petition the court to appoint you a *conservator* or *guardian* of the *estate* or *person*. In other cases, you can help such people by having them sign a *special* or *general* power of attorney.

The conservator or guardian of the *estate* handles all of the ward's personal or real property and money. The conservator or guardian decides what to spend, how to spend it, what investments to make. He or she also collects any money due, pays bills, and keeps records of all transactions.

Conservators or guardians of the *person* are responsible for the physical care and welfare of their ward. They may choose where that ward will live and may arrange for necessary medical and nursing care. He or she turns over all bills to the conservator of the estate; in some cases, the person may be conservator of the estate and/or person.

Most states allow any relative or a friend of the relative (other than a creditor) to petition the court for appointment as a guardian or conservator. The extent of inadequacy to determine need varies. In roughly half the states it's only necessary to prove that the person is unable to manage his or her affairs. In the remaining states proof must be established that the incapacitated person is "mentally incompetent" or a "spendthrift" according to the testimony of a doctor, other witnesses, or the person in question.

To be named a conservator or guardian, have your lawyer draw up the proper papers and file them with the court. Although you can get standard power-of-attorney forms (sometimes called "statutory short forms") from stationery and office supply stores, you might want a lawyer if you want to be named a *special* or *general* power of attorney. Remember, a *special* power of attorney limits you to one specific purpose: a *general* power of attorney authorizes you to transact business in general for the person. Power of attorney terminates at the death of an incompetent or sick person and is no substitute for guardianship or conservatorship or a will.

For further information, send $2.50 to the American Civil Liberties Union for a copy of "The Rights of Older Persons" (ACLU has offices in major cities). You can also order the book through Avon Books, Mail Order Dept., 250 West 55th St., New York, NY 10019. Add 25¢ for postage.

WHEN DO YOU NEED A LAWYER?

Unless you understand the law in these situations, you'd probably need a lawyer if:

■ You are in a business or setting up one and are involved with other people and with large sums of money.

■ You are injured (or you injure someone) through negligence and either sue or are sued.

■ You seek to recover a *large* sum of money from someone or someone seeks to recover money from you.

■ You make out a will or set up a trust or otherwise dispose of real property.

■ You are involved in any transaction involving large sums of money or any transactions covering a year or more in time. (Don't forget, contracts not to be performed in one year must be in writing.)

You should choose your family lawyer on the same basis you'd choose your family doctor. You'd want to select someone who would sympathize with your problems while respecting your pocketbook. If you don't have a family lawyer, here are some suggestions on finding the right one for you:

1. Ask friends whose judgment you respect, or ask your accountant, banker, insurance agent, stockbroker, union or association representative who might have frequent dealings with lawyers.

2. Call your local bar association. It may operate a "dial-law" telephone number that you can call to get basic information on legal problems. The bar association may also have a lawyer referral system that gives callers the names of qualified lawyers or may refer you to other sources of legal aid.

Some bar associations operate "fee panels" of lawyers who will work for the elderly for modest fixed fees.

3.   Send for these helpful booklets: "The American Lawyer: How to Choose and Use One" and "Your Rights Over Age 50" for $1 each from Order Billing, American Bar Association, 1155 E. 60th St., Chicago, IL 60637. For a tax-deductible $15, you can join HALT (a nationwide organization that is seeking to make our legal system more understandable, accessible, and responsive) and receive "Shopping for a Lawyer" and a series of other Citizens' Legal Manuals and a quarterly newsletter. Write HALT, Suite 319, 201 Massachusetts Ave. NE, Washington, DC 20002.

4.   Check out any lawyer in the *Martindale-Hubbell Law Directory* available at public libraries. This directory rates lawyers' abilities and notes key clients.

5.   Seek out legal clinics. Some 700 "legal supermarkets" have opened up around the country. They have staffs of several lawyers and offer legal advice on a high-volume, low-cost (30 to 35 percent below regular fees) basis. Also look for free legal clinics established by some university law schools.

6.   Contact your Area Agency on Aging (look in local telephone book and call nearest Office on Aging). These agencies have special funds and programs to offer legal services to older Americans. And they can refer you to other free or low-cost legal services in your area.

7.   Consider mediation and arbitration panels. With or without the help of a lawyer, you can negotiate a settlement yourself through a third party— often a lawyer. These panels are sponsored by courts, district attorney's offices, and nonprofit groups. For the name and address of a panel near you, write to Special Committee on Alternative Means of Dispute Resolution, American Bar Association, 1800 M St. NW, Washington, DC 20036.

At the first meeting with a lawyer, *discuss fees*. Abraham Lincoln once said: "A lawyer's time and advice are his stock in trade." The less advice a lawyer has to give, and the less time he has to spend on your case, the less it will probably cost you. (Most lawyers charge *about* $50 an hour for their time.)

You can minimize expenses by contacting your lawyer when facts are fresh, witnesses are available, problems are just beginning. The lawyer can prevent you from making costly mistakes, prevent the problems from growing, and bring the matter to a conclusion sooner.

If you have a complaint about legal fees, be sure to bring the matter to the fee arbitration panel of the state or local bar. The panel will hear both of you and decide on a proper fee.

WHERE TO GET LEGAL HELP

Many city and state offices on aging and many local senior centers have "lay advocates" or "paralegals," who have not been through law school but who do have legal training, to give advice and other assistance to seniors. Their services are either free or low-cost. Also see if your community has a legal clinic, which probably has a staff of several lawyers and can offer legal advice on a high-volume, low-cost basis. Some university law schools have established free legal clinics. Or you can call your local bar association (listed in telephone directory under "Lawyers" or "Lawyer Referrals") and see if they have a referral service. Under this arrangement you can get a half-hour consultation for around $25 that may resolve your case.

You can also get help from these *organizations*:

■ National Senior Citizens Law Center, 1709 W. 8th St., Los Angeles, CA 90017.

■ National Legal Aid and Defender Association, 2100 M St. NW, Washington, DC 20037.

You can also get these *books* from libraries or stores:

■ *The Family Legal Advisor* by Alice Helm (New York: Crown, 1982).

■ *What Everyone Needs to Know About Law* by Joseph Newman (Washington, DC: U.S. News Books, 1975).

■ *Handbook of Everyday Law* by Martin J. Ross (rev. ed., New York: Fawcett, 1982).

■ *Estate Planning Guide* by Sidney Kess & Bertil Westlin (Chicago: Commerce Clearing House, 1982).

■ *The Complete Guide to Estate Planning* by John J. Gargan (Englewood Cliffs, N.J.: Prentice-Hall, 1980).

■ *You and Your Will: The Planning and Management of Your Estate* by Paul P. Ashley (rev. ed., New York: McGraw-Hill, 1978).

■ *You, the Law, and Retirement*, available free from Administration on Aging, Publication Department, Rm. 4146, 330 Independence Ave. SW, Washington, DC 20201.

CAN YOU EVER ACT AS YOUR OWN LAWYER?

There are many situations in which you have the absolute legal right to represent yourself, but whether it is wise to do so is sometimes doubtful. However, there are two situations in which you may not need a lawyer:

SOCIAL SECURITY OR MEDICARE DISPUTES. If you disagree with a decision on Social Security or Medicare benefits, you may ask the Social Security Administration to reconsider. If after this reconsideration you're still not satisfied, you have 60 days to ask for a hearing by an examiner of the Bureau of Hearing and Appeals.

If your appeal concerns benefits for in-patient hospital, extended care, or home health services under Medicare, $100 or more must be involved.

You may or may not appear in person, and you have the option of being represented by an attorney or any other individual. You can also ask Social Security representatives to get help for you from the local bar association, Legal Aid Society, or other organization.

If you disagree with the hearing examiner's decision, you have *60 days* to ask for a review by the Appeals Council. You'll be notified in writing of whatever action is taken in your case. If you disagree with the Appeals Council action, you have 60 days to file a civil action in a U.S. District Court. However, if your appeal involves Medicare, $1,000 or more must be involved.

If you have any questions about your right to appeal decisions made on your claims, write, call, or visit your local Social Security office.

SMALL CLAIMS COURT. All states have Small Claims Courts, usually located in major metropolitan areas. Generally, these courts make *money judgments only*. They can't order anyone to return property to fulfill a contract. Most states set limits of about $750 in settling money claims.

It costs from about $5 to $20 to file suit in these courts, but you may have other costs, including sending a summons by certified mail or paying the sheriff or process server to deliver it. Most Small Claims Courts *bar lawyers*, although you may consult one before presenting your case. And you must take several steps yourself when you file a suit. For instance:

1. You must go to the clerk of the court, fill out a claim, and pay a fee. The court then sets a hearing date.
2. You either mail or send a summons to the defendant.
3. You may appear in court on a hearing day and present your case to a

judge or arbitrator. As plaintiff, you'll have to furnish concrete proof of wrongdoing and produce any necessary witnesses.

4. The judge or arbitrator then makes a decision (sometimes delayed for study). If you win, the defendant is ordered to pay you the money.

However, *collecting* the money might be a different story. According to a survey in *Consumers Union*, in at least one out of five cases *you won't be able to collect the money you won*. Whomever you sued might be broke or bankrupt or they may have skipped town. If the defendant is able to pay but refuses, you could have the court place a lien on the person's property or wages or bank account.

Small Claims Courts aren't perfect, but they do offer you the most handy means to collect money owed you or withheld, without paying attorney fees. To find the nearest Small Claims Court, check with your local library. You can also write to the U.S. Department of Justice, Office of the Attorney General, Washington, DC 20530, and ask for a copy of "Consumers Tell It to the Judge: Small Claims Courts and Consumer Complaints."

Alternatives to small claims and other courts have become so common that many telephone Yellow Pages now have listings for mediation and arbitration services. And here are major organizations that can help:

■ American Arbitration Association, 140 W. 51st St., New York, NY 10020.

■ American Bar Association, Special Committee on Alternative Means of Dispute Resolution, 1800 M St. NW, Washington, DC 20036.

■ Endispute, Suite 803, 11 Dupont Circle NW, Washington, DC 20036 (offices also in Chicago, Los Angeles, San Francisco).

■ The Center for Public Resources, 680 5th Ave., New York, NY 10019.

WHAT ARE SOME OTHER LEGAL AREAS THAT MIGHT AFFECT YOU?

Here are some other legal areas that specifically affect older Americans:

1. *The Age Discrimination in Employment Act.* The ADEA is designed to encourage the employment of people age 40 to 70. The ADEA applies to private employers who employ 20 or more people in an industry affecting commerce. Most federal, state, and local government employees are covered, as are employment agencies serving one or more covered employers, and labor unions representing 25 or more members or functioning as hiring halls.

Under the ADEA most employers cannot require employees to retire before they are age 70. Mandatory retirement at any age is forbidden for many government employees. In general, the act also prohibits discrimination in hiring, job retention, promotion, compensation, or other terms or conditions of employment.

Certain classes of workers are specifically exempted under the act: (a) executives who are entitled to retirement benefits of at least $27,000 annually; (b) elected officials and their staffs; (c) commercially scheduled airline pilots. The act also allows the following exemptions or "differentiations": (a) where age is a bona fide occupation qualification; (b) where differentiation is based on reasonable factors other than age; (c) to observe the terms of a bona fide seniority system, employee benefit plan, retirement pension, or insurance plan that does not subvert or evade the purposes of the act; (d) discharge or discipline of a person for "good cause."

2. *Age Discrimination Act.* The act forbids most age discrimination in programs and activities receiving federal financial assistance. The act contains some important exceptions: (a) it does not cover employment that is covered by the ADEA (above); (b) it permits age distinctions that are "necessary to the normal operation" of a program or "to the achievement of statutory objective." Other important exceptions in the act are that age distinctions are permitted when they are specifically provided for in state, federal, or local law; and that a program can use "reasonable factors other than age" as a basis for making decisions.

3. *The Equal Credit Opportunity Act.* This act prohibits discrimination in any aspect of a credit transaction because of sex, marital state, race, national origin, religion, or age. It also prohibits discrimination because of receiving payments from a public assistance program. It covers all creditors who regularly extend credit, including banks, small loan and finance companies, retail and department stores, credit card companies, and credit unions. The act does allow creditors to determine creditworthiness by considering such factors as income, expenses, debts, and the reliability of the applicant.

4. *The Employee Retirement Income Security Age.* In general, ERISA covers employee benefit plans, including pension and hospital plans. ERISA does not require any employer to establish plans, but those who do must meet certain standards. The law also provides that each employed person not covered by a plan be permitted to put aside, on a tax-deferred basis, a certain amount of compensation for retirement.

5. *Nursing Home Residents Rights.* All residents of Medicare and/or Medicaid-certified nursing homes are guaranteed the right to: (a) *dignity and*

privacy—to be treated with respect and dignity and have privacy in personal care and treatment; (b) *communication and association*—to meet and talk privately with spouses and others, participate in community activities, and send and receive unopened personal mail; (c) *information*—to be fully informed of all rights and responsibilities and all services and charges; (d) *medical treatment*—to be informed about their medical conditions, participate in planning medical treatment, and be free from physical and chemical abuse and restraint; (e) *personal and financial affairs*—to manage their personal financial affairs, use personal clothing and possessions, and express complaints without fear of reprisal; (f) *transfer and discharge*—to be released only for medical reasons, for personal welfare or the welfare of others, or for nonpayment, and to be given reasonable advance notice of any discharge. These rights are found in the Code of Federal Regulations. For further information, contact your local Office on Aging.

WHAT ARE SOME AREAS OF CONSUMER CONCERN FOR THE ELDERLY?

The Legal Counsel for the Elderly, 1909 K St. NW, Washington, DC 20049, puts out a "Legal Rights Calendar" ($4.95) that spells out many other areas of consumer concern including mail orders, credit information, billing disputes. And the Council for Better Business Bureaus, 1515 Wilson Blvd., Arlington, VA 22209, offers a free booklet, "Consumer Problems of the Elderly," that covers physical safety, shelter, economic security, companionship, and other areas.

The older we are, the more vulnerable we seem to be to some frauds and quacks. It's not that we're gullible, but when we retire on a fixed income, we often grasp at products or promises that might help us make or save money. In this complex, changing world, even experts find it hard to keep up with new laws, techniques, and products that might affect our health and wealth. Thus, it's harder than ever for the average consumer to avoid the pitfalls, especially when frauds are increasing at a rate of 12 percent a year.

Consumer specialists say that elderly persons spend over $2 billion annually on various frauds and quacks. Here's a rundown on various shady dealings; by knowing the "tricks of the trade," you should be able to avoid them—before it's too late.

HEALTH FRAUDS AND QUACKS. As we grow older, we may develop more internal illnesses than usual. If so, we may become prey to the modern "medicine man" who may be trying to sell everything from needless vitamins and mineral supplements to cancer and arthritis "cures."

As far as nutrition is concerned, most of us get adequate vitamins, minerals, and other nutrients from the foods we eat. If you eat properly from the Basic Four food groups, you usually won't need supplemental vitamins and minerals unless there is something organically wrong and your doctor prescribes them for the condition. If you take vitamin or mineral supplements, your body uses only those nutrients it needs, then gets rid of excess C and B complex and stores A and D. But an excess of vitamins A and D may prove harmful as does excess iron.

As most of us eventually develop some form of *arthritis*, this disease is a favorite tool of the health quack. Rheumatoid arthritis is made to order, as the pain comes and goes regardless of what you do or don't do for it. Fraudulent products to "cure or relieve" arthritis range from filtered seawater to magnetic bracelets; from radium baths to musical vibrations. If they "work," it's because the pain has gone away (remission) conveniently after the "cure" was applied.

Common aspirin is the best—and cheapest—medicine to relieve arthritic pain. Sometimes your doctor may prescribe cortisone or gold salts. These, combined with heat, rest, and sometimes surgery, are the only reliable means to control arthritic pain.

About half of most *cancers* can be treated and cured through surgery, radiation, and chemotherapy (the use of drugs). However, many quacks and frauds advertise cancer "cures" consisting of biological injections, special diets, plant products, powders and pastes, and corrosive or caustic agents that may prove dangerous or cause disfigurement. Machines and devices include everything from zinc-lined pine boxes (the patients sit in them to absorb "orgone energy") to a "magic spike" filled with barium chloride. None of these devices—diets, injections, powders, pastes, caustic agents—"cures" cancer, says the American Medical Association (AMA).

The AMA offers six rules to help spot a health fraud or quack:

1. Quacks often uses a special or "secret" formula or machine that is claimed to cure the disease.
2. They may promise or imply a quick or easy cure, or they may talk about "pepping up" your health.
3. They advertise, using "case histories" and testimonials from their "patients" to impress people.
4. They refuse to accept the tried and proved methods of medical research and proof. They clamor constantly for "medical investigation" and

recognition, but they avoid a test or stop short of giving the data needed for a scientific evaluation.

5.   They claim medical men are persecuting them or are afraid of competition.

6.   They claim their methods of treatment are better than surgery, X rays, and drugs prescribed by a physician.

EXTRA-INCOME SCHEMES. Knowing that older persons are often anxious to stretch their income, many fast-buck operators concentrate on "work-at-home" schemes. These operators advertise in classified sections of newspapers or magazines, pitching equipment or "instructions" to make money on everything from raising mushrooms to publishing songs. Here are favorite tricks of the "work-at-home" promoters:

1.   The "buy back" where the promoter pledges to buy back products if they are "up to standards." Unfortunately, none of your output will be "quite good enough."

2.   Worthless instructions or course materials at highly inflated prices. Often, the instructions or materials are meaningless or worthless.

3.   Worthless or "special equipment" for your project. Often the equipment is overpriced, needs repairs, is obsolete.

Beware especially of ads that promise huge profits on part-time earnings, use testimonials, and supply only a box number for a return address. If you're in doubt about an offer, contact your local Better Business Bureau, Small Business Administration office, banker, or lawyer *before* you accept an offer.

CON GAMES. Crooks have some 26 basic "games" they play to hoodwink people out of money, and the "pocketbook drop," the "bank examiner swindle," or the "handkerchief switch" are favorite ploys against the elderly.

1.   The "pocketbook drop." This game is played by a team of two women against a "lamb" who is almost always an elderly woman. The "pocketbook drop" centers on the story of one of the confidence women: It seems that she has just "found" an envelope or pocketbook containing a good deal of money. By the time the woman tells of this find, the lamb has been engaged in conversation by the other team member (usually at a shopping center).

The woman who found the money solicits the opinion of two "strangers" (one is actually the other team member). Finally, one of them suggests that

---

TAKE A BITE OUT OF CRIME

Many older people are not only afraid of crime, they are afraid to report crimes against themselves or other older persons. Yet reporting such crimes can help, as many state victim assistance programs depend on police notification. There are also many private assistance agencies in many regions of the country; to learn more about such resources, you can contact these agencies:

- NATIONAL ORGANIZATION FOR VICTIM ASSISTANCE, 1757 Park Rd. NW, Washington, DC 20010.

- FOOD AND DRUG ADMINISTRATION, BUREAU OF MEDICAL DEVICES, CONSUMER AND REGULATORY AFFAIRS BRANCH (HFK-131), 8757 Georgia Ave., Silver Spring, MD 20910.

- THE CRIME PREVENTION COALITION, Box 6700, Rockville, MD 20850 can send you the free brochure "Senior Citizens Against Crime," published by the U.S. Department of Justice.

- CRIMINAL JUSTICE SERVICES, AMERICAN ASSOCIATION OF RETIRED PERSONS, 1909 K St. NW, Washington, DC 20049.

Also, your local police or sheriff's office may have a crime prevention unit to provide assistance in your area.

---

the three "strangers" share in the money. They mention an imaginary "lawyer" whom they phone to solicit an opinion. Their lawyer agrees to the plan but suggests that each party put up several thousand dollars to show "good faith."

The "lamb" then goes to her bank, draws out the stipulated money, and gives it to the women to deliver it to the lawyer. The victim is told she can get her "good-faith" money and her share of the found money by calling at the lawyer's office. Of course, there is no such lawyer or office, and when the "lamb" tries to trace lawyer, office, women, or money, she realizes she has been "fleeced."

2. The "bank examiner swindle." In this scheme, con men usually select an older woman as a victim and learn all about her banking habits—and how much she has in the bank. Then the victim receives a phone call from a "bank examiner," who says that the bank believes one of its employees is stealing money, perhaps from her account.

The con man asks the victim if she'll cooperate by drawing out some of her money, wearing gloves so the "examiners" can check the teller's fingerprints. The "examiner" offers a handsome reward for the victim's coopera-tion.

The elderly woman then goes to the bank, draws out her money from the suspect teller, and turns it over to the "examiner," who is waiting outside. He disappears to check the "fingerprints" and never returns with her money.

3. The "handkerchief drop." This works like the "pocketbook drop" in that it involves three persons—two confidence men and their victim, who is usually a man.

One of the confidence men, posing as a sailor or military man looking for the address of a bawdy house, asks the "lamb" for instructions. The accom-plice approaches the lamb and other con man and tries to dissuade him from going to the house of ill fame on the grounds that he will probably get robbed.

The bogus seaman insists on going but says he'll leave his money (usually $500) with the "lamb," who looks like an "honest man." However, the "sailor" asks the "lamb" to put up $500 of his own money to be placed in a handkerchief with the seaman's money. "This way I know you won't lose the money," says the "seaman."

Once the lamb supplies his money, the confidence man ties up both bundles in the handkerchief and hands it to the lamb to carry. Before doing so, he instructs the victim how to "carry" the money safely. To demonstrate, he puts it inside his shirt. But when he "retrieves" the handkerchief he has substituted a similar one containing bits of paper. The victim then carries this bundle safely, only to find out later that the handkerchief with the real money has disappeared with the phony "sailor" (and his accomplice).

Older persons are also prey to phony "government" or Social Security examiners and inspectors. Sometimes the "examiner" will claim that the victim made an error on his (or her) Social Security form or "owes" money to Medicare.

The bogus inspector may ask for immediate payment to clear up the matter. However, remember this: Social Security officials *always carry identification* and *never ask for cash*. If you're in doubt, ask for his identifica-tion, then check with the local Social Security office. Apply the same checks to any other "inspectors" who may claim that you're violating some city ordi-nance and that your furnace needs "immediate repairs." Ask to see ID papers and check with local authorities.

Harder to stop are those door-to-door salesmen who may claim to be representing a well-known company and offer a "fabulous deal" to remodel your house, put up new siding, repair or replace the roof. A good rule of thumb: Most legitimate companies—except those that traditionally sell door to door (like Fuller Brush)—don't use door-to-door salesmen. Unless you know the salesman, don't buy anything or sign a contract (although the law may give you a "cooling-off period"). If you're in doubt, check with the local Better Business Bureau or chamber of commerce.

And if you're telephoned by anyone claiming to be a "bank examiner," security officer, Social Security official, FBI agent, and so on, don't give any information. Tell the person you'll call back. Then check with the "office" to see if the caller is "legitimate," or check with the local police or other authorities.

While the following may not be outright frauds, here are some other "deals" that leave you lighter in pocketbook and heavier in heart:

■ Dance studios and "lonely-hearts" clubs. Some dance studios and correspondence clubs take advantage of older persons' loneliness and milk them of hard-earned savings. Watch especially for these sales techniques: bogus contests, fanciful testimonials, "teams" of salesmen to batter down resistance, flattery and cajolery, false or misleading names or claims of "companions" or "pen pals."

■ Referral selling. In this scheme, you're led to believe that by giving the seller names of friends as prospects, you'll get a discount on the item being sold. Unfortunately, you often pay more for the product than if you bought it from a reputable merchant, and your chances of making "referrals" are often slim.

■ Vanity publishing. Certain book and song publishers will print anything if you pay them to do so. You send them a manuscript or song, and they write back that it's a "masterpiece" and just waiting for an eager audience. They ask you to sign a contract to help them produce and promote the product. Unfortunately, you usually put up *all* the money for a dubious printing and merchandising job. And although your manuscript may have merit, it will suffer from being produced and distributed by a "vanity" publisher. The rule here: If a legitimate publisher won't invest money in your work, it probably isn't worth publishing.

■ Unordered merchandise. Legally, you can be sent only two kinds of merchandise without your consent: (1) free samples that are clearly marked as such; (2) merchandise mailed by a charitable organization asking for contributions. In either of these cases, you can consider the merchandise as a gift. In all other instances it's illegal to send merchandise to anyone unless it has been previously requested.

If you do receive unordered merchandise, you don't have to pay for it, and it's illegal for the person or firm sending it to dun you for it or send a bill. If you have difficulty with unordered merchandise, complain to the local post office (if it's been mailed) or to the Federal Trade Commission.

■   Bait and switch. You might see a terrific ad in the newspaper advertising "TV sets for only $91." You rush down to the store, $91 in hand, only to be told that the merchandise has been "sold out" or was "really not very good." However, the salesman knows you're primed to buy and neatly tries to switch you onto a higher-priced item.

Your first line of defense is to shop around before you buy that "amazing" bargain. Your second line of defense is to protest when you have been "baited" then "switched." If the seller shrugs off the complaint, contact your local Better Business Bureau or chamber of commerce. And be sure to present all the evidence: the advertisement or flyer that offers the "fabulous" deal.

WHAT TO DO IF YOU'VE GOTTEN "GYPPED"

If you feel that you've been "taken," first go back to the seller, *armed with the facts*—receipts, letters, advertisements, bills, and so forth. Perhaps it's a simple misunderstanding that can be cleared up—especially if the seller sees you have "evidence" in hand. If this doesn't work, take your complaint to the local chamber of commerce or Better Business Bureau. Often, they can apply pressure on the seller, especially if it's a local merchant. Many Better Business Bureaus use arbitrators and offer tribunals to handle disputes.

Local newspapers and radio and TV stations often have "action" reporters or columns from which you might get help. And your local post office can file a complaint against mail-order merchandising.

Many major companies have "customer service," "consumer affairs," or similar officers who handle complaints. However, before going to them (or filing a formal complaint), ask what kind of facts they need to handle your problem.

If your problem involves products or services regulated or under the jurisdiction of the Federal Trade Commission or the Food and Drug Administration, you can file a complaint with the local office or with national headquarters.

If you need legal advice, you can get help through your local Legal Aid Society or Legal Referral Service or local bar association.

In many communities you can appeal to the district attorney. The highest legal official in your state is the attorney general, and your state might also have its own consumer protection agency. The highest consumer agency in the land is the Office of Consumer Affairs, New Executive Office Building, Washington, DC 20506. This office publishes the "Consumers' Resource Handbook," which is designed to help you locate the right source of assistance for a wide array of consumer problems. It includes a directory of federal agencies and is available free from Consumer Information Center, Dept. 5323, Pueblo, CO 81009.

WHERE YOU CAN GET FREE HELP

Free help is often a telephone call or postcard away. Here are resources of help in specific areas:

■ *Employment.* Take questions to the Equal Employment Opportunity Commission. This and other federal agencies are listed under "U.S. Government" in your telephone directory.

■ *Education and Training.* Direct questions to the Department of Education or to the particular government agency, such as the Department of Labor, that funds the program you are interested in.

■ *Other Rights Covered by the Age Discrimination Act.* Questions about the Age Discrimination Act should generally be directed to the Office for Civil Rights in the Department of Health and Human Services.

■ *Credit.* In general, you can direct questions to the Federal Trade Commission which has offices in major cities. And you can get a pamphlet, "The Equal Credit Opportunity Act," by writing to the FTC, Legal and Public Records, Rm. 180, Washington, DC 20580. Also, you can get "Your Guide to Consumer Credit and Bankruptcy" by sending $1 to Order Billing, American Bar Assn., 1155 E. 60th St., Chicago, IL 60637.

■ *Pensions.* The Department of Labor (offices in major cities) can provide you with extensive literature on the Employee Retirement Income Security Act (ERISA) and will answer questions on the act. One particularly useful pamphlet is "Know Your Pension Plan: Your Pension Plan Checklist," which will help you evaluate your pension plan. It is available from U.S. Department of Labor, Labor Management Services Administration, Washington, DC 20016. Another source for information and referrals is the Pension Rights Center, 1346 Connecticut Ave. NW, Rm. 1019, Washington, DC 20036. This organization publishes excellent "Pension Facts" pamphlets; write them for details.

■ *Social Security.* The basic resource for information is the Social Security Administration (consult your local telephone directory for listing of this office; contact can be made in person or by phone). Your local office can provide you with abundant literature explaining all parts of the system.

■ *Retirement.* The Area Agency on Aging should be able to refer you to resources that will help you plan for retirement and should have available free booklets on retirement-related subjects. Subject Bibliography SB-285, "Retirement," is a listing of more than 70 federal publications on retirement. It is available from the Supt. of Documents, U.S. Government Printing Office, Washington, DC 20402.

■ *Medicare.* The basic resource is the area Health Care Financing Administration. The basic publication, "Your Medicare Handbook," is available through your local Social Security office. Ask for publication 05-10050.

■ *Medigap Insurance.* An extremely useful publication is "Guide to Health Insurance for People with Medicare," developed jointly by the National Association of Insurance Commissioners and the Health Care Financing Administration, Health Care Financing Administration publication # 92110.

■ *Medicaid.* For information on the Medicaid program you must go to the public aid office in your area, as Medicaid is administered through the states.

■ *Housing.* You can get a "Retirement Housing" fact sheet and publications list from Publications, Administration on Aging, Dept. of Health and Human Services, Washington, DC 20291. Some housing questions can also be directed to the Department of Housing and Urban Development (HUD), Washington, DC 20410. However, much legislation pertaining to housing is in the form of local ordinances; call an appropriate branch of local government for more information.

■ *Tax Benefits.* The basic Internal Revenue Service publication for older Americans is publication #554, "Tax Benefits for Older Americans." It is available from your local IRS office.

■ *Insurance.* All forms of consumer insurance are regulated at the state level by State Insurance Commissioners, usually located in state capitals. Check with your state capital telephone directory assistance for the telephone number (also listed in "Consumer Resources Handbook").

Also send for the "Consumer Information Catalog", a listing of free and low-cost consumer information available from the federal government. Many federal and state agencies have 800 (toll-free) numbers to help you report or receive information fast. You can get a listing of these state and federal 800 numbers by writing: "Direct Contacts for Consumers," Consumer Information Center, Pueblo, CO 81009.

SENIOR POWER PACKS A WALLOP AT THE BALLOT BOX

Although seniors (age 65 and older) account for only around 11.5 percent of the U.S. population, they form almost 16 percent of the voting population. And Census Bureau figures show that the elderly exercise their right to vote in greater proportion than other age groups. Of the elderly, 75 percent register and 65 percent actually vote, while only 65 percent of the general population registers and 59 percent vote in general elections. Thus, even now the *elderly can swing any election and elect any candidate* they really want. And this power will explode with even greater force in the future as the proportion of elderly is expected to reach over 13 percent of the population before the end of the century, and the proportion of the voting population is expected to almost double.

Individual votes are fine, but mass "clout" is better. You can multiply your senior power if you and your friends agree on a specific issue or candidate, contact other senior organizations and centers, and see if you can ally yourselves to get joint action. Senior groups such as the National Council of Senior Citizens, American Association of Retired Persons, Gray Panthers, National Alliance of Senior Citizens, and others have put together sophisticated lobbies well versed in Social Security, Medicare, subsidized housing, and other programs of particular interest to seniors.

To magnify your senior power, here are some steps in the POLITICAL PROCESSES:

POLITICAL PROCESSES

HOW TO ACCOMPLISH A POLITICAL OBJECTIVE

- Know what you are seeking and why you are seeking it. Know the opposing position.

- Know who is in charge—who can help you, who can hurt you. Know the decision-making machinery in your community.

- Inform the public through every educational and public relations facility.

- Approach your campaign of action with enthusiasm, sincerity, and determination—but not grimness.

HOW TO ELECT YOUR CANDIDATE

- *On the firing line* you can assemble campaign kits, distribute literature, organize rallies, write speeches, seek contributions, do research or stenographic or clerical work, clip newspaper items, organize registration drives.

- *At home you can* do telephoning, write newspaper editors or radio and TV stations, answer or send personal letters, hold coffee hours.

- *During election day* you can help get voters to the polls, organize transportation, baby-sit while mothers go to polls, be a poll watcher or election official.

HOW TO HELP ENACT LEGISLATION

- Write to your representative or senator and send him a pamphlet or a newspaper clipping dealing with an issue that interests you.

- Meet with your legislators when they are back home; make sure you're on their mailing lists.

- Find out what committees they serve on and try to attend meetings.

- Express your views through your organization—which can convey your message through meetings and lobbying with key legislators.

SOME HANDY LEGAL TERMS

ACCEPTANCE   The act of accepting an offer that results in a binding contract.

ADMINISTRATOR   One appointed by a probate court to administer the estate of a deceased person.

ASSAULT   An attempt or threat to beat or otherwise harm another, made without touching the person.

ASSIGNMENT   The transfer to another of real or personal property, including contract rights.

BATTERY   Any unlawful physical contact inflicted on a person without consent.

BENEFICIARY   One who is to receive property under a will; also one who is to be paid the proceeds of an insurance policy.

BINDER   Usually a short, fairly simple memorandum of major points of agreement between seller and buyer of re-alty, to bind the parties to enter into a formal contract.

CHATTEL MORTGAGE   An agreement to make personal property security for a debt or performance of an obligation.

CODICIL   An instrument made subsequent to a will and modifying the will in some respect; must be executed and witnessed like a will.

CONDITIONAL SALE   One in which seller retains title to goods as security for payment of the purchase price.

CONSIDERATION   The return a party to a contract makes for whatever is given to the other party.

CONTRACT   A promissory agreement between 2 or more persons that creates, changes, or terminates a legal relationship and grants rights enforceable at law.

CONTRIBUTORY NEGLIGENCE The negligence of a person claiming damages for harm from negligence of another, with the claimant's negligence a contributing cause.

COVENANT An agreement by deed by which either party pledged to the other that something is or will be done, or not done, or that certain facts are true.

DEED OF TRUST The conveyance of legal title to realty to a third party, as security for payment of a debt owed by the real owner. The practical effect is the same as a mortgage.

EARNEST MONEY The small sum put up by the buyer when signing a binder.

EASEMENT A liberty, right to use, or privilege of access given to one person in relation to the land of another.

ESCROW Money, property, or a document held by a third person for delivery to one of the parties upon fulfillment of certain obligations.

EXECUTOR One appointed through a will to administer it on the testator's death.

GUARDIAN One invested with the power and duty to take care of the person and property of another.

HOLOGRAPHIC WILL One entirely hand-written by the maker (testator).

INTESTATE Having died without a will.

NEGLIGENCE The omission to do something reasonably prudent people would do or commission of an act they would not do.

PROBATE The judicial determination of the validity of a will.

TESTATOR One who makes a will.

TORT A private or civil wrong to a person's health, liberty, reputation, or property.

WARRANTY A representation or promise, expressed or implied in a contract, as in insurance policies, deeds, sales.

WILL A legal declaration or testament of one's wishes for the disposition of property after death.

ZONING The restrictions placed by local government on the use to which land can be put, setting aside areas for business and residences, specifying the kind, size, and location of buildings on the land.

PART V.

THERE'S
NO PLACE LIKE
HOME

Your housing is as personal as your dreams, as practical as your pocketbook. It's your biggest asset and greatest liability, taking the lion's share of your budget (about one third) and dictating where and how you live.

With increased leisure time and/or retirement, your home becomes your recreation and entertainment center, perhaps your office and convalescent ward. How you are old is more important than how old you are in determining your housing needs and wants. For instance:

DO YOU WANT HOUSING FOR ACTIVE LIVING? If so, your housing should allow you to enjoy activities inside and out. The structure should be as trouble-free as possible, attractive and roomy enough to entertain business and social friends.

DO YOU WANT MORE PRIVACY? You might want housing that's a snug harbor, to which you can retreat, enjoy and relax in security, read, watch television, do hobbies, listen to music, rest without being bothered. You'd need adequate lighting, furniture, and household equipment for protection and comfort.

DO YOU WANT TO ALLOW FOR POSSIBLE CONVALESCENCE? Accidents and illnesses happen at any age or stage of living; at some point we'll all need medical attention. Often the option of remaining at home or moving to a hospital or nursing home depends on how adequate your housing is for convalescent needs. Do you have a separate bedroom or sleeping alcove to permit nursing care? Do you have adequate heating and cooling in all rooms for year-round comfort in sickness and health? Can you control sound to eliminate outside noises while enhancing indoor sounds for better listening? Are doorways and halls wide enough to permit a wheelchair? Are there any stairs or thresholds? All these are important considerations for convalescence.

185

One point is certain: Whatever your housing needs today—they'll change tomorrow when children leave; there's a death in the family; the breadwinner changes jobs or retires. . . . So keep an open mind—think of your housing needs when and if you change your present house. It's not *where* you live but *how* you live that dictates your housing needs and wants.

SHOULD YOU MOVE OR STAY PUT?

About 70 percent of us retire in the place we now live. Of those who move, about 20 percent move to a smaller place in the same general area—only about 10 percent actually leave their home state. Those who do move are usually apartment dwellers and renters; people with no real community ties but maybe with money, social status, and good health. Even those who don't move often dream of it; a recent study showed that about 60 percent of recent retirees "considered" moving.

What might make you want to move or stay put? Let's first examine the reasons you might want to *stay put*:

■ *It's familiar.* You know the repairmen, storekeepers, bus drivers, mailmen, neighbors. You've found a doctor and a lawyer who sympathize with your problems and respect your pocketbook; grocers and druggists who deliver. And you've long jumped that hurdle from stranger to neighbor (which often takes months and even years!). Think how it would be if you and your spouse moved as a couple and one died, leaving the other a stranger in a strange environment!

■ *It's within your budget.* It usually takes two to three years to find best buys in any area, especially food, repairs, services. If you moved, you'd have to buy new furniture or pay dearly to move older furniture (that might not fit smaller housing). Also, in order to be eligible for the many personal and property tax advantages most states offer to persons 60 and over, you'd have to live in the area for a year or more. Your old will may not be valid in the new state, and if you own property in one state but reside in another, both states may have a claim (for estate taxes) on your property.

■ *It's a sentimental shrine.* Your housing is often the lure that brings children and grandchildren "home" for the holidays or vacations. It's the place you and they feel you belong.

TO MOVE OR STAY PUT?

Whether you move or stay put depends largely on how adequate your present housing is for present and future living needs. Will the home have too much room after the children leave? Will the home free you or tie you down? Can it serve as your recreation and entertainment center as well as your office or convalescent ward? Are you proud (and will continue to be) of your neighborhood? These are just a few of the questions to ask: The more "Yes" answers you give, the happier you'll be staying put. But if you answer "No" or can't think of ways to improve your present housing, consider moving.

QUESTIONS ABOUT HOUSING AT PRESENT   YES   NO

  1. Are you happy and comfortable where you live?   ——   ——

  2. Is your home paid for, and are expenses under control? ——   ——

  3. Is housing easy to maintain, repair?   ——   ——

  4. Are you friendly with neighbors; do you like area? ——   ——

  5. Is transportation adequate for all needs?   ——   ——

  6. Are your children near and can you visit often? ——   ——

  7. Are you active in civic, social organizations? ——   ——

  8. Are you near places of worship and recreation centers? ——   ——

  9. Is community stable, safe, likely to remain so? ——   ——

10. Is home suitable for entertainment, recreation? ——   ——

11. Would home be suitable if anyone got sick and required convalescent care? ——   ——

12. Is housing in good repair, or could it be easily fixed up? ——   ——

13. Are property taxes stable? ——   ——

14. Are property values rising? ——   ——

This makes sense if you like your present life, neighborhood, and feel it gives you leeway to adapt to new ventures. But if you want to break with the past and explore the future, you may find these reasons for *moving*:

■ *Neighbors and neighborhoods change.* Even your best friends, relatives, doctor, lawyer, and merchants die or move away; you'd miss them as much as if you had moved. Neighborhoods decline (especially older ones), and your present housing may not seem like "home" anymore.

■ *The older home may not be suitable for retirement.* Your older home may not have the adequate heating, lighting, or safety features you need and want. Stairs may be too hard to climb, upkeep too difficult, yard work too much trouble. The roof may start to leak, and the furnace may need repairs.

■ *You may want to start a new way of life.* A move could give you a new way of life . . . fresh challenges and opportunities to "be somebody." A move lifts you out of a rut and gets you involved in new pursuits, friendships, life-styles. If you want to break with the past, a move commits you to the future.

What to Look for in Any Housing

Whether you move or stay put, your housing and location should offer you the following social and psychological advantages. You should:

■ be near people you like and love and who feel the same about you;

■ feel that you belong in the community;

■ know that you can live to the fullest despite any handicaps;

■ have all the services and facilities that allow you to live fully;

■ feel physically safe and mentally at ease.

These social and psychological factors become even more vital in retirement. You may not enjoy your former social prestige or financial status. You may no longer be asked to serve on civic committees or run for office. You may not be invited to as many parties or be able to afford to entertain as you once did.

In terms of general layout, your housing should include these features:

■ *all rooms on one floor*—no thresholds or walking hazards;

■ *doors and halls wide enough* to accommodate a wheelchair;

■ *lighting*—perhaps three times as much lighting as for younger families, including good lighting in all hallways, near stairs, and dark places;

■ *nonslip surfaces*—unglazed ceramic tile, unwaxed vinyl or vinyl asbestos in kitchen and bathroom, rugs and carpets firmly anchored;

■ *railings and supports*—handrails by any stairs or inclines, grab rails or supports in bathroom, kitchen, or near other hazardous areas;

■ *heating and cooling*—central heating and cooling to supply 70 to 75 degrees F. heat (or cooling) in each room;

■ *sound control*—some provision to muffle outside noises but to enhance indoor acoustics.

In short, your housing should be suitable for comfortable living in both health and sickness. Here are some room-by-room requirements:

BEDROOM. You should have one or more bedrooms (or a sleeping alcove) to allow privacy and permit sick care. There should be enough room around the bed so it can be made easily, and there should be a direct line—with no obstacles—between bedroom and bathroom.

BATHROOM. Doors should be wide enough and bathroom fixtures so arranged to accommodate a wheelchair. There should be grab bars or strong rails to help you get in and out of the bathtub. All fixtures should be strong enough for support.

KITCHEN. This room should be large enough and pleasant enough to eat in. Within the work area, the best arrangement is a continuous flow from refrigerator-sink-counter-range-service. Cupboards should not be over 63 inches from the floor, and storage bins shouldn't be below 27 inches (to eliminate excessive reaching and stooping).

What If You Decide to Remain in Your Present Housing?

Here's how you might make your present housing more suitable for retirement living:

1. *Danger-proof the old homestead.* Falls are especially likely and hazardous as we grow older. Your center of gravity changes somewhat as you grow older, and you may lose your balance more easily. If so, you're more

likely to break a limb, which would take longer to mend than when you were younger.

According to the National Safety Council, more than 43 percent of accidental injuries occur in and around the home. Falls are the major problem, followed by burns, cuts, and poisonings.

To avoid falls, *keep traffic lanes free of hazards.* Anchor scatter rugs firmly or place a nonslip mat underneath . . . wipe up grease, milk, or water before it spills you . . . install grab bars in slippery tubs or shower stalls.

Use common sense and good safety practices to avoid burns, cuts, poisonings. Have a good family health guide or first-aid manual handy in case of emergencies. Also, keep the telephone numbers of your police and fire departments, doctors, poison control centers, clinics, and hospitals handy.

2. *Shut off rooms to save on heat, lighting.* By shutting off certain rooms—or an entire floor—you could save on lighting, heating, and other maintenance expenses. You'd also eliminate certain housekeeping chores, reduce some hazards, and concentrate your living on one level, avoiding stairs.

3. *Rent out certain rooms or a floor.* If zoning regulations permit (inquire at your city hall), you could rent out rooms or even an entire floor. You can get FHA-insured loans to do any necessary remodeling or fixing up, and you'd get a tax break because of depreciation deductions on property used to produce income. The extra income could go a long way to help meet retirement expenses.

If You Decide to Move, Should You Buy or Rent?

During the course of many moves, I've rented, sampled, and bought at least 10 different types of housing: apartments, studios, flats, single-family houses, condominiums and co-ops, mobile homes, adult communities. Here's how I rate the advantages and disadvantages of renting and buying these various units.

RENTING ADVANTAGES: I had more freedom to move and travel, fewer initial and monthly payments, repairs, or other maintenance problems and expenses. DISADVANTAGES: I always felt cramped by other people and by my surroundings; I didn't maintain the place as well as I should have because I lacked pride of ownership. I was even reluctant to hang pictures or to put up personal items that might have made the place more mine. And I never built up equity by renting.

HOW TO TAKE THE HEADACHES OUT OF MOVING

Moving is a personal and practical headache. It's more trouble than you realize and costs more than you think (and they estimate). There's no easy way to move, but you can save trouble and money by following these tips from those (including me) who have moved several times:

1. Use moving as an excuse to throw out half your possessions (books, unused toys and games, heavy furniture and appliances, and so on). Also, do as much of your own packing as possible, and try to do as much moving yourself as possible.

2. If possible, try to schedule your move outside the peak months—early May until mid-October—when most business moves are being made and more problems may arise.

3. Get estimates from *at least three* movers and study the handbook "Your Rights and Responsibilities When You Move" that the Interstate Commerce Commission (ICC) requires every interstate mover to give prospective customers. Also request "Guide to a Satisfactory Move" from American Movers Conference, P.O. Box 2302, Arlington, VA 22209.

4. Try to pick the best mover for you. There are many intangible factors involved in picking a mover, but you do have some guidelines. The ICC has required that every moving company hand each potential customer a copy of its performance report for the previous year, and this must be done when the salesman comes to your home to estimate your move. While past performance is only one gauge to measure a mover, it may help to narrow your selection.

OWNING ADVANTAGES: I always had more room, privacy, and feeling of security and comfort. I took better care of the place (pride plus practical economics), I had substantial tax advantages, and I built an equity. DISADVANTAGES: I tied up a lot of cash in down payments and monthly payments. I was bombarded with unexpected repairs and expenses, time-consuming gardening, and general maintenance. And I'm strictly not a do-it-yourself type. It often cost me 10 percent of the value of the house for yearly operating and maintenance expenses.

But from a dollars-and-cents standpoint I discovered: *Home owning was cheaper if I lived in a place at least three to four years before selling.* I had gone through the first flush of fixing up the place to make it more livable (and profitable to sell), the house had normally increased in value (about 10 percent or more a year), and I always made a profit selling—reducing our monthly payments.

TAX ADVANTAGES OF SELLING YOUR HOUSE

If you are age 55 or over and sell or exchange your home for a profit, you may avoid taxes on profits up to $125,000. To claim this exclusion, you must have owned and occupied the house as your principal residence for at least *three out of five years* preceding date of sale (the time doesn't have to be consecutive).

The profit on the sale is the difference between its "adjusted sales price" and its "adjusted cost basis." *Adjusted sales price* is the gross selling price minus sales costs such as real estate sales commission, transfer tax, and other selling expenses. *Adjusted cost basis* is the sum of (1) the purchase price; (2) the closing costs that were not tax deductible at the time of purchase; (3) capital improvement costs added during ownership, minus any casualty loss or depreciation (for business use) deducted during ownership. The adjusted cost basis must also be reduced by any previously deferred gains.

The once-in-a-lifetime exemption also applies to cooperative apartment ownership tied to stock ownership, and to condominiums. However, you don't have to apply for the exclusion if you reinvest the money within two years in a new home as expensive as or more than the adjusted sales price of your old home.

For further information, ask the Internal Revenue Service for its free publication #523, "Tax Information on Selling Your Home."

In a recent study, *Tax-Guard* (a tax-oriented newsletter at Suite 202, 320 Walnut St., Philadelphia, PA 19106) compared homeownership to rental costs over 30 years of a $70,000 house. Assuming an annual inflation rate of 8 percent and an annual investment yield of 12 percent on money saved by buying, in 30 years the house would be worth $704,000, while the renter's investment of any saving would have grown to only $524,000. If you're in doubt about whether to buy or rent, you can get a dollars-and-cents analysis from Equivalent Rent Analysis, 108 Myr Hall, Cornell University, Ithaca, NY 14853. Write to them for details. You can also get a free four-page fact sheet titled "Should You Rent or Buy a Home" from the field offices of Housing and Urban Development (HUD) in major cities or write HUD at Washington, DC 20410. The U.S. Bureau of Labor Statistics puts out a bulletin (#2016), "Rent or Buy? Evaluating Alternatives in the Shelter Market." Write to BLS at Washington, DC 20212, for information. And for $2 you can get a bulletin, "Homeowner or Tenant: How to Make a Wise Choice," from American Institute for Economic Research, Great Barrington, MA 01230.

Is There Any Way to "Try It Before Buying It"?

It's always wise to rent, lease, or *swap* homes in your new community while renting, leasing, or swapping your home "back home." This gives you a chance to evaluate your new home at your leisure and still have the option of returning if you aren't satisfied. Here are four organizations that will list your home for a fee of around $15, then let you exchange letters and make arrangements. Note that deadlines for listings are about six months in advance of the time you might want to swap:

Vacation Exchange Club
12006 111th Ave., No. 12
Youngtown, AZ 85363

Interchange Home Exchange
P.O. Box 3975
San Francisco, CA 94119

Holiday Home Exchange Bureau
P.O. Box 878
Belen, NM 87002

Inter Service Home Exchange
P.O. Box 87
Glen Echo, MD 20812

WHAT ARE YOUR HOUSING OPTIONS?

At the beginning of this section I discussed the three different housing options you may want at various stages of retirement living: (1) activity, (2) privacy, (3) convalescence. Here are options under the three possibilities:

■ *Active living.* You would want housing that would allow you to enjoy activities both in- and outdoors. The structure should be as trouble-free as possible and attractive and roomy enough to entertain business and social friends. *Housing possibilities:*

single-family homes
adult communities

retirement clubs, residences, hotels
mobile or modular homes

■ *Privacy.* You might want housing that's a snug harbor, to which you can retreat and enjoy and relax in security. You could read, watch television, do hobbies, listen to music, rest without being bothered. You'd need adequate lighting, furniture, and household equipment for protection and comfort. *Housing possibilities:*

apartments
co-ops

condominiums
town houses

■ *Convalescence.* Accidents and illnesses happen at any age or stage of

How Do the Various Types of Housing Compare?

First, let's compare housing for *activity:*

HOUSING	AVERAGE COST	ADVANTAGES	DISADVANTAGES
2-bedroom, single-family homes	$60,000	More privacy, more space, bigger rooms	More expensive, more maintenance and repairs
Adult communities	$55,000	Security, recreation, and maintenance provided, sociability	Age segregation, "fun and games" may pall as you grow older; community often run by cliques
Retirement clubs, hotels, residences	$600 monthly (room & some meals)	Convenience of hotel living; maid service; recreation; meals	Sometimes must share room or toilet facilities; food not always good; no medical care
Mobile homes	$20,000 plus $75 or more per month rental	Lowest cost and upkeep; privacy; variable location	"Sardine can" social swim; cramped quarters and space; high depreciation; strict park rules

Now let's compare housing for *privacy:*

HOUSING	AVERAGE COST	ADVANTAGES	DISADVANTAGES
Apartments	$350 monthly rent for private landlord; 1/4 income for subsidized	Some services & conveniences; no upkeep or repairs	Often shoddy buildings; rent raises; long waiting lists for nonprofit units
Co-ops	$55,000 for unit; plus $100 mo. and up maintenance	Nonprofit management; payments include taxes, maintenance, and recreation	Any buyer must be "approved"; if anyone defaults, other owners must pay up; can't rent out units

	Cost	Advantages	Disadvantages
Condominiums	$65,000 for unit; $100 and up mo. maintenance	Title to units, tax advantages, equity buildup, can sell or rent or will more freely	Parking problems; maintenance and recreation fees escalate; some frauds and sometimes shoddy construction
Town houses	$55,000	Advantages of single-family dwelling with lower costs	Common walls may cause noise problems; rooms generally smaller than in detached units

Now let's compare housing for convalescence:

	Cost	Advantages	Disadvantages
Life-care facilities	$5,000 to $60,000 up entrance fee; $400 up mo. for meals, medical care, recreation	Comprehensive services for living in health or sickness; constant care	"End of road" housing with average age in 70s & 80s; in some cases must sign over all assets including Social Security and other income
Multitype facilities	(see above)	Greater variety of accommodations, from regular housekeeping apts. to nursing home; may consist of single high-rise building or cluster of separate units	(see above)

living; at some point we'll all need medical attention. Often the option of remaining at home or moving to a hospital or nursing home depends on how adequate your housing is for convalescent care. That's why you should have at least a *separate* bedroom (if you are a couple) so one person could be taken care of at home at a fraction of the cost of hospital or nursing care. *Housing possibilities:*

multitype facilities   life-care facilities

WOULD YOU LIKE A RETIREMENT COMMUNITY?

Formerly located in outlying areas of the South and West (mainly Florida, Arizona, and California) and geared mainly to retirees, "adult communities" are now located all over the country and cater to couples "age 45 and older." They offer varied housing, including single-family homes, garden apartments, co-ops, and condominums. Housing generally starts around $60,000, and other charges (maintenance and recreation) might add an extra $100 to $200 a month. They are geared to "active retirement" living, which could grow tiresome if your primary concern is peace and privacy.

Most adult communities are shaped by the people who live there; spend time getting to know the people, the "cliques" and problems. It usually takes about seven years for a community to "shake down," so go slow about buying into any newly developed place. And have the contract checked by a local real estate lawyer. Be especially aware of escalator clauses for maintenance and recreation. Here are the *good* and *bad* about a retirement community:

GOOD	BAD
People your own age—peer support	Age segregation
Organized activities and recreational facilities	Isolation—often far from city
Easy housing maintenance	Lack of transportation to city
Usually good in-community transportation	Monotony in housing design
Good housing value	Sometimes escalating maintenance and recreation costs
Stress on active living	Less civic pride and responsibility
Attractive surroundings	Lack of privacy

GOOD	BAD
	Less intellectual stimulation
	Not suitable as you grow older and more passive
	Widow may be out of place in couple-oriented community
	Keeping up with "Retiree Jones"
	Restrictions on landscaping and altering housing
	Good hospitals often not close

Many retirees prefer a *college town* for its stimulating environment, low-cost living, attractive atmosphere, and cultural activities. Among the favored towns:

Ann Arbor, Mich.   Gainesville, Fla.
Austin, Tex.   Ithaca, N.Y.
Berkeley, Calif.   La Jolla, Calif.
Chapel Hill, N.C.   Madison, Wis.
Bloomington, Ind.   Portland, Ore.

What Are Some Problems in Buying Retirement Land?

Probably more retirees have been bitten by a "land shark" than any other critter. Basically, the problems are these:

■ *Most people buy for speculation—not building.* Less than 5 percent of those who buy retirement land ever build on it. They buy for *speculation* because they get inflated reports on the true value of the land. Much of the land lies in remote parts of the South and West (Florida, New Mexico, Arizona) and is sold in the East and Midwest (anyone who knows the land wouldn't pay the price, which is sometimes 100 times what the land is really worth).

■ *Most of the land doesn't have basic services.* Some of this land is so remote and so "raw" that it doesn't have power, water, roads, sewers, and so forth. If these services were to be put in, you would be assessed for your share of such developments. And you would be assessed for your share of power (at approximately $12,000 a mile for telephone and power lines) and for water (approximately $9,000 to dig a well—if there is water to be had), and a septic tank (approximately $1,000). In some cases you'd even need a bulldozer to get to your land or a power boat (some land gets flooded at high tide).

■ *If services are in, there could be a mountain of debt.* Usually, you don't get your deed until you've made all your payments. When you get your deed, you may find that there's a mountain of hidden debt against the land because the builder has created a "special service district" that has broad quasi-government powers to levy taxes and assessments on property owners. Sometimes the developer even gets a "piece of the action" by contracting for any provided services.

How Can I Avoid Getting Bitten by a "Land Shark"?

■ *Don't buy a site unseen.* As noted, most of this land is sold far from the site, in towns of the Midwest and East during the winter. The land company lures you in with a "free banquet" and after wining and dining you, shows you a film of a "core" area of the project that has been carefully cultivated to look "livable." But outside the core area, this land (the lots you'd buy) is barren and worthless. The pressure is on you to buy "right now" after the glow of dinner and the luster of the film. The land company may have even planted "shills" at your table (there's always a sales rep at each table) to "talk up" the land and its value. And the down payment and monthly payments are so low, that it hardly seems worthwhile to inspect the land. But there's no substitute for a sober appraisal of the land site. And even if you think you *might* possibly visit the land during a seemingly safe "money-back-guarantee" period, how do you know you'll be able to make the trip and meet all the specifications for getting back your money?

■ *Don't take "promises" for granted.* The promoters may promise to develop shopping centers, recreation areas, golf courses, and so forth, but they're under no obligation to provide these unless they say so in writing. Also, find out about the costs of any recreational facilities the developers provide. A favorite stunt is to "subsidize" these facilities for a certain length of time, then lease them to the landowners for an inflated fee.

Under the law, developers having subdivisions containing 50 lots or more must: (1) file a statement of record with the Office of Interstate Land Sales, listing information about the ownership of the land, the state of its title, its physical nature, the availability of roads and utilities and other matters; (2) furnish each purchaser a printed property report at least 72 hours before signing an agreement for purchase or lease; (3) must not use fraud or misrepresentation in the sale or promotion of the land.

The Office of Interstate Land Sales says it gets some 5,000 complaints on land sales each year, from people who say they have been "swindled." This office has obtained refunds in several instances. For further information, write Office of Interstate Land Sales, Department of Housing and Urban Development, Washington, DC 20410.

WHERE DO OLDER PEOPLE LIVE NOW?

About half (45 percent) of persons age 65 and older live in seven states: California, New York (each with over 2 million older persons), Florida, Illinois, Ohio, Pennsylvania, and Texas (each with over 1 million seniors).

The 65 + group is 12 percent or more of the total population in 16 states:

Florida (17.6%)	Kansas (13.1%)
Arkansas (13.9%)	Massachusetts (12.8%)
Iowa (13.6%)	Maine (12.7%)
Rhode Island (13.6%)	North Dakota (12.5%)
South Dakota (13.4%)	West Virginia (12.4%)
Missouri (13.3%)	Wisconsin (12.2%)
Nebraska (13.2%)	Connecticut (12.0%)
Pennsylvania (13.2%)	Minnesota (12.0%)

About 32 percent of the elderly live outside of metropolitan areas compared with 20 percent of all other age groups. And the rural elderly population is growing twice as fast as the metropolitan elderly population.

Are Older People Living in "Ideal" Places?

Not necessarily. Any "ideal" place would have to meet these standards:

1. *Climate and environment.* A good climate and environment would have:

no sharp changes in temperature	mild seasons
lots of sunshine	no heavy snowfalls or bitter cold
gentle blowing breezes	minimal threats of hurricanes, tornadoes, floods
minimum dampness and pollution	

The ideal place would have more days when the temperature is 66 degrees F. and the humidity, 55 percent. Days like this allow the body chemistry to function without strain; the more days you have like this, the better you feel. Outside these "ideals" you could have these variations:

Winter—an average of 65 to 72 degrees F. with a relative humidity of 35 to 40 percent. Indoors it would be between 67 and 68 degrees F.

Summer—an average of 70 to 78 degrees F. with a relative humidity of 55 to 65 percent. Indoors it would be around 71 degrees F.

The *temperature-humidity index* (a measurement of summertime discomfort resulting from the combined effects of temperature and humidity) should be *under* 72. Above that you begin to feel uncomfortable.

2. *Medical facilities.* Semiprivate hospital rooms should cost less than $200 daily (average cost in 1984), and there should be at least 5 hospital beds per 1,000 residents. There should also be at least 1 doctor per 750 residents. And there should be convalescent facilities in the community, along with adequate community homecare facilities (meals on wheels, visiting nurses, homemakers, and so forth).

3. *Cost of living.* Retired couples should be able to live on $12,000 a year or less and pay less than 10 percent of income for state and local taxes. There should be part-time jobs available and some job counseling for older people. Food costs should be in line with other communities, and locally grown produce and meats should be available. Or you should even be able to hunt or fish for your supper. Services and energy costs should be reasonable.

4. *Housing availability and cost.* You should be able to get a variety of two-bedroom units for $60,000 and up, and rentals should be available from about $400 a month and up. Property taxes should be 2 percent or less of market value.

5. *Leisure-time activities.* A writer, artist, or musician should at least feel comfortable. There should be libraries, museums, theaters, FM classical music stations, good TV reception (including cable), adult education classes, houses of worship, senior centers, service clubs, Ys or fitness centers, craft and hobby courses and facilities, swimming pools, parks, tennis courts, golf courses, saddle horses, bike and hiking trails, gardens and gardening facilities, a variety of socially compatible people.

6. *Special services for seniors.* Besides senior centers, there should be local or area agencies on aging. The community should offer personal and property tax exemptions (exemptions for renters, too), discounts for seniors (entertainment, medicines, food, personal items), transportation facilities (minibuses, dial-a-ride, limousine or tax services), and a daily hot meal program. You hope civic and service groups will also offer other programs and services for seniors.

How Do the Various Regions of the U.S. Compare?

Here is how the various regions of the United States compare in quality of life (S = South; W = West; NC = North-Central; NE = Northeast):

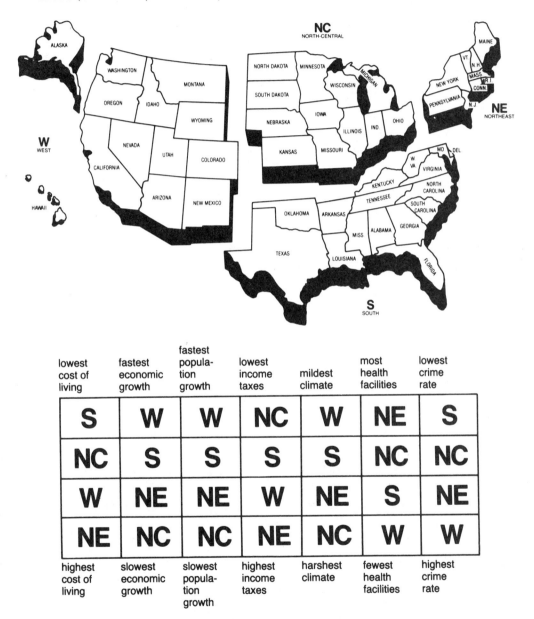

lowest cost of living	fastest economic growth	fastest population growth	lowest income taxes	mildest climate	most health facilities	lowest crime rate
S	W	W	NC	W	NE	S
NC	S	S	S	S	NC	NC
W	NE	NE	W	NE	S	NE
NE	NC	NC	NE	NC	W	W
highest cost of living	slowest economic growth	slowest population growth	highest income taxes	harshest climate	fewest health facilities	highest crime rate

As you can see, no one climate has all the good or bad.

What Are the Economic Factors to Consider?

Chase Econometrics, a subsidiary of Chase Manhattan Bank, lists 10 economic factors to rate a state for retirement during the 1980s. The economic forecasting organization also assigns "points" to indicate the importance of each factor, as follows:

1.   *Unemployment* (10 points). Where unemployment is high, retirees find part-time or full-time work to augment their retirement incomes scarce. Projections in this area were made to 1985 to eliminate effects of the present business cycle.

2.   *Nonmanufacturing Employment Growth* (10 points). Nonmanufacturing growth over the decade was used because retirees generally will not be working in manufacturing or other industrial jobs. This is a vital factor if inflation persists.

3.   *Ratio of Elderly to Working-Age Population* (10 points). If the ratio of retirees to the working-age population is low, there is a greater ability to fund social services for the elderly and less competition for part-time jobs.

4.   *Property Tax Loads* (10 points). High property taxes are always a threat to people living on fixed incomes, especially with property values constantly increasing.

5.   *Living Costs* (10 points). General living costs are very important to the fixed-income retiree. The assumption is that high-income areas tend to have high living costs, and vice versa.

6.   *Housing* (10 points). Total housing starts per capita were used as a measure of housing "tightness." The higher the number of starts relative to the population, the easier it should be to find suitable housing.

7.   *Growth of Retired Population* (5 points). Growth in the number of retirees in an area is often an indication of its desirability. However, some retirees simply cannot afford to move or don't wish to. Thus, it has a low value.

8.   *Weather Conditions* (15 points). A good climate, without the hardships of heavy snow and one with generally warmer temperatures is desirable. This also means low heating bills. You can live without air conditioning, but not without heat.

9.   *Utility Rates* (10 points). Good weather can lose some of its attractiveness if it means high utility rates. In order to capture the trend in a state's utility costs, the rates expected to prevail in 1985 have been used.

10.   *Metropolitanization* (20 points). This measures the percentage of a state's population residing in metropolitan areas. It is a catchall measurement that includes medical facilities, cultural and leisure activities, public transpor-

tation, social services, and so on. It is assumed that highly rural states have fewer of these kinds of services available. Some retirees, of course, don't mind living in rural areas if a well-developed urban area is nearby.

For each factor, the Chase experts rewarded or penalized a state according to how it varied from the norm. A state that scored higher was given more points; one that ranked lower had more points subtracted. Thus these scores that varied from the norm of 110 points.

Adding up the score, here is how the states rate:

STATE	POINTS	STATE	POINTS
Utah	305	Nebraska	−138
Louisiana	295	Ohio	−160
South Carolina	280	Wisconsin	−170
Nevada	260	Delaware	−195
Texas	230	Indiana	−195
New Mexico	200	Illinois	−223
Alabama	185	Missouri	−225
Arizona	175	Pennsylvania	−230
Florida	160	South Dakota	−235
Georgia	155	Iowa	−240
Colorado	140	Michigan	−245
North Carolina	110	Montana	−250
Tennessee	100	Minnesota	−265
Kentucky	88	North Dakota	−280
Virginia	75	Connecticut	−285
Washington	40	New Hampshire	−300
California	35	New York	−355
Oklahoma	30	Rhode Island	−373
Maryland	−5	Vermont	−385
Idaho	−15	New Jersey	−390
Oregon	−15	Maine	−428
Kansas	−20	Massachusetts	−498
Arkansas	−63	(Hawaii and Alaska were omitted	
Mississippi	−70	because of insufficient data. Negative	
West Virginia	−103	values result from scores below	
Wyoming	−130	average.)	

What Are Other Factors to Consider?

In researching for my three books, *Sunbelt Retirement, Retirement Edens: Outside the Sunbelt,* and *Travel and Retirement Edens Abroad,* I rated and compared places as measured against certain *subjective* factors as well as the objective factors above. Subjectively, a state like Utah may not rank as high if you didn't accept or appreciate the influence of the Church of

Jesus Christ of Latter-Day Saints (Mormon). Fully 60 percent of the residents are Mormons and the church's presence is felt in the legislature (90 percent Mormon) and in businesses controlled by the church—ranging from sugar mills to finance companies, textile mills, hotels, an airline, hospitals, radio and television stations. The church also regulates morality and social behavior. While liquor is available, it isn't easy to get. Yet the church also encourages a respect for age and such traditional values as strong family ties and self-reliance.

PSYCHOLOGICAL WELL-BEING IN THE UNITED STATES. The Institute for Social Research asked people in the nine regions of the United States to rate their lives in six major areas. A low number indicates higher well-being: a 1 would indicate best outlook on life, most positive feelings, fewest negative findings, highest personal competence, and highest overall satisfaction. Factors that make up the six areas: (1) *outlook on life*—whether interesting or boring; (2) *stress*—is life easy or hard; feelings of being tied down, worried about bills, mental health; (3) *positive feelings*—whether people have felt excited, pleased, on top of the world; (4) *negative feelings*—the number of yes answers people give in response to whether they have felt very lonely, so restless they couldn't sit still, bored, depressed, upset; (5) *personal competence*—certainty that life and problems will work out and that planning is better than luck; (6) *overall satisfaction*—degree of satisfaction with neighborhood, home life, education, health, friendships, family life, standard of living. The nine regions, with their rankings on the six scales, are listed in order of their overall psychological well-being.

AREA	OUTLOOK ON LIFE	STRESS	POSITIVE FEELINGS	NEGATIVE FEELINGS	PERSONAL COMPETENCE	OVERALL SATISFACTION
West South-Central	2	1	3	7	3	2
West North-Central	7	2	4	1	2	3
New England	1	7	7	2	5	1
Mountain	6	6	1	4	1	6
Pacific	5	3	2	8	4	8
South Atlantic	4	4	5	5	7	5
East South-Central	9	8	6	9	6	7
Middle Atlantic	8	9	8	6	8	9

HOW DO STATE INCOME TAX BURDENS COMPARE?

Although there may be some variation in state income taxes, here is how the states compared in 1983 in *overall* income tax burdens, in order of highest burden;

New York	Idaho
Massachusetts	Kansas
District of Columbia	South Carolina
Maryland	New Hampshire
Wisconsin	Ohio
Minnesota	Missouri
Michigan	Arizona
Delaware	Montana
New Jersey	Oklahoma
Rhode Island	Arkansas
California	West Virginia
Hawaii	Alaska
Vermont	Alabama
Oregon	New Mexico
Connecticut	Mississippi
Virginia	Indiana
Pennsylvania	South Dakota
Nebraska	North Dakota
Maine	Washington
North Carolina	Texas
Illinois	Florida
Colorado	Tennessee
Iowa	Nevada
Utah	Louisana
Kentucky	Wyoming
Georgia	

For a list of tax sources, see section on State Property Taxes that follows.

How Do U.S. Property Taxes Compare?

In 90 major cities, you can expect to pay a property tax at an average of 1.8 percent of the market value of your home ($1,080 on a $60,000 house). Cities with more than 100,000 people levy lower taxes than cities of 50,000 to 100,000—1.6 percent compared to 1.9 percent.

You'll find property taxes steepest of all in Northeastern states (averaging 4 percent of market value), and lowest in Southern states (averaging 1 percent of market value). In the Midwest, Detroit levies the highest property taxes—3 percent of market value. Elsewhere in the Midwest, however, the tax rate is much lower, averaging 1.8 percent of market value. Western cities rarely have a tax rate over 2.5 percent of market value; most in fact are lower than 1.5 percent of market value.

But although states set the overall tax structure, towns, cities, and counties usually set the property taxes and any additional sales taxes. So you must pinpoint taxes on a particular house in a particular neighborhood in a particular town. Chambers of commerce, local realtors, and my books (which give tax rates for most retirement areas) can help. You can also contact:

■ Tax Foundation, 1875 Connecticut Ave. NW, Washington, DC 20009

■ Commerce Clearing House, 4025 W. Peterson Ave., Chicago, IL 60646. It publishes the State Tax Handbook and Tax Guides to various states.

■ American Association of Retired Persons, 215 Long Beach Blvd., Long Beach, CA 90801, also publishes federal and state tax booklets that are updated annually.

■ State Tax Departments and State Units on Aging (see listing toward end of this book) located in state capitals but may have metropolitan offices, can give you specific tax information as it applies to you. Seniors usually get both personal and property (rental) tax exemptions and deferrals, but you must be a resident for tax purposes. This usually requires remaining in the state for six months or more; establishing a home, business, or profession; registering to vote; or meeting some other requirement. Also you must apply by a certain date (often January 1) before the tax year to be eligible. And some exemptions may require several years' residence before becoming eligible.

What About Retiring to Foreign Lands?

Although most of us retire in the United States, perhaps not too far from where we live now, the Social Security Administration sends some 320,000 checks overseas each month to Americans who have retired abroad. And some 2 million Americans live or make extended stays beyond our borders. This number will double or triple in the next 10 years, predicts Thomas Boylston Adams, treasurer of the American Academy of Arts and Sciences. And a recent Harris poll shows that some 12 percent of Americans, if given the chance, would emigrate.

Why the exodus? "A better life-style at lower cost" chorus the expatriates, who know that a strong U.S. dollar can cut retirement costs in half. For instance, you can rent a retirement home for under $200 a month in Mexico or

Costa Rica or buy for under $40,000; buy land for another 5 cents an acre in Australia; get free medical care in Canada, Britain, and Scandinavia; full-course meals for under $5 in Italy, Spain, Portugal, and Greece; double or triple your money on the Hong Kong and Singapore stock exchanges; pay *no* income or capital gains tax in Andorra, the Bahamas, Bermuda, Cayman Islands, Monaco, Nauru, and New Hebrides.

Most popular countries with American retirees (in order):

Mexico	Israel
Canada	Ireland
Italy	Portugal
Philippines	Spain
Greece	Norway
Germany	France
United Kingdom	Sweden

Some other countries with large numbers of American retirees and residents (in alphabetical order):

Australia	Dominican Republic
Austria	Japan
Brazil	Peru
Colombia	Venezuela
Costa Rica	

So you would have lots of American company in most parts of the world. And you don't have to put down roots to plant money and watch it grow; in most countries, if you don't stay more than six months at a time, you aren't taxed as a resident. So think of overseas retirement as an *extended vacation* that would cost you less than if you remained at home.

Using both subjective and objective factors noted in this chapter, I have discovered about 800 "Retirement Edens" throughout the world. I define a "Retirement Eden" as ". . . a place you would love to visit and like to live in . . . a haven where you can be happier, healthier, and wealthier than you are now . . . a place where you can make as well as save money . . ." Some *possibilities* detailed in my books:

Abita Springs, La.	Ashland, Ore.
Algarve, Portugal	Bad Homburg, Germany
Amherst, Mass.	Blount County, Tenn.

Boulder, Colo.

Branson, Mo.

Bucks County, Pa.

Camden, Me.

Campione, Switzerland

Cedar City, Utah

Cooperstown, N.Y.

Corfu, Greece

Chapel Hill, N.C.

Coeur d'Alene, Idaho

Costa del Sol, Spain

Covington, La.

Dalkey, Ireland

Devils Lake, N.D.

Door County, Wis.

Durango, Colo.

Eureka Springs, Ark.

Easton, Md.

Escazu, Costa Rica

Fairhope, Ala.

French Riviera

Great Barrington, Mass.

Golden Isle, Ga.

Hanover, N.H.

Hemet, Calif.

Hesse Spas, Germany

Jekyll Island, Ga.

Kerrville, Tex.

Lahaina, Maui, Haw.

Lake Chapala, Mexico

Land Between the Lakes, Ky.

Lihue, Kauai, Haw.

Malmo, Sweden

McAllen, Tex.

Mt. Dora, Fla.

Montserrat, B.W.I.

Muskogee, Okla.

Muskoka Area, Canada

Neosho, Mo.

New Jersey Shore Area

Nevada City, Calif.

Okanagan Valley, Canada

Oaxaca, Mexico

Perth, Australia

Pomfret, Conn.

Port Orford, Ore.

Prescott, Ariz.

Ramona, Calif.

Roswell, N.M.

Sandpoint, Idaho

San Miguel de Allende, Mexico

San Remo, Italy

Sedona, Ariz.

Siena, Italy

Sonoma, Calif.

St. George, Utah

St. Barthelemy, F.W.I.

St. John, U.S.V.I.

Torquay, England

Tryon, N.C.

Vero Beach, Fla.

Upper Arlington, Ohio

Winona, Minn.

Wytheville, Va.

Woodstock, Vt.

Zermatt, Switzerland

How Can I Size Up Any Community for Retirement?

Selecting retirement housing is like selecting a spouse: there are many possibilities but few that are right. To find the right housing for you:

■ Try to pinpoint the area you'd like to settle in. Also, write the Administration on Aging, Dept. HEW, Washington, DC 20201, and the U.S. Dept. of

Housing and Urban Development (HUD) Information Center, Washington, DC 20410, for housing suggestions. If health is a factor, check with your doctor.

■ After you've pinpointed an area, write to the specific state units on aging (see list in the directory section). Ask about location and availability of housing; cost of living and taxes; climate and environment; special facilities for seniors, including tax exemptions. Be as specific as possible.

■ Write to the many sources below, as well as the Retirement Research and Welfare Association (an affiliate of the American Association of Retired Persons), 215 Long Beach Blvd., Long Beach, CA 90802, for a free listing of such facilities in the states of your choice. There is a limit of three lists per person.

■ Write to the chambers of commerce of the various cities and towns you're interested in. No street address is necessary, but get zip codes from your post office or library. Again, specify what you're looking for. A friendly (or no) answer from the chamber of commerce will give you an idea if the welcome mat is out.

■ Subscribe to weekly or Sunday papers to learn about the area's business; social life; cost of food, clothing, appliances; and real estate prices.

■ Vacation there—off season as well as on. Get the pulse of the town; is it brisk in the morning but dull in the evening? Are weekdays somber and weekends lively?

■ Get to know the people—the postman, grocer, real estate agent, librarian, chamber of commerce people, as well as the people you meet in clubs, town meetings, houses of worship. Are they friendly or do they avoid strangers? How long would it take to go from "stranger to neighbor"? (Two years is about average.)

■ Rent before buying. Rent a house, apartment, mobile home, and so on (the type of housing you'd like) before buying. Rent your home "back home." If you decide you don't like your new community, you'll always have a place to retreat.

HOW TO ADAPT TO A NEW ENVIRONMENT

In my book *Travel & Retirement Edens Abroad* (New York: E. P. Dutton, 1983) I discussed the problem of "culture shock" in adapting to a new environment. Basically, here are the various stages any newcomer goes through on leaving "home" for a new place to live:

1. *Elation.* At first you may be delighted at the difference in your new place and how you have escaped the "rat race" back home. This may be called the "spectator" phase when you aren't forced to participate.

2. *Satisfaction.* In this stage you seek out a few basic satisfactions that brought you to the new place. If you find these within the first year or two of moving, you'll be motivated to stay. If not, you're likely to pack your bags and head "back home."

3. *Identification.* At this stage you've mastered any language differences and are referring to the people and your new place as "we" or "our." During this stage you feel more like one of the natives than as an outsider.

As I said, all this should take place within the first two years. To keep abreast of social activities as well as climate, medical facilities, housing, and other costs, and general business developments, subscribe to the local weekly newspaper. It will keep you up to date while you're contemplating a move. Then, probably your best way to go from stranger to neighbor is to join a club, house of worship, volunteer group, or civic enterprise of your choice. Better still: transfer membership in a national organization (Rotary, Lions, Kiwanis, Boy and Girl Scouts, Cancer Society, League of Women Voters, and so on) to the local chapter in your new community. Fortunately, many communities with high percentages of retirees have more civic, service, and social clubs and organizations than other towns. And if you have picked your new place because you like it and it likes you, you'll find more people of similar backgrounds and interests. So you should have an instant group of new friends.

For further information write to these *organizations:*

■ American Association of Homes for the Aging, 1050 17th St., Washington, DC 20036.

■ Manufactured Housing (Mobile Homes) Institute, 1745 Jefferson Davis Hwy., Arlington, VA 22282.

■ Mobile Home Consumer Affairs Council, Box 3163, Anaheim, CA 92803.

■ National Association of Home Builders, 15th and M Sts. NW, Washington, DC 20005.

■ National Homeowners Association, 1906 Sunderland Pl. NW, Washington, DC 20036.

CHECKPOINTS FOR PICKING A RETIREMENT SPOT
Rate each item from 0 to 5 in each column. Multiply A, B, and C by
Importance (first column).

ITEM OR FACTOR	IMPORTANCE TO YOU	PLACE A	PLACE B	PLACE C
1. Climate, geography, scenery	_____	_____	_____	_____
2. Health and medical facilities	_____	_____	_____	_____
3. Cost of living, housing	_____	_____	_____	_____
4. Family, friends, and associates	_____	_____	_____	_____
5. Religious and social facilities	_____	_____	_____	_____
6. Recreation and sports facilities	_____	_____	_____	_____
7. Cultural and historical advantages	_____	_____	_____	_____
8. Accessibility to important things	_____	_____	_____	_____
9. Employment opportunities	_____	_____	_____	_____
10. Type and size town preferred	_____	_____	_____	_____

TOTALS: Add columns.

■ Farmers Home Administration (rural housing), 14th and Independence Ave. SW, Washington, DC 20250.

For further information, get these *books* at libraries, bookstores, or send for them.

■ *Sunbelt Retirement* by Peter A. Dickinson (New York, E. P. Dutton, 1983 ed.).

■ *Retirement Edens: Outside the Sunbelt* by Peter A. Dickinson (New York: E. P. Dutton, 1981).

■ *Travel and Retirement Edens Abroad* by Peter A. Dickinson (New York: E. P. Dutton, 1983).

■ *Where to Retire on a Small Income* by Norman D. Ford (New York: Harian, 1979).

■ *Finding Your Best Place to Live in America* by Thomas Bowman and George Giuliani (New York: Red Lion Books, 1982).

■ *How to Avoid the Retirement Trap* by Leland and Lee Cooley, (New York: Popular Library, 1973).

■ *Retirement in the West* by Morie Morrison (San Francisco: Chronicle Books, 1976).

■ *Where Will You Live Tomorrow?* by Michael and Marika Sumichrast and Ronald Shafer (Homewood, Ill.: Dow Jones–Irwin, 1981).

■ *The Fannie Mae Guide to Buying, Financing, and Selling Your Home*, ed. Curt Tuck (rev. ed.; New York: Dolphin Doubleday, 1978).

■ *Condominium Living* by Dennis Le Croissette (Montrose, Calif.: Younghusband Co., 1980).

■ *An Insider's Guide to Owning Land in Subdivisions: How to Buy, Appraise and Get Rid of Your Lot*, $2.50 from INFORM, 25 Broad St., New York, NY 10004.

■ *Where to Live for Your Health* by Norman and Madelyn Carlisle (New York: Harcourt Brace Jovanovich, 1980).

■ *Consumer's Guide to Mobile Home Selection* by Cora McKown, free from Agriculture Publications, Agriculture Experiment State, University of Arkansas, 72701.

■ *Mobile Home Buyers Guide*, Dept. of Commerce, Consumer Protection Div., 33 N. Grant Ave., Columbus, OH 43215.

And you can send for *catalogs* of retirement housing by writing to:

■ Strout Realty, P.O. Box 2757, Springfield, MO 65803.

■ United Farm Agency, 612 W 47th St., Kansas City, MO 64112.

For information on *time sharing* (the purchase of a vacation home in increments of a week or more by a number of buyers), you can get these booklets and books:

■ *Resort Timesharing—A Consumer's Guide*, $1 from the American Land Development Association, 1000 16th St. NW, Suite 604, Washington, DC 20036.

■ *Resort Timesharing* by Keith W. Trowbridge (New York: Simon & Schuster, 1982).

■ *The Buyer's Guide to Resort Timesharing* by Carl Burlingame, $7 from CHB Company, P.O. Box 184, Los Altos, CA 94022.

Good Books on Investing in Real Estate

■ *How You Can Become Financially Independent by Investing in Real Estate* by Albert J. Lowry (New York: Simon & Schuster, 1982).

■ *Real Estate Turnaround: Craig Hall's Investment Formula That Makes Millions* by Craig Hall (Englewood Cliffs, N.J.: Prentice-Hall, 1982).

■ *How We Made a Million Dollars Recycling Old Houses* by Sam and Mary Weir (Chicago: Contemporary Books, 1980).

■ *The Condominium Book: A Guide to Getting the Most for Your Money* by Lee Butcher (Homewood, Ill.: Dow Jones–Irwin, 1980).

■ *Questions About Condominiums: What to Ask Before You Buy*, free from Consumer Information, Dept. 602G, Pueblo, CO 81009.

■ *Designs for Low-Cost Wood Homes*, $1.30 from Supt. of Documents, U.S. Government Printing Office, Washington, DC 20402. Order stock No. 001-001-0019-1.

Also, you can order these helpful government publications from the Consumer Information Center, Pueblo, CO 81009. Enclose check or money order for amount indicated:

Buying Lots from Developers ($1).
Finding and Keeping a Healthy House ($1.25).
Home Buyers Vocabulary (free).
Questions and Answers on Condominiums (free).
Rent or Buy? (free).
Selecting and Financing a Home ($1.10).
When You Move—Do's and Don't's (free).
Wise Home Buying (free).

PART VI.

TIME—

THE MONEY OF

YOUR LIFE

MEANINGFUL USE OF TIME

George Bernard Shaw once said: "A perpetual holiday is a good working definition of Hell." And from another sage: "Killing time is suicide on the installment plan." Yes, time *is* the money of your life. You have just so much time to spend; how well you spend it determines the quality of your life.

When you're retired, you'll have at least an extra 50 hours a week to spend *when* you want and *how* you want. You'll find that you can't fish this time away or rest it away, because whatever you do for long must have meaning—must pay some reward. And whatever the reward, it will satisfy some basic need or want that remains constant throughout life.

What Do We Want from Spending Time?

As the value of the dollar goes down, the value of time goes up. All time isn't the same. A moment of awe in religion, ecstasy in love, is more of an experience than a moment riding a bus, shoveling snow, or eating beans. So we should consider the *quality* as well as the *quantity* of time.

Also consider *variety*. You'll want more than one activity to suit your needs and desires. Sometimes you'll want to be alone . . . other times to be with people. At times you'll want to be entertained or informed . . . creative or meditative . . . play for "fun" or for exercise . . . strive to win or sit back and watch.

You'll probably do different things for different reasons. One person might do something to "make money." Another person might do the *same thing* because "it's fun" . . . "I want to learn" . . . "I want to impress people" . . . "I want to get across my ideas." Perhaps other people's experiences can help illustrate these points. The Institute of Gerontology at the University of

Michigan surveyed older people to find their formulas for remaining active, useful, and happy in retirement. They said:

1. Keeping busy isn't enough; neither is just a hobby.
2. Plan some activities with other people.
3. Continue learning—no matter what your age.
4. Stay in touch with younger people.
5. Try out your activities *before retirement.*

WHY DO WE SPEND TIME NOW THE WAY WE DO?

Most of our thoughts and actions were shaped by our background, social class, present surroundings. These include:

■ *Cultural background and present environment.* We're all a mixture of cultural heritage, parental influence, social class, education, present environment. If your grandmother ever said, "The devil will find work for idle hands," that made an indelible stamp on your mind. Lack of education hinders leisure; some of us have more time on our hands than we have the knowledge, interest, and curiosity to handle. We've been regulated by clocks; regimented by school, work, and TV schedules. Our fellow employees, bosses, friends, and neighbors influence what we do. Often, we do something because we feel that it's "expected" of us or it's "the thing people want us do."

■ *The demands of the job.* If you must be at work early in the morning, you're not going to stay out late at night "making whoopee." If your job is physically demanding, you're not going to pound rocks for fun. On the other hand, if you're desk-bound, you'll probably want to bowl, hunt, or fish for recreational activity. Unfortunately, work is geared to earning to live . . . not learning to live. Figuratively, we're still punching a time clock, whether we're at work or play. We use our leisure as a release from work, and we don't let leisure interfere with working. And while we may be experts at work, we usually are amateurs at play.

■ *How much or little money we have.* We often choose leisure activities on the basis of what they cost. If we don't have much money we pick activities that are free or don't cost much money; if we have lots of money, we may pick something to "impress our neighbors" rather than to please ourselves.

■ *Physical and mental limitations.* A broken leg and a dull mind may limit activities; psychological "hangups" influence what we think and do, too.

■ *The nearness of activities.* If the corner saloon is nearer than the public library, we may opt for the former. However, seniors get discounts on public transportation, and many senior centers, schools with adult education classes are easily accessible.

WHAT ARE SOME OF THE REWARDS YOU WANT FROM SPENDING TIME?

Generally, you'll want a *reward* for spending time—perhaps something you can jingle in your pocket (money), paste in your scrapbook (recognition) or at least etch in your memory. These basic needs and wants—which will remain the same whether or not you're retired—fall into the following classifications:

■ *Recreation and relaxation*—the rewards for a hard day's or life's work.

■ *Self-expression*—new levels of accomplishment in old and new pursuits.

■ *Recognition*—a "pat on the back" for individual accomplishments.

■ *Participation*—to serve others while helping yourself.

■ *Adventure*—new experiences, sights, knowledge for mind and body.

■ *Learning*—practical reasons and methods to keep up to date.

■ *Activity*—new dimensions in sports and games.

■ *Security*—the rewards (rather than a paycheck) for useful work.

Can I Get These Rewards as Well in Retirement?

Yes. First realize that you're going to want the same rewards in retirement that you sought through work. But there's an interplay between work and leisure, and many of us have developed skills on the job that are ideally suited to leisure. In *Social Aspects of Aging*, I. H. Simpson found that many people with jobs oriented around *people* showed the greatest continuity in style from pre- to postretirement. Simpson suggested that retirement and leisure roles, in particular, might offer greater opportunities for practicing these interpersonal skills, or whatever other skills you learned on the job.

And many of our work goals are related to *participating* in something that's rewarding. Participating is related to *belonging*—which is related to the desire to *serve* and to feel needed. This, in turn, brings *recognition* of individual talents, interests, and the contributions that each of us can make.

In fact, in retirement you can often get better *recognition* as an individual doing his or her "thing" than as a member of a group doing "their thing." And as you'll be able to work at your own pace, you'll be more productive and do a better job at leisure than at work.

How Can I Select Activities to Satisfy My Basic Needs and Wants?

Realize the importance of being you. You are unique; there has been no one on earth like you, and there will be no one like you when you leave. So you should select activities to satisfy *you* and you alone.

Then, realize that we seldom change our likes and dislikes. You're going to want the same things in retirement as you do now. You are what you were and what you will be; the *past* is the key to the present as well as a clue to your future. So successful leisure—like successful retirement—may depend more on the renewal of *past* pursuits than on seeking new activities. Perhaps you should ask yourself:

- What did I *like* to do when I was a youngster?

- *How did I like* to earn money (not what you had to do)?

- *What do I like* to do in my spare time?

- *What have I always wanted* to do but never had time to do?

Also, you could contact an organization like Constructive Leisure, 511 N. La Cienega Blvd., Los Angeles, CA 90048, for professional advice on selecting activities.

According to a recent survey by the Louis Harris organization and the National Council on Aging, here is what older people do in their leisure time, ranked in degree of popularity:

1. Socializing with friends
2. Gardening or raising plants
3. Reading
4. Watching television
5. Sitting and thinking
6. Caring for younger or older members of the family
7. Participating in recreational activities
8. Going for walks
9. Participating in fraternal or community organizations or clubs
10. Sleeping
11. Just doing nothing
12. Working part- or full-time
13. Doing volunteer work
14. Political activities

IS THERE SOME SORT OF FORMULA THAT CAN HELP YOU SELECT ACTIVITIES?

Yes, you can use the ACHATES formula developed by my friend, Robert Peterson, in his book *New Life Begins at Forty* (New York: Trident Press, 1967). The letters in the formula spell the name *Achates*, which means "a faithful friend" (Achates is the friend of Aeneas in Vergil's *Aeneid*).

> A = Arts
> C = Crafts
> H = Humanitarianism
> A = Armchair Pursuits
> T = Travel
> E = Education
> S = Sports

This formula can prove a faithful friend to guide you to activities that can satisfy your basic needs and wants. Let's examine each of these seven headings:

A = ARTS. You're an artist everytime you do something—anything—that makes you proud to say "I made it" or "I did it." This can be anything from flower arranging to writing best-selling novels. The secret is to judge your accomplishment in the light of *your* past, not that of some recognized expert. If you take up the piano in retirement and learn to play "Chopsticks," you've created—you've risen to new levels of accomplishment. And you're just as much an artist as Rubinstein (who once learned to play "Chopsticks" and just went on from there).

Also, realize that you can become an artist at any age or stage of life. Did you realize that Grandma Moses didn't take up painting until she was age 78—and only then because she had arthritis that was so bad she couldn't do farm chores. The doctor thought that the painting might be good for her hands.

To learn painting, you can enroll in courses in schools, colleges, Ys, senior centers, art museums, and private studios. For further information on art and painting, check your local library for the books and courses available.

And here are some other creative, artistic endeavors:

■ *Gardening* satisfies your creative needs in many ways. When you garden, you foster life, create beauty, gain peace of mind, and get in tune with nature. Gardening offers challenges and opportunities in plant breeding, specializing, grow for resale, introducing new plants, collecting the rare and unusual. To get started, ask questions of friends and neighbors and then contact a nearby nurseryman. You can also get information from these sources: *Senior Gardening*, *Gardens for All*, 180 Flynn Ave., Burlington, VT 05401. *Your Home Garden*—a selected list of publications available from the Government Printing Office. Ask for it from Public Documents Distribution Center, 5801 Tabor Ave., Philadelphia, PA 19120. U.S. Dept. of Agriculture, Research Service, Federal Center Bldg., Hyattsville, MD 20782. Ask for free booklets on mulches, soils, compost, fertilizer.

■   *Writing* helps you to clarify your thoughts, express your ideas, vent your emotions. Everyone has something to write about, and it doesn't necessarily require formal training: more important are purpose, persistence, and patience. To find outlets for your writing, consult *Writer's Market*, a directory of over 4,000 outlets for all kinds of writing—articles, novels, short stories, plays, gags, greeting card verse, and so forth. The book should be available at most libraries or bookstores; the same company, *Writer's Digest*, publishes similar market directories for songwriters, photographers, artists, and craftworkers.

■   *Theater* has a part for you, whether you perform onstage or backstage. Amateur theater groups welcome past experience and present aspiration, and there's a role for an older person in almost every play. For example, Judith Lowry, at age 80, was wowing New York audiences in *The Effects of Gamma Rays . . .* her replacement was 82-year-old Annie Ives.
    To locate theater productions in your area, watch newspapers for try-out announcements and check community centers, chambers of commerce, libraries, Ys, and bookstores for notices of upcoming little-theater productions.

■   *Music* rewards you mentally, physically, emotionally, and socially. You can reap rewards in many ways: playing musical instruments, singing, composing, conducting, and *appreciating*, really listening to, music. Some think learning to play an instrument is difficult, but it isn't, provided you really *want* to. An experiment at Boston University proves the point: in 18 months, young students taught 45 seniors to play concert pieces on the piano. And music teachers say that within a year seniors can learn to play relatively difficult tunes on an organ, guitar, accordion, or recorder. If you'd rather sing than play, almost every town or city has some sort of church or community choral group. A good book: *Never Too Late* by John Holt (New York: Delta, 1980, $4.95)—a saga about learning to play the cello after age 50.

C = CRAFTS. Whatever your taste or aptitude, there's a creative craft to satisfy it. Two out of every five Americans engage in woodworking, weaving, pottery, ceramics, or other craft for pleasure as well as profit. In fact, some 16 percent of those engaged in crafts are earning over $1,000 a year, and 9 percent of them are earning over $5,000 a year.

Most of us prefer creative crafts that don't require intricate detail or physical strength, and the crafts best suited for the later years include weaving, rug making, plastics molding, sewing, ceramics, knitting, woodworking, and leathercraft.

Where can you learn about crafts? Your library has may good crafts books including those listed below. Magazines like *Woman's Day*, *McCalls*, and *Family Circle* often feature craft ideas. Many specialty magazines (available at libraries and some newsstands) like *Handweaver and Craftsman*, *Modern Carpentry*, *Family Crafts Ideas* can give you many suggestions. And you can even start a craft using kits available from:

- Dick Blick, P.O. Box 1267, Galesburg, IL 61401.

- C.C.M. Arts and Crafts, Inc., 9250 Baltimore Ave., College Park, MD 20740.

- Economy Handicrafts, 47-11 Francis Lewis Blvd., Flushing, NY 11361.

- Sax Arts and Crafts, 207 N. Milwaukee St., Milwaukee, WI 53202.

Write to them for catalogs and prices.

One of the best overall crafts organization is the American Craft Council, 401 Park Ave. S., New York, NY 10016. It sponsors the American Craft Museums at 45th and 53rd Streets in New York City, publishes the bimonthly magazine *American Craft*, operates a nationwide audiovisual service, and has a subsidiary, American Craft Enterprises, that covers crafts markets in various parts of the country.

Some 400,000 Americans are now associated with more than 1,200 crafts organizations nationwide, and there are about 6,000 arts and crafts events staged in the United States each year. And in a report, "The Handcrafts Business," available at Bank of America branches, the nation's biggest bank says there is a vast and growing market for original works in metal, leather, wood, glass, clay, paper, and many other media. However, the bank warns that going from amateur to entrepreneur requires a number of assessments. For example, expenses will probably exceed income for months and possibly years. However, the Internal Revenue Service says that if you do *anything* (especially crafts) that can produce an income, and *make an effort to sell it;* you can write off all the expenses associated with producing that item. This includes the space used for a shop in your home; all tools, equipment, materials; courses and classes; advertising and other selling expenses. And many senior centers, elder craftsman shops, and craft exchanges are set up to give you an outlet to sell your merchandise. You might also want to refer to pages 130 to 132 and 151 and 152 for more information.

Here are some good publications to help you get started:

■ *Artists' Market*, $11.95 postpaid, from Writer's Digest Books, 9933 Alliance Rd., Cincinnati, OH 45242.

■ *Career Opportunities in Crafts* by Elyse Sommer (New York: Crown, 1977), $10.95 hardcover; $5.95 paper.

■ *The Crafts Business Encylopedia* by Michael Scott (New York: Harcourt Brace Jovanovich, 1979), $10.50 hardcover; $4.35 paper.

■ *How to Earn More Money from Your Crafts* by Merle Dowd, $6.95 from The Writing Works, 7438 S.E. 40th St., Mercer Island, WA 98040.

■ *Craftsmen in Business—A Guide to Financial Management*, $7.00 postpaid from American Craft Council, 401 Park Avenue S, New York, NY 10016.

■ *Craftworker's Market*, $12.95 from Writer's Digest Books. See address above.

H = HUMANITARIANISM. This is a fancy name for *volunteering*. But often you *get* more than you give when you volunteer. You meet new friends, learn new skills, and can enhance your place in the community. Even more, some 17 percent of those who go into volunteer work end up in paying jobs stemming from the volunteer activity. And many people retire successfully in their own or a new community by joining a prestigious volunteer organization *before* they retire (often using the leverage of their job and company to get a top-rung volunteer post)—then continuing this activity in retirement.

If you live in an urban area, you can contact several central bureaus that act as clearinghouses for nonprofit agencies in need of voluntary help. These clearinghouses operate under the name "Volunteer Service Bureau" or something similar. You can usually find them in the telephone book under "United Way," "Community Chest," "United Funds," "Health and Welfare Council," "United Appeal," "Council of Social Services" or "Community Service Council."

In smaller towns or rural areas, contact the Cooperative Extension Service, the educational branch of the U.S. Department of Agriculture. There are some 3,000 such offices, each headed by a county agricultural agent or a home economist. Located in the county seat, they are listed in the telephone book under such titles as "Extension Service," "U.S. Cooperative Extension Service," or your county's "County Extension Service."

And here are addresses of other organizations that can find you a volunteer spot, many paying a small stipend:

ACTION (Retired Senior Volunteer Program, Senior Companion, Foster Grandparents), offices in major cities and Washington, DC 20525.

Green Thumb, Suite 600, 1012 14th St. NW, Washington, DC 20005.

Service Corps of Retired Executives (SCORE), Small Business Administration, 1441 L St. NW, Washington, DC 20416.

Senior Aides, National Council of Senior Citizens, 1511 K St. NW, Washington, DC 20005.

National Center for Voluntary Action (private clearinghouse for information on local volunteer centers), 1214 16th St. NW, Washington, DC 20036.

National Council on the Aging, 600 Maryland Ave. SW, Washington, DC 20024.

Veterans Administration, Voluntary Service Office, 810 Vermont Ave. NW, Washington, DC 20420.

Association of Volunteer Bureaus of America (national network of private organizations that help to place volunteers), 801 N. Fairfax St., Alexandria, VA 22314.

National School Volunteer Program (places teaching assistants in classrooms), 300 N. Washington St., Alexandria, VA 22314.

The International Executive Service Corps (experienced executive assistance in overseas projects), 622 Third Ave., New York, NY 10017.

Second Career Program (locates both volunteer and for-pay work), 4929 Wilshire Blvd., Los Angeles, CA 90010, and 61 Chambers St., New York, NY 10017.

Peace Corps, 806 Connecticut Ave. NW, Washington, DC 20526. Call toll-free 800 424-8580. In Florida 1-800 241-3862.

National Park Service (coordinates volunteer projects in federal recreation areas), U.S. Dept. of Interior, Washington, DC 20240.

A = ARMCHAIR What is the number-one armchair activity? *Watching television!* However, a Cornell University study found that 6 out of 7 senior citizens watching television would rather be doing something else—if they only had a better idea.

Rather than abusing television, many seniors are *using* it in these ways:

1. *As a springboard to action.* When there's a documentary on, they invite friends and neighbors over, review the program, then plan some action stemming from the program—whether it's working with guide dogs for the blind or improving safety conditions.

2. *For monitoring political activity.* In a recent election, groups of older people would monitor programs to see that their candidate got equal time.

3. *For improving the image of older people.* Although older people comprise over 10 percent of the population, only about 1 percent of the roles feature older people. When we do appear, we're usually ugly, senile, whining, and seeking help from competent younger people. However, a group of seniors felt that some characterizations of older people were unfair, and they have been effective in changing the image of older people as portrayed in television programs.

4. *For getting an education.* Besides simply learning from the many informative programs offered by the Public Broadcasting Service (PBS) and some cable TV stations, many seniors are going back to school via the tube. A new program developed by the National University Consortium lets them earn a bachelor's degree from one of seven colleges in their own living rooms. Students must live within the reception area and register with a college that is a consortium member. Among current members are California State University at Dominguez Hills; Iona College (New York); Linfield College (Oregon); the University of Maryland; University College at Pennsylvania State University; Southern Vermont College; and the University of Tennessee at Chattanooga, and more colleges and television stations are signing up. For information on participating schools and stations, write to: National University Consortium, University of Maryland, College Park, MD 20742.

And many seniors are turning to *collecting hobbies* for pleasure and profit. You can collect almost anything—coins, books, buttons, clocks, bottles, dolls, old prints, sheet music. Some of the most popular collecting hobbies (with addresses for further information) are:

Stamps. The Philatelic Foundation, 270 Madison Ave., New York, NY 10016.

Coins. American Numismatic Association, P.O. Box 2366, Colorado Springs, CO 80901.

Buttons. National Button Society of America, Box 116, Lamoni, IA 50140.

Dolls. International Doll Association, 10920 Indian Trail, Suite 302, Dallas, TX 75229.

Miniatures. National Association of Miniature Enthusiasts, P.O. Box 2621, Anaheim, CA 92804.

Trains. National Model Railroad Association, 4602 4th St. NW, Canton, OH 44708.

Watches. International Watch Fob Club, 5892 Stow Rd., Hudson, OH 44236, and National Association of Watch & Clock Collectors, 514 Poplar St., Columbia, PA 17512.

T = TRAVEL. There are many reasons that you might want to travel in retirement. Travel helps you to:

1. *Break a routine.* Travel gets you out of the rut of a "do-nothing" retirement, gives you new challenges and opportunities, makes you think and plan.

2. *Gain a new perspective on yourself.* Travel takes you out of familiar surroundings and away from familiar people and makes you relate to strange people and places (and they to you). This helps you gain a fresh perspective from which to think and plan.

3. *Gain a sense of personal history.* We owe it to ourselves to visit the land of our ancestors. This helps to give you a sense of your place in this world, and will help you either to shed a preconceived image of the "old country," or to gain a new perspective on your own country.

4. *Strengthen your hobby.* Wouldn't it be more interesting to play golf at St. Andrew's in Scotland? Paint along the banks of the Seine? Take pictures at the Vatican? For people who *participate*—do things like hobbies—travel means the adventure of exciting new places, people, and experiences.

5. *Take advantage of time.* Remember: time is money; money is time. When you travel to most parts of Europe and Asia, you can live for less than you would back home. And the longer your trip—and the more off season— the lower your costs.

Seniors are eligible for many *discounts* in traveling, among them:

Domestic airlines. Congress has passed a law that permits airlines to offer senior discounts that can average about a *third of the cost* of a one-way ticket. Most require advance reservations of at least 24 hours, and you must show legal proof of age. Airlines offering such discounts include American, Delta, Pan American, and many others. *Always ask about discounts* when you call any airlines or contact any travel agent.

Buses. Greyhound and Trailways offer 13 percent discounts to seniors on many trips.

Trains. Some trains have 25 percent "Golden Opportunity Discounts" on regular one-way coach fares of $40 or more. These apply particularly to *Amtrak*.

Hotels. Over a dozen hotel chains in the United States offer discounts to seniors, and many individual hotels and resorts offer seniors discounts of 10 percent and more, especially the Days Inns chain. *Ask at any hotel* if they offer discounts; you can write to the Days Inns September Days Club for membership information: P.O. Box 4042, Atlanta, GA 30302.

Auto Rentals. Most senior organizations offer auto rental discounts to members. Among them are the American Association of Retired Persons (1909 K St. NW, Washington, DC 20049) or National Council of Senior Citizens (1511 K St. NW, Washington, DC 20005).

Travel Agencies. Grand Circle Tours (555 Madison Ave., New York, NY 10022) specializes in tours for people 55 and older. On these escorted tours, some 60 to 70 percent of the older travelers are single (usually women). The company does a lot of matching of clients so they can avoid the single supplement charge. Travel Mates (56 West 45th St., New York, NY 10036) also arranges tours for the "over 50" set, and helps match up travelers to cut costs. Also contact Saga ("Holidays for the Over 60s"), Park Square Bldg., Suite 1162, 31st St. James Ave., Boston, MA 02116.

National Parks. The National Park Service issues a free Golden Age Passport for those age 62 or over. This gives you free entrance to U.S. parks, recreation area, and monuments. For details, write: Public Inquiries, National Park Service, Washington, DC 20240.

And for a free leaflet with useful travel advice, write Travel Tips for Senior Citizens, Public Information Service, Room 4827-A, Dept. of State, Washington, DC 20520. A very helpful book that pulls much of this information together is the newly revised edition of the *Discount Guide for Travelers Over Fifty-Five* by Caroline and Walter Weintz (New York: E. P. Dutton, 1983), $5.75.

Discounts also apply to *foreign* travel, with Switzerland, Japan, Spain, and Canada all offering discounts, mainly on travel within the country. Ask your travel agent for details. Or you can send for a free copy of "Sources of Tourist Information on Foreign Countries" from the U.S. Department of Commerce, U.S. Travel Service, Washington, DC 20030.

If you're worried about health care overseas, you can contact these organizations for lists of English-speaking doctors overseas:

International Association for Medical Assistance to Travelers, 736 Center
St., Lewiston, NY 14092.
Intermedic, 777 Third Ave., New York, NY 10017.

For top value overseas, plan to stay at Grade B or superior second-class
hostels. Usually, the higher the floor and the smaller the room, the lower the
price. Rooms in older wings or facing inside courts are also cheaper. And in
northern Europe, a room without a private bath is considerably less expensive. Most foreign countries list and rate their hotels; you can get these lists
through the various government tourist offices located in New York or San
Francisco (the reference department of your local library has the addresses).
If you're going to Spain, be sure to ask about the *paradors* and in Portugal the
pousadas. These are luxury hotels subsidized by the government, which offer
resort accommodations (for good price) in converted castles, monasteries, and
other historic buildings.

E = EDUCATION. Someone once said: "It's a shame to waste education on
the young." You have many practical reasons for continuing learning. First,
the mind can't stagnate—it either moves forward or backward. Then, in this
changing world, we need up-to-the-minute information to make or save
money, participate in community affairs, find suitable housing, hobbies,
activities.

It's never too late to learn. The one organ we can depend upon to last us
into old age is the brain: even at age 80 we can learn at the speed of a 13-year-
old—if we really want to. And we've got the *wisdom, experience*, and *time* to
learn and to apply what we learn for personal and practical reasons.

Never before have there been so many formal and informal ways to
learn. In a recent survey, the Adult Education Association found that almost
4,000 agencies of all sorts—schools, libraries, churches, park districts, adult
education classes—offer learning programs for older people. If there's a high
school, university, or college nearby, most likely its extension division will
offer classes. And most community colleges will offer classes not on their
calendar for adults whenever 10 or more students sign up for one.

Over 600 colleges, universities, folk schools, and other educational institutions in 50 states, Canada, Great Britain, Mexico, Bermuda, Scandinavia,
Holland, France, Germany and Italy offer special low-cost, short-term residential academic programs for older adults. They are open to people over 60
or to those whose spouse qualifies. Most programs begin on a Sunday evening
and end the next Saturday morning and are limited to 35 to 45 elders. For a

catalog of these courses, write to: Elderhostel, 100 Boylston St., Suite 200, Boston, MA 02116.

Here are other educational possibilities for seniors:

College Level Examination Program (CLEP) gives older students the opportunity to earn credit toward a degree. The standardized test is accepted by many colleges and universities across the country. For further information: College Level Examination Program, P.O. Box 582, Princeton, NJ 08540.

Correspondence courses. The National University Extension Association, Suite 360, 1 Dupont Circle, Washington, DC 20036, will send you a guide to the institutions offering independent study programs by mail. And the National Home Study Council, 1601 18th St. NW, Washington, DC 20009, will send you a copy of their "Directory of Accredited Home Study Schools."

Other sources of information include:

Adult Education Association of the U.S., 810 18th St. NW, Washington, DC 20006.

National Association for Public Continuing and Adult Education, 1201 16th St. NW, Washington, DC 20036.

Association for Continuing Higher Education, P.O. Box 207, N. Dartmouth, MA 02747.

American Library Association, Adult References and Services Div., 50 E. Huron St., Chicago, IL 60611.

American Association of Community and Junior Colleges, 1 Dupont Circle NW, Suite 410, Washington, DC 20036.

National Clearinghouse on Aging, Washington, DC 20201. Ask for free fact sheet: "Educational Opportunities for Older Persons."

Education Network for Older Adults (provides information on courses available in a particular subject), Suite 624, 36 S. Wabash Ave., Chicago, IL 60603.

Lifelong Learning (travel/study programs to all parts of the world), University Extension, University of California, Berkeley, CA 94720.

Institute of Lifetime Learning, 1909 K St. NW, Washington, DC 20049.

Interhostel (overseas university programs), University of New Hampshire, 6 Garrison Ave., Durham, NH 03824.

International Summer Schools, Warnborough College, Boars Hill, Oxford OX1 5ED England.

The Academy of Senior Professionals (membership organization with options for residential living and life-care, along with intellectual, cultural, and service activities), Eckerd College, St. Petersburg, FL 33733.

National Center for Educational Brokering, National Institute for Work and Learning (counseling to help define goals and evaluate alternatives), 1211 Connecticut Ave., Washington, DC 20036.

Chautauqua Institution (minihostel program for older adults of New York and surrounding states), Chautauqua, NY 14722.

And you can send for these *publications:*

Lifetime Learning Publications (books and materials to fit the special needs of the continuing education learner), 10 Davis Dr., Belmont, CA 94002.

Back to School: The College Guide for Adults (step-by-step guidance to college experiences for older adults), Peterson's Guides, P.O. Box 2123, Princeton, NJ 08540.

Dropping Back In: How to Complete Your College Education Quickly and Economically by Miriam Hecht and Lillian Traub (New York: E. P. Dutton, 1982), $8.95.

And for those who want to learn by *audio cassette* (self-improvement, foreign languages, history, politics, businesses, entertainment, literature) write for catalogs from:

Audio Book Co., Box 9100, Van Nuys, CA 91409.

Audio Forum, On the Green, Guilford, CT 06437.

Books on Tape, Box 7900, Newport Beach, CA 92660.

Knight Education, Box 57231, 2406 W. 7th St., Los Angeles, CA 90057.

Spoken Arts, 310 North Ave., New Rochelle, NY 10801.

Your library might have copies of these books:

Princeton's Directory of Information and Services for Older Adults.

The New York Times Guide to Continuing Education in America.

Directory of U.S. College and University Degrees for Part-Time Students.

In fact, many libraries offer "minicourses" of particular interest to adults, as do many senior centers, Ys, churches, synagogues, and other community organizations. And they may have *talking and large-print books* for those who have a hard time seeing. For further information you can write: Library of Congress, Division for the Blind and Physically Handicapped, Washington, DC 20542.

For those who are *deaf*, a number of states provide schools and adult education programs. The federal government provides free educational films and materials on loan, as well as commercial films with subtitles. You must be certified as eligible for this film service; find out by applying to Captioned Films for the Deaf, U.S. Office of Education, Washington, DC 20202.

s = SPORTS. It's possible to "play your way to better health" if you do it the right way. As noted in the section on Physical Health, the best exercises are those that are rhythmic, continuous, and build you up to a steady level of exertion. Unfortunately, most games are not very good exercise because they are a series of starts and stops. But you can get better exercise and enjoy your activities more if you *walk* instead of ride between golf shots, and switch from singles in tennis, which is a series of stops and starts, to doubles, which is a more leisurely and sociable game and actually gives you better exercise. *Cycling, swimming*, and *skiing* can all give you the exercise you need, too. These are covered in detail in the "Health Means Wealth" section. If you think skiing is only for youngsters, note that the Eastern division of the U.S. Ski Association has added a 75-year-plus category to its senior racing program, and the Senior PEP (Physical Exercise Pays) League is enrolling increasing numbers in free cross-country skiing clinics and workshops. The Senior PEP clinics are designed to introduce people over age 50 to the sport.

For more information on senior skiing (in or out of season), contact these organizations:

■ 70 + Ski Club: c/o Lloyd Lambert, 104 East Side Drive, Ballston Lakes, NY 12019.

■ Senior PEP League: U.S. Ski Association, Box 777, Brattleboro, VT 05301.

■ Alpine Seniors Competitions: U.S. Ski Association, Box 727, Brattleboro, VT 05301.

■ NASTAR: National Standard Race Program has a 50-plus category; information is available from ski schools at participating ski areas or from World Wide Ski Corporation, P.O. Box 4580, Aspen, CO 81612.

Note that many ski areas offer lift ticket discounts to skiers over 65 but do not publicize this or include themselves on the 70 + Club list. You can find out by checking with the area's ski manager or marketing department.

You can even combine sports with travel. The National Senior Sports Association conducts golf, tennis, fishing, and bowling tournaments at popular resort facilities across the country. Prices are kept low by scheduling events in the off-season and using group rates. For further information contact NSSA at 1900 St. NW, Washington, DC 20036.

Once I've Selected Activities, How Can I Stick with Them?

Like any plan, your leisure schedule must have some objectives or goals. Give yourself incentives by:

1. *Planning activities at fixed points of the day.* If you have nothing planned that you really *want to do* after lunch or dinner, it's too easy just to let down or let go. So plan something. This will give you the momentum to continue on until dinner. Then, if you want, have something planned for after dinner as well.

2. *Paying a fee* for a class or activity. You'll follow through to get your money's worth.

3. *Committing yourself to your plan* by telling others about it. You'll be encouraged by their enthusiasm and your own sense of accomplishment.

4. *Involving other people* so you won't let them down. Sharing experiences makes any activity more enjoyable.

What If I Don't Want to Do Anything?

A little girl I know showed her grandfather a picture book of photographs of animals and words. One page showed a polar bear lying on its back with its paws dangling. On the upper part of the same page was a seal, halfway in and halfway out of the water. Underneath was an inscription from Samuel Butler,

"All animals except man know that the chief business of life is to enjoy it."

Most of us were born poets but we haven't learned to enjoy the poetry of our lives. And while you might want to spend most time "being active," there will be times when you won't want to "do" anything. One grandfather told his grandson: "My favorite thing to do is to sit on *this* sand dune and stare at *that* tree."

More and more of us are finding that *contemplation*—pondering, meditating, or thinking—is a creative force. The ancient Greeks said that contemplation was the *activity of leisure* because it merges life, knowledge, freedom, and love.

How do you contemplate? Like anything else, you can cultivate philosophical thinking. Ideally, you should be physically and mentally at ease, released from distractions and everyday cares. At first your mind might be occupied with everyday thoughts and problems. But after a while your mind might "idle" and roam to new areas.

Whatever your thoughts, you are pondering, weighing, analyzing. You are developing a process, a philosophy that will help you live more fully within yourself and for others. You are not loafing! You are in tune with yourself and nature.

But however you choose to spend your leisure time, you might find it worthwhile, every now and then, to remind yourself of this poem by Robert Browning:

> *When a man's busy, why, leisure*
> *Strikes him as wonderful pleasure;*
> *Faith and at leisure once is he?*
> *Straightway he wants to be busy.*

EPILOG:
THE REST
SHOULD BE
THE BEST

Retirement or "renewment" is not only a way of life, it's a sought-after way of living. More and more of us are retiring early because never before have we had so much security, confidence in our past and present, and faith in our future:

SECURITY. With increases in Social Security benefits, Medicare, other public and private programs, we can now look forward to a more economically secure future as well as a happier and healthier one.

CONFIDENCE. Those of us in our fifties and sixties have experienced a lot, seen much, and learned to live through it all. Nothing is new or startling; in facing the future we can calmly ask: "What else is new?"

FAITH. Through knowledge and exposure to the challenges and opportunities, we realize that everybody "wins" in retirement. For instance, when someone retires, people get promoted up and down the line. New jobs and opportunities open up, perhaps even for our children and grandchildren. We realize that we can promote ourselves to a better way of living, and we have many organizations and individuals who have pioneered and cleared the way for us.

The Government Leads the Way

Every major department of the federal government has programs affecting older Americans (some 150 individual programs). The U.S. Administration on Aging (AOA) of the U.S. Department of Health and Human Services serves as the federal focal point, working with other federal agencies and with national voluntary organizations. The AOA also administers the Older

237

Americans Act, which provides for state and community grants, nutrition programs, research and development, model programs, manpower, and training. The AOA also assists the Federal Council on Aging, which is appointed by the president.

The National Clearinghouse on Aging, Dept. HHS, Washington, DC 20201, 202/245-0188, is a fountainhead of information on aging programs at the *federal* level as are the individual *state* Agencies on Aging (see list below) on the state level. And the National Institute on Aging, Dept. HHS, Bethesda, MD 20205, can tell you about physical and mental health programs on aging. And for a chart book on Federal Programs on Aging, write to Care Reports, 6529 Elgin Lane, Bethesda, MD 20817.

1981 WHITE HOUSE CONFERENCE ON AGING RECOMMENDATIONS

A survey of the 2,200 delegates of the White House Conference on Aging produced a list of the Top 10 recommendations for action in this decade:

    1.   Preserve the financial integrity and stability of the Social Security System.

    2.   Develop a national health policy for all Americans.

    3.   Preserve current levels of Medicare, Medicaid, Social Security funding, the minimum benefit, and cost-of-living increases.

    4.   Expand Social Security to all gainfully employed persons; do not move toward a voluntary social insurance system.

    5.   Eliminate discrimination against older workers by ending mandatory retirement and emphasizing flexible work schedules.

    6.   Include long-term community-based care in a national health plan, and expand Medicare and Medicaid to include in-home mental and social services. Protect the rights and independence of institutionalized elderly.

    7.   Use general fund financing to fund Social Security if necessary.

    8.   Assure appropriate and affordable housing for older persons.

    9.   Expand home-health- and in-home health-care services.

    10. Control inflation through macroeconomic measures.

The National Council on Aging, 600 Maryland Ave. SW, Washington, DC 20024, is a private organization that works with both public and private organizations in developing programs on aging. And the Gerontological Society, 1411 K St. NW, Suite 300, Washington, DC 20005, includes professionals and practitioners in all disciplines in the aging field. The International Federation on Aging, 1909 K St. NW, Washington, DC 20049, is a private, nonprofit organization that transfers and disseminates practical information for older people and serves as an advocate on an international level.

Some other organizations that act on a national level and offer various services, including insurance programs, travel, advocacy programs, and local chapters (write to them for details on membership and services) are:

- American Association of Retired Persons, 1909 K St. NW, Washington, DC 20049. Membership Center, 215 Long Beach Blvd., Long Beach, CA 90801.

- Action for Independent Maturity (for preretirement), 1909 K St. NW, Washington, DC 20049; also 215 Long Beach Blvd., Long Beach, CA 90801.

- Gray Panthers, 3635 Chestnut St., Philadelphia, PA 19104.

- National Alliance of Senior Citizens, 101 Park Washington Court, Falls Church, VA 22046.

- National Association of Mature People, 2212 NW 50th, P.O. Box 26792, Oklahoma City, OK 73112.

- Institute for the Puerto Rican/Hispanic Elderly, 105 E. 22nd St., New York, NY 10010.

- National Association of Retired Federal Employees, 1533 New Hampshire Ave. NW, Washington, DC 20036.

- National Council of Senior Citizens, 925 15th St. NW, Washington, DC 20005.

- National Association for Retired Credit Union People, P.O. Box 391, Madison, WI 53701.

- ILGWU Program, 201 W. 52nd St., New York, NY 10019.

- Older Women's League, 600 Maryland Ave. SW, Washington, DC 20024.

- UAW Program, 8731 East Jefferson Ave., Detroit, MI 48214.

STATE COMMISSIONS AND OFFICES ON AGING

State commissions and offices on aging are responsible for coordinating services for older Americans. They can provide information on programs, services and opportunities for the aging.

ALABAMA
Commission on Aging
2853 Fairlane Drive
Bldg. "G," Suite #63
Montgomery, 36130
(205) 832-6640

ALASKA
Office on Aging
Department of Health &
   Social Services
Pouch H, OIC
Juneau, 99811
(907) 465-4903/04/05/06

AMERICAN SAMOA
Territorial Administration
   on Aging
Government of American
   Samoa
Pago Pago, 96799

ARIZONA
Aging and Adult
   Administration
1400 W. Washington
   Avenue
P.O. Box #6123
Phoenix, 85007
(602) 255-4446

ARKANSAS
Office on Aging and Adult
   Services
Department of Human
   Services
1428 Donaghey Building
7th and Main St.
Little Rock, 72201
(501) 371-2441

CALIFORNIA
Department of Aging
Health & Welfare Agency
1020 19th St.
Sacramento, 95814
(916) 322-5290

COLORADO
Division of Services for the
   Aging
Department of Social
   Services
1575 Sherman St.
Denver, 80203
(303) 866-2586

CONNECTICUT
Department on Aging
80 Washington St.
Hartford, 06115
(203) 566-7728

DELAWARE
Division of Aging
Department of Health &
   Social Services
Delaware State Hospital,
   CT Building
New Castle, 19720
(302) 421-6791

DISTRICT OF COLUMBIA
Office of Aging
Office of the Mayor
1012 14th St. NW,
   Suite #1106
20005
(202) 724-5623

FLORIDA
Aging & Adult Services
Department of Health &
   Rehabilitative Services
1321 Winewood Blvd.,
   Building 2, Rm. 328
Tallahassee, 32301
(904) 488-2650

GEORGIA
Office of Aging
Department of Human
   Resources
618 Ponce de Leon Ave.
   NE
Atlanta, 30308
(404) 894-5333

GUAM
Office of Aging
Social Service Dept. of
   Public Health
Government of Guam
P.O. Box 2816
Agana, 96910

HAWAII
Executive Office on Aging
Office of the Governor
State of Hawaii
1149 Bethel St., Room 307
Honolulu, 96813
(808) 548-2593

IDAHO
Idaho Office on Aging
Statehouse, 700 West
   State St.
Boise, 83720
(202) 334-3833

ILLINOIS
Department on Aging
421 East Capitol Ave.
Springfield, 62706
(217) 785-2870

INDIANA
Commission on Aging and
   Aged
115 North Pennsylvania
   St.
Consolidated Bldg.
Indianapolis, 46204
(317) 232-7006

IOWA
Commission on Aging
415 West 10th St.
Jewett Bldg.
Des Moines, 50319
(515) 281-5187

KANSAS
Department on Aging
610 West 10th St.
Topeka, 66612
(913) 296-4986

KENTUCKY
Division for Aging Services
Bureau of Social Services,
   6th Floor, West
275 East Main St.
Frankfort, 40621
(502) 564-6930

LOUISIANA
Office of Elderly Affairs
Office of the Governor
4528 Bennington Dr.
Baton Rouge, 70898
(504) 925-1700

MAINE
Bureau of Maine's Elderly
Department of Human
   Services
State House, Station 11
Augusta, 04333
(207) 289-2561

MARYLAND
Office on Aging
State Office Bldg.
301 W. Preston St., 10th
   Floor
Baltimore, 21201
(301) 383-2100

MASSACHUSETTS
Department of Elder
   Affairs
38 Chauncey St., 2nd Floor
Boston, 02111
(617) 727-7750/51,52

MICHIGAN
Office of Services to the
   Aging
300 East Michigan
P.O. Box 30026
Lansing, 48909
(517) 373-8230

MINNESOTA
Minnesota Board on Aging
204 Metro Square Bldg.
7th & Robert Sts.

St. Paul, 55101
(612) 296-2544

MISSISSIPPI
Council on Aging
802 North State St.,
   Rm. 301
Jackson, 39201
(601) 354-6590

MISSOURI
Office of Aging
Department of Social
   Services
Broadway State Office
   Bldg.
16th Floor
P.O. Box 1337
Jefferson City, 65102
(314) 751-2075

MONTANA
Aging Branch
Budgets and Contracts
   Bureau
Department of Social &
   Rehabilitation Services,
   Community Services
   Division
P.O. Box 4210, Rm. 204
Helena, 59604
(406) 449-5650

NEBRASKA
Commission on Aging
State House Station 95044
Lincoln, 68509
(402) 471-2307

NEVADA
Division for Aging Services
Department of Human
   Resources
505 East King St.
Rm. 101
Carson City, 89710
(702) 885-4210

NEW HAMPSHIRE
Council on Aging
14 Depot St.
Concord, 03301
(603) 271-2751

NEW JERSEY
Division on Aging
Department of Community
   Affairs
363 West State St., CN807
Trenton, 08625
(609) 292-4833

NEW MEXICO
State Agency on Aging
Chamisa Hill Building
440 St. Michaels Dr.
Santa Fe, 87501
(505) 827-2802

NEW YORK
Office for the Aging
Agency Building #2
Empire State Plaza
Albany, 12223
(518) 474-5731

NORTH CAROLINA
Division of Aging
Department of Human
   Resources
708 Hillsborough St., Suite
   200
Raleigh, 27603
(919) 733-3983

NORTH DAKOTA
Aging Services
Social Service
   Board of N.D.
State Capitol Bldg.
Bismarck, 58505
(701) 224-2310

OHIO
Commission on Aging
50 West Broad St., 9th
   Floor
Columbus, 43215
(614) 466-5500, 5501

OKLAHOMA
Special Unit on Aging
Department of Human
    Services
P.O. Box 25352
Oklahoma City, 73125
(405) 521-2281

OREGON
Office of Elderly Affairs
Human Resources
    Department
772 Commercial St. SE
Salem, 97310
(503) 378-4728

PENNSYLVANIA
Department of Aging
Rm. 404 Finance Bldg.
Harrisburg, 17120
(717) 783-1550

PUERTO RICO
Gericulture Commission
Dept. of Social Services
P.O. Box 11398
Santurce, 00910

RHODE ISLAND
Department of Elderly
    Affairs
79 Washington St.
Providence, 02903
(401) 277-2880

SOUTH CAROLINA
Commission on Aging
915 Main St.
Columbia, 29201
(803) 758-2576

SOUTH DAKOTA
Office of Adult Services
    and Aging
Department of Social
    Services
Richard F. Kneip Bldg.
Pierre, 57501
(605) 773-3656

TENNESSEE
Commission on Aging
703 Tennessee Bldg.
535 Church St.
Nashville, 37219
(615) 741-2056

TEXAS
Texas Department on
    Aging
Capitol Station
P.O. Box 12786
Austin, 78711
(512) 475-2717

UTAH
Division of Aging
Dept. of Social Services
150 W. North Temple, 3rd
    Floor
Salt Lake City, 84102
(801) 533-6422

VERMONT
Office on Aging
103 S. Main St.
Waterbury, 05676
(802) 241-2400

VIRGINIA
Office on Aging
830 E. Main St.
Suite 950
Richmond, 23219
(804) 786-7894

VIRGIN ISLANDS
Commission on Aging
P.O. Box 539
Charlotte Amalie
St. Thomas, 00801

WASHINGTON
Bureau of Aging & Adult
    Services
Dept. of Social & Health
    Services
OG-43G
Olympia, 98504
(206) 753-2502

WEST VIRGINIA
Commission on Aging
State Capitol
Charleston, 25305
(304) 348-3317

WISCONSIN
Bureau on Aging
Dept. of Health & Social
    Services
Division of Community
    Services
1 W. Wilson St.
P.O. Box 7851
Madison, 53707
(608) 266-2536

WYOMING
Commission on Aging
401 W. 19th St.
Cheyenne, 82002
(307) 777-7986

The Universities Launch Their Own Projects

Many universities have established institutes of gerontology, councils or special programs on aging, and are conducting research projects in all phases of the developing fields of *gerontology* (the social science of aging) and *geriatrics* (the medical science of aging). These colleges and universities are offering special certificates and degrees in these fields and are attracting many young, dedicated students. Pioneers in this area have been University of Michigan–Wayne State University, University of Southern California, Duke University, Syracuse, University of Georgia, Penn State, University of Oregon, and many others.

Some universities have even developed *retirement-planning programs*, along with the many organizations listed above. Most preretirement planners belong to the International Society of Preretirement Planners, El Monte Plaza, Box 196, 3500 Clayton Rd., Suite B, Concord, CA 94519. This organization has found that the most important areas for early retirees to consider are (in order of those responding):

SUBJECT AREA	PERCENTAGE RESPONDING*
Finances	85
Use of leisure time	35
Health insurance	19
Recreation	15
Company benefits	15
Personal assessment	12
Psychological impact of retirement	4
Where to live	4
Estate planning	4
Reason for retiring	4

*Percentage total exceeds 100 because some respondents provided more than one answer.

You can get membership information and a list of organizations in preretirement planning from the ISPP above. Some other organizations active in preretirement planning programs:

- American Guidance Service, Publishers Building, Circle Pines, MN 55014.

- American Management Association, 135 W. 50th St., New York, NY 10020.

- Dartnell, 4660 Ravenswood Ave., Chicago, IL 60640.

- Hope Publishing and Training Center, 807 N. 50th St., Omaha, NB 68132.

- Manpower Education Institute, 127 E. 35th St., New York, NY 10016.

- Pre-Retirement Planning Institute, 11762 W. 34th Ave., Wheat Ridge, CO 80033.

- Retirement Program Services, 157 E. 57th St., New York, NY 10022.

- RETIRE (Retirement Education and Training Information and Resource Evaluation), Genro Bldg., 444 Sherman St., Denver, CO 80203.

- Retirement Advisors, 919 3rd Ave., New York, NY 10022.

- Retirement Services, Inc., P.O. Box 5325, Eugene, OR 97405.

- TIAA-CREF, 730 3rd Ave., New York, NY 10017.

What Some Companies Are Doing

Hewitt Associates, a benefits consulting firm, recently issued a report on "Company Sponsored Retiree Programs Beyond Pensions and Group Insurance." This research paper profiled retiree programs in ten companies across the country and is a sampling of what some companies are doing for their retirees (these and other companies also have retirement-planning programs):

- *Bucyrus-Erie.* This program has been in operation for over 30 years and is housed at its own clubhouse with recreational facilities, bar, cafeteria, and dining room. Employees become automatic members at no cost when they retire. Activities include semiweekly meetings, monthly dinners, daily activities, holiday dinners or picnics, and a variety of day trips for members.

- *Exxon.* Has 40 to 50 clubs with over 22,000 retirees. More clubs will be set up as needed and communications will be expanded to include a quarterly newsletter, informational pieces from the company, meetings with senior management, and improved processing of health benefit forms.

- *Gerber Products.* This program is available mainly to retirees near corporate headquarters (where most Gerber retirees are located). In addition to periodic social functions Gerber provides a toll-free telephone hot line for counseling and assistance on benefit claims, personal counseling on retirement-related problems, and membership in retiree organizations.

- *Honeywell.* Retiree Volunteer Project started in 1978 for headquarters-area retirees, but similar programs are in the works for two other locations. This program is primarily service-oriented, with retirees giving assistance to a variety of community agencies.

■ *Illinois Bell.* This company has 13,000 retirees with another 800 retiring each year. Illinois Bell has 20 Benefits Representatives busy with systematic contact with each retiree at least once annually. The representative is also available for telephone counseling at any time. The company has a financial assistance program and free or discounted telephone service for retirees.

■ *International Minerals and Chemicals.* Has two area location programs and a number of social functions for retirees and employees throughout the year. Options under consideration or in planning include a toll-free telephone hot line, a newsletter, and a home visitation program.

■ *S.C. Johnson.* In addition to free picnics, recreation programs, and so forth, the company provides for 50 percent of the cost of numerous other activities, including day and overnight trips, theater parties, dinners, free stays at a company-owned resort, educational expense reimbursement, community services programs, and personal counseling.

■ *Levi Strauss.* The Retirement Services Department has compiled a nationwide "Directory of Volunteer and Community Services," which lists local volunteer opportunities, as well as personal assistance resources. The company pays a stipend and expenses for the retiree volunteers to make monthly visits to over 600 retirees, organize social functions, and assist with pension claims and other benefits. The company also sponsors a retiree newsletter and a telephone hot-line.

■ *Northwestern Mutual Life.* The program emphasis is primarily social, with a newsletter, company-sponsored clubs, sports events, trips, cultural events, parties, retiree gifts. A Quarter Century Club and Administrative Management Association also provide a variety of social and cultural opportunities.

■ *Textron.* A Textron Advisory Group is composed of 35 retired executives whose consulting activities are underwritten by the company. The basic idea is to allow group members to "use their extensive experience to benefit others." Consulting assignments can range from part-time to full-time temporary assignments and are charged at competitively priced fees.

Many Media to Choose From . . . .

Even if you don't belong to an organization offering pre- or postretirement planning programs, you have many resources to draw on. Some of the media active in this field include the Public Television program "Over Easy" (check local PBS listings) and the insurance company Mutual of Omaha's radio program "The Best Years." The American Association of Retired Persons has a 15-minute interview and talk show syndicated in 465 markets called "Prime Time."

Most of the associations listed above have magazines or house organs. I am the founding editor of *Harvest Years* (now *50 Plus*), which is the major independent magazine in the field, you can write to *50 Plus* at 850 Third Ave., New York, NY 10017. I am also the founding editor of *The Retirement Letter*, *the Money Newsletter for Mature People*, which is published 16 times a year. For subscription information, write to *The Retirement Letter*, 7315 Wisconsin Ave. #1200 N, Bethesda, MD 20814.

Some other publications of interest to seniors:

■ *Mature Years*, The United Methodist Church, 201 8th Ave. S., Nashville, TN 37202.

■ *Retired Officer*, The Retired Officers' Association, 201 N. Washington St., Alexandria, VA 22314.

■ *Retirement Planning Strategist*, 10076 Boca Entrada Blvd., Boca Raton, FL 33433.

■ *Senior World*, Senior World Publications, 4640 Jewell St., San Diego, CA 92109.

■ *United Retirement Bulletin*, United Business Service, 210 Newbury St., Boston, MA 02116.

■ The Public Affairs Committee, 381 Park Ave. South, New York, NY 10016, puts out a series of 25 booklets ("Packet on Aging"). Write to them for listing and latest price.

Besides the many books listed in various sections of this book, some general books on the subject include:

■ *The Best Years Book* by Hugh Downs and Richard Roll (New York: Dell, 1982).

■ *The Prime of Your Life* by Joseph Michaels (Boston: Little, Brown, 1983).

■ *Life Plans: Looking Forward to Retirement* by Grace Weinstein (New York: Holt, Rinehart & Winston, 1979), $4.95 (softcover), postpaid from the author, Grace Weinstein, 283 Maitland Ave., Teaneck, NJ 07666.

■ *Over 50: The Definitive Guide to Retirement* by Auren Uris (New York: Chilton, 1981).

Community Agencies Link Problems With Solutions

All states and most communities have now established Information and Referral (I & R) offices that link seniors with the services they need. Many I & R offices are staffed by Community Welfare Councils or United Fund Agencies. You'll find your I & R office listed in your telephone directory under these agencies or under "Area Agency on Aging" or "Information and Referral."

The I & R people can tell you about any local programs that might interest or help you. They will refer you to the proper place and can even make an appointment to help solve your problem. Some places you might like to know about: senior centers and clubs, local human resources agencies, religious organizations, professional societies.

Labor unions often run I-&-R-type services for their members, as do some civil rights groups. Branch offices of the Social Security Administration also advise about rights and procedures, and state employment agencies have older-worker specialists to help seniors find jobs.

Through this book, you should have all the information you'll need to start "renewment" today. To start you on your way:

1. Decide now what you really want to do to make the rest of your life the best of your life.

2. Review the sections on health, money, housing, leisure, and legal matters to see what you need and want to accomplish your goals.

3. Set goals for *now* and in the future. Remember, your plans should enrich your present as well as assure your future.

4. Start today to live and practive your new life-style. You can test and develop it today; polish and perfect it tomorrow.

Remember, I "retired" at age 45, and now, some 11 years later, I'm happier, healthier, and wealthier than I was before. You, too, will have many *happier tomorrows—if you start your retirement planning today!*

RETIREMENT READINESS QUIZ

Respond to each item by circling the corresponding letter of the phrase that best completes the partial statement.

1. The two chief sources of income for most retired persons today are:
   a. Social Security benefits and personal savings.
   b. Private pensions and Social Security benefits.

    c. Social Security and Supplemental Security Income benefits.

    d. Social Security benefits and wages and salaries.

2. It is a fact that older people:
   a. May be more easily upset than younger people by the learning of new tasks.
   b. Are considerably more resistant to change than younger people.
   c. Can learn new tasks just as well as younger people, if not better, even though it generally takes them longer to do so.
   d. Both a and c.

3. Gerontologists have found that the one type of leisure activity that is best for older persons to engage in is:
   a. Arts and crafts.
   b. Armchair activities (reading, TV, crosswords, and so on).
   c. Any activity that is easily mastered and requires limited skills.
   d. Not generally determinable.

4. The amount of monthly Social Security benefits that the retired person receives depends on:
   a. Average annual earnings during work life.
   b. Age at the time you start to collect.
   c. Age at the time you start to collect, and earnings at the time you claim benefits.
   d. Both a and c.

5. A person reaches his or her biological maturity:
   a. Between the early forties and mid-sixties.
   b. During the mid- to late twenties.
   c. Between age 60 and 75.
   d. Not at any particular age, as maturity varies from one individual to another.

6. Today, the largest percentage of retired persons:
   a. Live in nursing homes and institutions.
   b. Live with their children or relatives.
   c. Maintain their own households.
   d. Live in residential hotels or retirement homes.

7. A retired person's eligibility for Supplemental Security Income will depend on:

    a. The amount of monthly income the person receives or earns.

    b. The value of certain personal assets owned by the person.

    c. The person's age at the time he or she claims, the amount of monthly income the person receives or earns, and the value of certain personal assets owned by the person.

    d. Both a and b.

8. Two expenses that are likely to decrease because of retirement are:

    a. Personal and food expenses.

    b. Clothing and food expenses.

    c. Housing and personal expenses.

    d. Clothing and transportation expenses.

9. According to the Bureau of Labor Statistics, the percentage of a retired couple's annual budget that comprises housing costs is nearest to:

    a. 35%

    b. 25%

    c. 55%

    d. 15%

10. To claim Social Security benefits, a retired person must furnish the local Social Security office his or her:

    a. Social Security number and birth certificate.

    b. Social Security card.

    c. Social Security number, federal income tax withholding statement (form W-2) for the previous year, and birth certificate.

    d. Social Security card and federal income tax withholding statement (form W-2) for the previous year.

Respond to each of the following items by circling either the word *True* or *False*.

11. The person who chooses not to move to a different geographic region in retirement has few options for maintaining his or her preretirement standard of living.

        True   False

12. Asking a doctor to prescribe drugs by their generic name, rather than by a specific brand name, can often help the retired person save on drug costs.

        True   False

13. Because retirement income is limited, most retired people have little choice in the type of housing and locale they inhabit.

       True   False

14. The retired person who claims Social Security benefits at age 62 will receive monthly payments that are 20 percent lower than the full benefit received at age 65.

       True   False

15. Because older people need good nutrition to stay healthy and free of chronic ailments, it is virtually impossible for them to reduce their food expenses.

       True   False

16. Because Social Security payments may be periodically adjusted to compensate for increases in the general cost of living, inflation does not affect retirees.

       True   False

17. Older people are no more introspective than any other age group, even when they are living alone.

       True   False

18. The most important factors for a retired person to consider when deciding a move to another geographic region are the locale's climate and cost of living.

       True   False

19. It is a fact that in solving problems older people are no less apt to be creative and experimental than younger people.

       True   False

ANSWERS TO QUIZ: 1 (b); 2 (d); 3 (d); 4 (c); 5 (b); 6 (c); 7 (a); 8 (c); 9 (a); 10 (c); 11 False; 12 True; 13 False; 14 True; 15 False; 16 False; 17 True; 18 False; 19 True. *How many answers did you get right?* If you read this book thoroughly, you should have scored 100 percent. If not, go back to the sections of the book covering those questions you answered wrongly. Then you should be ready to launch a *successful retirement*—to retire to a happier, healthier, and wealthier life than you have now.

INDEX

academic programs, 229–230
"activated patient" programs, 73
Adams, Thomas Boylston, 206
Administration on Aging (AOA), U.S., 56, 237–238
Age Discrimination Act, 169
Age Discrimination in Employment Act (ADEA), 168–169
age of retirement, see retirement age
aging:
  diet and, 60
  federal offices on, 237–239
  myths of, 28
  physical, 17–18
  skin care and, 31–32
  state offices on, 166, 239–242
air travel, 227
alcohol, consumption of, 66
Alzheimer's disease, 48
American Association of Retired Persons, 246
American Craft Council, 223
American Depositary Receipts (ADRs), 116–117
American Medical Association (AMA), 44, 171–172

annuities, 122–124, 140–141
  foreign-currency denominated, 120
  home ownership and, 124–125
  life insurance and, 124, 140–141
  taxes on, 135, 140, 161
antenuptial (prenuptial) agreements, 42, 149
antiques, investments in, 113–114
appraisals:
  art and antique, 113
  health-risk, 19–20
armchair activities, 225–226
art, investments in, 113–114, 123
arteries, hardening of, 62
art hobbies, 221
arthritis, 48–50, 62, 73
  foot discomfort and, 36
  prevention and treatment of, 49–50, 75, 171
  quack "cures" for, 49–50, 171
aspirin, 171
auctions, art and antique, 113–114
audio cassette lessons, 231

autographs, as investments, 113–114
auto rentals, 228

back problems, 34–36
  prevention of, 35–36
Baker, Samm Sinclair, 44
"bank examiners," phony, 173–174
banks:
  commercial, 122, 162
  as executors of wills, 158
  foreign, 115–117
  money management overseen by, 162
  savings, 97, 99, 122, 158
basal cell cancer, 31
baseball, 59
bathing:
  foot care and, 36
  skin care and, 31
Better Business Bureau, 113, 170, 172, 175, 176–177
Blue Cross–Blue Shield, 67–68, 70, 74
bonds, 95, 122
  in closed- or open-end funds, 107
  convertible, 103

251